BLACK BOYS APART

Black Boys Apart

RACIAL UPLIFT AND RESPECTABILITY IN ALL-MALE PUBLIC SCHOOLS

Freeden Blume Oeur

University of Minnesota Press

Minneapolis

London

Portions of chapters 1, 3, and 4 were originally published as "The Respectable Brotherhood: Young Black Men in an All-Boys Charter High School," *Sociological Perspectives* 60, no. 6 (2017): 1063–81, https://doi.org/10.1177/0731121417706071. Portions of chapters 2 and 5 were originally published as "Recognizing Dignity: Young Black Men Growing Up in an Era of Surveillance," *Socius: Sociological Research for a Dynamic World* 2 (2016): 1–15, https://doi.org/10.1177/2378023116633712. Portions of chapter 4 were originally published as "It's Not How Regular Boys Are Supposed to Act: The Nonnormative Sexual Practices of Black Boys in All-Male Public Schools," in *Gender and Sexualities in Education: A Reader*, ed. D. Carlson and E. Meyer, 357–69 (New York: Peter Lang, 2014).

Published by the University of Minnesota Press
111 Third Avenue South, Suite 290
Minneapolis, MN 55401-2520
http://www.upress.umn.edu

Printed in the United States of America on acid-free paper

The University of Minnesota is an equal-opportunity educator and employer.

22 21 20 19 18   10 9 8 7 6 5 4 3 2

Library of Congress Cataloging-in-Publication Data
Names: Blume Oeur, Freeden, author.
Title: Black boys apart : racial uplift and respectability in all-male public schools / Freeden Blume Oeur.
Description: Minneapolis : University of Minnesota Press, [2018] | Includes bibliographical references and index.
Identifiers: LCCN 2018001569 | ISBN 978-0-8166-9638-3 (hc) | ISBN 978-0-8166-9646-8 (pb)
Subjects: LCSH: African American boys—Education—Social aspects. | African American boys—Social conditions. | Single-sex schools—United States. | Sex differences in education—United States.
Classification: LCC LC2771 .B58 2018 | DDC 371.829/96073—dc23
LC record available at https://lccn.loc.gov/2018001569

Dedicated to the memory of Al Moser

CONTENTS

Reform, Respectability, and the Crisis of Young Black Men

On a winter day in 1990, the city of Detroit convened a "Saving the Black Male" conference. It was democracy in action. Parents, school officials, and other community members passed a resolution demanding that elected officials intervene to "reverse the tide of failure among urban males."[1] A city task force responded with the bold proposal of opening several unique all-male public elementary schools. The proposed schools would innovate by recruiting Black male role models and by adopting African-centered curricula. Detroit's efforts came closely on the heels of another Rust Belt city, Milwaukee, seeking to open its own Black male academies. As one newspaper observed at the time, Milwaukee's proposal represented "the most drastic educational approach aimed at saving the next generation of young Black men from the social maelstrom now devouring much of the current generation."[2]

The schools faced heavy opposition. Some believed they were another form of racial segregation because they further isolated Black boys from their peers. Kenneth Clark, the psychologist whose research steered the U.S. Supreme Court in its monumental decision to desegregate public schools in 1954, called these Black academies "nonsense."[3] Meanwhile, feminist organizations argued that these academies posed a threat to Black *girls* by denying this population similar opportunities. A Detroit court sided with these opponents, and the city was required to enroll girls as well as boys in the new schools. The most well known of these schools, the Malcolm X Academy, was then subjected to cruel acts of racism. Protesters spray-painted "white power" on the school and demanded that the children go through security checks.[4] Yet this hostility only emboldened supporters, who felt that Black communities should have the right to design schools as they wished. In their eyes, schools that taught Black boys apart from their peers represented "islands of hope in a sea of indifference."[5]

A major restructuring of U.S. public education today has renewed hope in all-boys public education. Anchored by the 2002 No Child Left Behind law and propelled by the free-market doctrine of neoliberalism, this restructuring has embraced innovation and freedom of choice in schools. This second wave of Black male academies has benefited from the support of courts and civil rights organizations that had earlier been skeptical of these schools.[6] While firm numbers are elusive, there were an estimated 106 entirely single-sex public schools in 2014, up from just a handful during the 1990s.[7]

Why have Black communities turned to all-male education today? How do these schools make and reform Black manhood? How do these institutions help and harm? These are the questions that guide *Black Boys Apart*.

My research for this book took me to the large East Coast city of Morgan, one of the country's first major laboratories for choice and experimentation in public schools.[8] On a sweltering day in September 2009, I arrived at Northside Academy, a charter high school, and made a beeline for the school's lunchroom. An assembly was about to start. I stood near the back row next to Jeremiah, a ninth grader.

"Do you teach here?" Jeremiah asked. Like many of his classmates, Jeremiah had attended a charter middle school before enrolling in Northside. He lived with just his mother. He wanted to be the first person in his family to attend college. He loved comic books.

"No, I'm a researcher," I responded. "I'm here to learn more about your school. I'm Mr. Oeur."[9]

We shook hands, but Jeremiah looked skeptical. He then flashed a grin and said, "I'm learning about the school, too. I can be your assistant!" I chuckled. Jeremiah was already certain of one thing. "What you should *know* is that we *need* some girls in here!"

Trevor Green, the school's new principal, walked to the front of the room. The young Black men, members of the school's newest cohort, sat up dutifully and quietly, just as the school's strict culture of discipline required. "Good is the enemy of great," Mr. Green started. "Our focus is to be great at everything we do." He kept the details to a minimum that morning and instead relayed big messages that would be a hallmark of the school's weekly assemblies: "Prove society wrong." "Respect your brothers." "College is your pathway." Mr. Green frequently paused to ask, "Is that clear?" "YES!" the boys shouted in unison.

Around the same time, across town, Perry, a combined middle and high school, was also preparing for the new school year.[10] Just a few years before, Perry High had been one of the first public schools in the country to adopt an all-boys model. The implementation had been rocky, however, and the school struggled for years with staff turnover. Yet there were new reasons for optimism. Perry had won a large federal grant to support new initiatives, and several veteran administrators had been recruited to help lead the school. Perry lacked Northside's flexibility as a charter school (free to determine its own curricula and governance structure and to hire its own teachers), but there was a palpable sense of hope that the all-boys model could still work.

A spectacular marble staircase beckoned inside the front lobby, but the students entered instead through a small side entrance. There, they passed through a metal detector with a sign overhead that read, "ONLY YOU CAN TAKE THE 'U' OUT OF TRUANCY." Once inside, the students headed straight for the auditorium. On my way there, I ran into Laura Wheeler, a middle-aged white Spanish teacher I had met the week before in a faculty meeting.

The look on her face read, *I'm already stressed!*

"Busy morning, Ms. Wheeler?"

"A new year, a new start, Mr. Oeur!"

She was one of several staff members who had made a mid-career transition into teaching. As luck would have it, her siblings were already teachers, and they helped her secure her first teaching gig at an all-boys Catholic school.[11] When she looked into working in public schools, she found that the school district in Morgan was desperate for language instructors. So Ms. Wheeler had her pick of schools. Discovering that Perry High was all-boys, she jumped at the opportunity to work there. She would replace a long-term Spanish substitute teacher who, to her students' dismay, did not speak any Spanish.

Inside the auditorium, Lavar Bradley, the principal, welcomed the students to a new school year. While normally a jovial person, Mr. Bradley's smile quickly disappeared. The tone of his message matched that of Mr. Green's over at Northside Academy:

> Our school is on a serious mission this year. There needs to be a sense
> of urgency. All the statistics show that Black boys have no business
> being successful. But we're in the business of showing that those
> statistics are wrong!

For one school year, I traveled back and forth between Perry High School and Northside Academy. I observed classroom lessons and assemblies, hung out with the boys throughout the school, and spoke with parents, teachers, and other school officials. The young men had much in common: they came from many of the same racially segregated and class-disadvantaged neighborhoods. They came of age in a neoliberal conjuncture, a "contradictory moment of political struggles, victories, defeats and transformations" that constructs specific race and gender formations.[12] The young men found themselves at the center of major local and federal school reform in a time marked by the increased policing of their communities, state disinvestment, and a Great Recession that had crippled Black wealth. And they faced grim realities. Black boys are three times more likely than their white peers to receive an out-of-school suspension.[13] In 2013, the high school graduation rate for Black boys nationwide was 59 percent, compared to 80 percent for white boys.[14] Health indicators are similarly discouraging.[15]

Perry High School and Northside Academy also differed in significant ways. Without a clear plan of action, Perry High found itself stuck, so to speak, between the two waves: the school was determined to adopt the role-modeling mission of its earlier counterpart schools in Detroit and Milwaukee, but it was unable to achieve the respectable character for which it also yearned. Northside Academy, on the other hand, exemplified the second-wave model. Blessed with resources that Perry lacked and a mission to attract academically oriented students, the school aimed for nothing less than to join the ranks of the city's elite schools. Miscalculations and poor planning dogged Perry High, while Northside Academy quickly gained admirers across the city. Yet *Black Boys Apart* is not primarily concerned with what makes these schools successful. Black male academies are likely to succeed for reasons that other public schools succeed, such as the presence of a rigorous academic curriculum, caring adult-student relationships, and strong leadership.[16] A different question is what these schools judge to be success, and how they mold Black male identity to meet those goals. This book therefore interrogates all-boys schools as a matter of masculinity politics, or "those mobilizations and struggles where the meaning of masculine gender is at issue, and with it, men's position in gender relations."[17] This approach departs from the view of Black male academies as primarily a school-reform effort, or a way to "fix" schools to meet the needs of young men of color.[18] Instead, I examine these schools through the framework of governmentality, or the techniques and knowledges that manage the conduct of citizens and make them into appropriate gendered and racialized subjects.[19] In this view, Black male academies are not so much about reforming schools. Instead, they join a long political history of social institutions—including schools, churches, families, the media, and the criminal justice system—seeking to reform Black men and boys.

Educational researchers have rightfully been skeptical of the term "crisis," as it implies a temporary episode for something that is actually chronic.[20] I find, however, that two meanings of the term are central for a story on sex-separate education. First, the history of schooling in the United States reveals how perceived crises—"real" or not, temporary or not—have had real effects for gender arrangements, the distribution of resources, and the shaping of life outcomes. Second, the term "crisis" has profound valence in a history of Black political struggle. In the inaugural (1910) issue of *The Crisis,* the periodical of the National Association for the Advancement of Colored People (NAACP), W. E. B. Du Bois wrote that the newspaper "takes its name from the fact that the editors believe that this is a critical time *in the advancement of men.*"[21] Du Bois, a cofounder of the NAACP and one of the twentieth century's towering intellectual-activists, was not merely referring to dire statistics; rather, *crisis* was intended to motivate Black communities and their allies to take political action. *Black Boys Apart* will return often to Du Bois and his ideas. Conducted exactly a century after Du Bois penned these words, my research heeds the call to make sense of today's "critical time" in the advancement of Black boys.

From Resilience to Respectability

No statistical data show that single-sex schools benefit young men of color.[22] Yet qualitative work provides a more optimistic outlook on these schools. Edward Fergus, Pedro Noguera, and Margary Martin's book *Schooling for Resilience* is most representative of this approach. This study argues that the primary aim of male academies is to create "protective environments" in order to cultivate in the young men *resilience,* or the various capacities (such as optimism, self-confidence, and perseverance) that are needed to overcome adversity and to improve well-being. I refer to this as the *resilience perspective.* The thesis that these academies represent a "new wave" of school-reform efforts intended to "save" young men by instilling in them the resilience to overcome structural challenges (a lack of access to mainstream institutions) and cultural deficits (such as popular stereotypes and harmful cultural beliefs and behaviors) has been taken up enthusiastically by other scholars. In one study, graduates from a Black male academy cultivated resilience in order to not "let the neighborhood win."[23] In another, an all-male school cultivated *imara* (meaning "perseverance" in Swahili) in their students.[24] Black male academies are exalted for encouraging their students to "never quit" and to "never give up."[25]

While the resilience perspective is commendable for focusing attention on how young men of color are empowered agents in their schooling, this research overlooks the very social dynamics that motivate academies to promote resilience in the first place. Without an understanding of this wider context and history, resilience passes uncritically as a commonsense, virtuous quality. It is protected by the good intentions of school staff members. As Kenneth Saltman has argued, the admiration of resilience echoes controversial efforts to cultivate "grit" in disadvantaged children:

> Resilience studies ask not how the social conditions of poverty and violence can be transformed or how students can learn to comprehend and act to change what oppresses them. Instead resilience studies identifies the rare student who survives, graduates, and goes to university despite the social disinvestment, violence, targeting by the criminal justice system, despair, and poverty. Resilience studies focuses on the exceptional "success against all odds story." . . . Grit shares with resilience studies a deeply conservative refusal to address radical disparities in social investment, the historical policy legacy that reproduces a racialized class hierarchy, the ways there are clear winners and losers and the political pressure that maintains such radically unequal public spending patterns.[26]

The various study participants in the resilience framework resemble what Loïc Wacquant has called "paragons of morality," or honorable protagonists who narrate moral tales where they use their resilience to fend off an overwhelmingly threatening social landscape.[27] Across this scholarship, the barometer for school success is the degree to which students demonstrate the individual willpower, effort, and hope needed to transcend a racial subject position marked mostly by its defects.[28] All-male academies (and the students, families, and staff they represent) view their school as a possible "solution" to an external environment characterized as a monolithic problem. In this view, the schools are variously described as seeking to "protect," "inoculate," and "buffer" young men from neighborhood factors (the oft-cited gangs, drugs, and violence), while the community environment is reduced to a set of risks that need to be "countered" and "undone."[29] The study participants in *Schooling for Resilience* see themselves as fighting "a battle between good and evil."[30] Derrick Brooms explains how his respondents view themselves as "winners," but he is silent about who the "losers" are in this moral tale.[31] This framing accepts as an unassailable virtue precisely that which needs to be historically situated in these schools: the growing need to "protect" a respectable male identity from deviant features of Black masculinity and Black urban life.[32]

As Stuart Hall has written, common sense "represents itself as the 'traditional wisdom or truth of the ages,' but, in fact, it is deeply a product of history."[33] *Black Boys Apart* roots commonsense resilience in history to draw out issues of privilege, power, and politics. Indeed, the resilience perspective has overlooked the respectable character of Black male academies because—quite curiously—it has largely overlooked a long history of separating boys and girls in schools.[34] This history includes recent attempts to embrace Black all-male education, and a longer history of how Black children have been implicated in sex-separate public schooling since the Jim Crow era. The resilience perspective elides the historical antecedents to today's academies.[35] Had these authors compared today's all-male academies to efforts in the early 1990s (in Detroit and Milwaukee, which comprise what I call the first-wave Black male academies) they would have found that these original educators also sought to instill resilience in their young men. Without acknowledging this history, this research has failed to compare today's schools to their first-wave counterparts and therefore cannot specify precisely what makes today's academies distinctive.

This book departs from endorsements of Black male academies as school-reform efforts that seek to instill resilience and instead views these schools as efforts to reform Black male character by cultivating respectability.[36] Early Black leaders in the latter part of the nineteenth century promoted a "politics of respectability" that conformed to middle-class values in order to reject racist discourses of African Americans.[37] However, these politics proved troubling as they focused on reforming Black men's behavior—the embrace of moral discipline, self-restraint, and obedience—while taking "the emphasis away from structural forms of oppression."[38] A respectability politics therefore divided Black communities when upwardly mobile Black men "constructed their own status against that of the Black 'unrespectable' poor."[39] In an era of deteriorating Black wealth—exacerbated by state austerity measures and the Great Recession, which rocked the country shortly before my research started in 2009—a respectability politics has reemerged. As Fredrick Harris observes, these politics have become a common sense in Black communities and are pushed by high-profile Blacks from the comedian Bill Cosby, to CNN anchor Don Lemons, to even President Barack Obama. They have demanded that Black youth correct their behavior. Meanwhile, conservatives tout modern finishing schools and other educational programs that teach good manners to poor youth as a way of lifting them out of poverty.[40] A respectability politics demands correcting one's conduct in a "post-racial" America.

While Black all-male secondary institutions are relatively new, elite Black institutions such as the all-male Morehouse College continue to promote a respectability politics. Saida Grundy writes that Morehouse "embrace[s] conformity to mainstream middle-class gender constructs to produce and sustain normative patriarchal citizenship and 'respectable' Black males" and in doing so draws clear symbolic boundaries against those Black men most in "crisis."[41] Today's second-wave academies show evidence of institutionalizing respectability. Whereas the first attempts to open all-male schools were African-centered, the second-wave academies have established rigorous college-preparatory curricula grounded in the classics. At Chicago's Black all-male Urban Prep Academies, which have been lauded for their exemplary college-placement record, students wear blazers and ties and call one another by their surnames.[42]

Black Boys Apart complicates the "sociosexual binary of respectability versus deviance . . . by exploring the political and cultural imperatives *for perpetuating it.*"[43] Following Lester Spence, Michael Dumas, Fredrick Harris, and others, I link a respectability politics to a "neoliberal turn in Black politics."[44] Neoliberalism is a pervasive social policy doctrine that turns to the market for answers. To achieve greater innovation and efficiency, it demands deregulation and the transfer of the handling of goods and services from democratic institutions to the private sector. As part of this transition, Black communities emphasize "technical, entrepreneurial interventions" over "political organization as the imagined solution" to socioeconomic inequality.[45] Neoliberalism was codified into educational law in 2002 with the passage of No Child Left Behind, a sweeping set of school reforms that loosened restrictions on single-sex education.[46] *Black Boys Apart* demonstrates that this neoliberal turn marks a return to historical attempts to reform Black male subjectivity. Only by understanding how Black male academies are oriented to the past can we assess whether they can carve a hopeful path forward for their young men.

Crises of Masculinity

To understand why communities have turned to single-sex education for Black boys, we first need to grasp the historical precedent of turning to sex-separate education as a strategy to defend and restore gender and racial hierarchies. The concept of hegemonic masculinity can help us chart these strategies. Hegemonic masculinity refers to the web of practices, relations, and regulations that ensure men's dominance over women in a larger gender order. It is the most exalted form of manhood in a specific historical and social context.[47] Hegemonic masculinity exists in relation to other marginalized masculinities, which vary by race, class, sexuality, ability, and other lines of difference. Hegemonic masculinity is not simply a matter of brute force; rather, people consent to its practices. It is less a stable system and more a "mobile relation" that is always on guard, monitoring and responding to challenges to its authority.[48] Throughout U.S. history, dominant groups have resisted the encroachment of others—including women and nonwhites—by framing young white men as victims in crisis.[49]

These strategies appear at the very start of coed schooling in the United States. In the mid-nineteenth century, calls for more cost-effective schooling and a thriving evangelical movement helped to spread coeducation across the country.[50] Early school leaders explained that coeducation would not disrupt an existing gender hierarchy grounded in the belief in natural differences between men and women.[51] Boys and girls could physically mix in schools—just as they did in the home and the church—but this would not violate their "separate spheres." Girls were groomed to be dutiful wives and mothers while schooling helped boys cultivate a genteel respectability that was the "source of men's strength and authority over both women and the lower classes."[52] Gender relations were defined by a principle of "different and unequal." Given entrenched views of gender difference, coeducation was hardly controversial.[53]

The growing success of girls sparked concerns of a "crisis" of boys. The psychologist G. Stanley Hall warned that the "feminine environment" of schools would strip young boys of their essential "savage" nature.[54] The progress of the nation—perhaps civilization itself—was at stake, since boys needed to channel their aggressive tendencies for the nation to advance as a global superpower.[55] Critiques that schools were both failing and feminizing young men were nested in larger fears of threats to dominant white masculinity during this time. As Michael Kimmel writes, the ideal of the "Self-Made Man" was under siege. A corporate workforce threatened to stifle men's "primal" tendencies and inhibit their autonomy, while women's suffrage threatened to unsettle men's hold on political power.[56]

For Blacks during the Jim Crow era, gendered divisions took shape through a project of racial uplift. Black elites pushed for a "Talented Tenth" of men to lift up the race by pursuing a college education and by adopting the Victorian ideals of temperance, refined manners, and industriousness.[57] Meanwhile, the Black church pushed for the training of respectable Black girls who would enter occupations such as nursing, missionary work, and domestic work in white homes.[58] This separate educational track for Black girls illustrates how "sex segregation sought to replicate gendered norms as a strategy for gaining white respect."[59] Most Black men and boys, on the other hand, were met with fear—rooted in "controlling images" of Black men as sexual predators—and were deprived of these educational opportunities.[60] As Verna Williams describes, Black men were thus denied access to breadwinning roles and came to be viewed as failed patriarchs.[61]

With the U.S. Supreme Court's mandate of racial integration in schools in the case of *Brown v. Board of Education* (1954), white communities would turn to sex segregation as a strategy to confine Black boys. Desegregation sparked fears that Black boys would socialize with white girls. Some schools in the South, which had led coeducation efforts some one hundred years earlier, now devised strategies to create single-sex schools as new options for white parents. Today's skeptics cite these "last-gasp attempts of segregationists" as evidence of the racist undertones in the history of expanding school choice for parents, now a key feature of neoliberal education.[62] Responding to the decision to open separate boys' and girls' schools in one Mississippi district, the school board's sole Black member flatly remarked, "The idea is to keep the Black boys from having any contact with the white girls—pure and simple."[63] Demanding the deference of dangerous Black men would help preserve the sanctity of white womanhood, while white men retained control of white women's bodies.[64]

A new boy crisis emerged on the eve of the twenty-first century. In the absence of much comprehensive research on masculinity in schools, anxious educators and parents have turned to trade publications concerned with "saving boys."[65] This "boy-industry" genre—including Dan Kindlon and Michael Thompson's *Raising Cain* (2000) and especially William Pollack's *Real Boys* (1998)—claims that young men now suffer from depression and low self-esteem. Pollack explicitly writes that coed schools favor girls over boys. A strong theme across boy-industry literature is that schools inappropriately feminize young men and therefore engage in a form of reverse gender discrimination.[66] Single-sex schooling proponents have their own reading list of "how-to" books, all of which stress that coed schools are increasingly not "boy friendly," by authors such as Leonard Sax and Michael Gurian.[67] According to this perspective, while boys and girls remain essentially different, this difference has nothing to do with inequality. Rather, inequality is the "naturally occurring outcome of difference."[68] By tailoring schools to the unique needs of boys and girls, sex-separate education embraces the increasingly dominant principle that the sexes are "different but equal." Indeed, the first-wave Black male academies emphasized the idea that "being equal does not mean being the same" and that hyperactivity and aggressiveness were "accepted as normal" among the boys at the school.[69] To be sure, young women do outperform young men on a range of measures. They earn, on average, higher grades in high school, and they graduate within four years at a higher rate.[70] Yet women and girls remain structurally disadvantaged relative to men, as educational success has not translated into full economic equality. Sociologist Philip Cohen has rebuked hand-wringing over the "end of men" by reminding us that women remain, despite incremental progress, a tiny minority "in the top echelons of wealth and power."[71] Men also continue to possess far greater symbolic control than women in cultural domains such as athletics.[72] Yet the "boy crisis" narrative persists because a new "soft essentialism" allows sympathizers to focus on the costs to boys while overlooking men's overall advantage in a gender order.[73]

There has been mounting criticism of essentialist claims. Researchers have dubbed such claims "pseudoscience" and an "essentialist myth."[74] The neuroscientist Lise Eliot explains that the best scientific evidence available shows that the "basic brain mechanisms of learning and memory do not differ between boys and girls."[75] Yet school districts continue to draw explicitly on these trade publications in crafting the "best practices" behind single-sex schooling.[76] The American Civil Liberties Union (ACLU) has led the charge against these practices. In 2012, its campaign, Teach Kids, Not Stereotypes, collected data on single-sex programs in a number of states.[77] The ACLU argued that most of the districts in their report drew on the flawed logic of hardwired brain differences between boys and girls and had repackaged sex stereotypes. The organization found that one middle school taught images of men as "warrior, protector, and provider." These beliefs reflect those in the boy-industry literature, which blend a "pining for an idyllic past" with "a spiritualist view of masculinity as inherent in a biology created by God."[78]

The feminist legal scholar Juliet Williams observes that a belief that boys and girls are "different but equal" not only spares proponents from having to explain historical patterns of sexism, but strategically distances them from the more insidious "separate but equal" doctrine associated with de jure racial segregation.[79] In fact, the boy-industry camp has selectively used the language of "disadvantaged boys" to advance its own agenda. Williams shows how texts in the boy-industry literature acknowledge the disproportionate harm that young men of color face, but still prioritize gender as the explanatory variable in children's educational inequalities.[80] Differences between Black boys and white boys are treated as matters of "nuance" and are generally subsumed under the perceived commonalities of young men.[81] In another example, Williams observes how Leonard Sax and others have increasingly invoked the language of "social justice" to defend the right to single-sex public education. In appropriating a phrase associated with civil rights struggles, "boys not traditionally associated with disadvantage" are able "to partake in a language of redress."[82] For example, the original name of the Sax-led National Association of Single-Sex Public Education was the National Association *for the Advancement* of Single-Sex Public Education, curiously reminiscent of the Black civil rights organization, the National Association for the Advancement of Colored People (NAACP). This is especially ironic because the NAACP rejected Black all-male schools when they were first proposed in the early 1990s. Why, then, would communities today support schools that historically have been used as a strategy to reinforce gender and racial hierarchies? To gain some purchase on this question, I turn to W. E. B. Du Bois himself, a cofounder of the NAACP.

The Black Nationalist Defense of All-Boys Education

Reflecting on Milwaukee's efforts to open male academies in the early 1990s, the NAACP warned that these schools would only replicate the damaging effects of segregating Black boys in punitive spaces such as special education rooms and disciplinary schools.[83] Benjamin Hooks, the executive director of the NAACP, asserted "that it would be a backward step with untold consequences to embrace the notion of officially sanctioned, state-sponsored racial segregation."[84] This view was consistent with the organization's long-standing commitment to *integrationism,* a racial ideology that rejects "any form of institutional separation based on racial categories" and fights "for full civil and political rights within the existing system of capitalist democracy."[85] This ideology became a foundation of Black emancipatory struggle following de jure segregation of public institutions under Jim Crow. In the inaugural (1910) issue of *The Crisis,* the NAACP's monthly periodical, Du Bois decried efforts to open racially segregated schools. Separate schoolchildren by race, the scholar warned, and "the result is war."[86]

It is startling, then, that Clifford Watson and Geneva Smitherman, two of the chief architects of this first wave of Black academies, identified Du Bois as a guiding light.[87] However, to use to the words of gender studies scholar Roderick Ferguson, these Black reformers were "incited" to different "norms, concepts, and ideals" associated with Du Bois.[88] The school reformers had used Du Bois strategically for achieving specific political goals. In a development that has received little attention in existing research, Black male academies have drawn inspiration from elite Black colleges. Watson and Smitherman were incited to a Du Bois who was giving a lecture at Fisk University (Du Bois's alma mater) in 1933. Du Bois now argued emphatically that Black-controlled educational institutions were necessary in the face of deepening racial segregation. Writing a year later in *The Crisis*, Du Bois advocated for voluntary separate schooling for Blacks (for the "race-conscious Black man cooperating together in his own institutions and movements"), but for the eventual integration of Blacks into mainstream society.[89]

Today's all-boys schooling proponents align with various intellectual and political traditions (such as Critical Race Theory and Black progressive education), but they are linked by Black Nationalism.[90] This ideology stresses Black agency and self-determination. It seeks "to strengthen in-group values while holding those promoted by the larger society at arm's length."[91] A Black Nationalist ideology has fought for community control over schools.[92] The community control tradition reveals that the "commitment to desegregated schooling" among Black families "is complex and certainly not unwavering."[93] Rather than offer unconditional support for integrated schools, actors in this tradition have yearned for "momentary" strategies amid an "educational terrain over which they have had little control."[94] In response to failed integration efforts in the 1960s and 1970s, community schools have fought to empower Black families to control *where* and *how* their children learn. For example, the first-wave Black male academies were built around two innovations that were rare in public schools at the time.[95] One was academic: the schools immersed themselves in Afrocentric themes, pedagogies, and curricula to challenge the Eurocentrism of public schooling. The other centered on the nature of within-school relationships, or forms of belonging. The schools recruited Black men to serve as mentors and role models for the Black boys.[96] In a 1991 issue of *The Crisis,* a Detroit school official emphasized "that community support for the academies' original all-male concept was overwhelming."[97] The district received twelve hundred applications for five hundred available spots.

More recently, Clarence Terry and colleagues have maintained that "stakeholders concerned with the education of African American students are well within their rights to call for more sympathetic, intentional, and effective schooling practices directed specifically at Black males."[98] Their inspiration? A brief 1935 article by Du Bois entitled "Does the Negro Need Separate Schools?" "God knows he does," was Du Bois's response.[99] White-dominated schools, Du Bois felt, possessed "unsympathetic teachers" and were marked with "hostile public opinion."[100] In 2006, a decade and a half after the Milwaukee and Detroit experiments, and now well into the era of No Child Left Behind, the NAACP reversed course and offered mild support for all-boys education. Theodore Shaw, the president of the organization's Legal Defense and Educational Fund, hinted strongly at the neoliberal logic behind this change of heart. "I believe," Shaw said, that "the crisis among Black males is so severe we have to have some room to experiment."[101]

Black Manhood and Governmentality

Black Boys Apart examines how in this contemporary neoliberal moment, Black leaders and Black institutions use Du Bois as a cultural and historical reference for fashioning a desirable Black manhood. My intention here is not to valorize Du Bois or to "discover" or "reject" him.[102] I do not mean for Du Bois's lessons on Black politics and education to be the final word on Black single-sex schooling. Rather, it is precisely the wide-ranging and revisionist nature of Du Bois's ideas on education, race, and gender that accentuate the promise *and* perils behind Black all-boys education, as well as the contradictions within this form of schooling.[103]

To gain traction on the formation of neoliberal subjectivities, I draw on Michel Foucault's notion of governmentality. In his observations of neoliberalism's ascendancy, Foucault developed this concept to refer to the ensemble of technologies and practices that regulate conduct and make people into appropriate subjects and citizens.[104] Unlike sovereign power, which secures domination through fear and terror, governmentality actively shapes a way of life—habits, sensibilities, and manners—in a more "gentle" fashion.[105] As David Garland writes, governmentality is not a coercive form of power that acts on docile subjects; rather, governmentality

> constructs individuals who are capable of choice and action, shapes
> them as active subjects, and seeks to align their choices with the choices
> of governing authorities. This kind of power does not seize hold of the
> individual's body in a disciplinary grip or regiment individuals into
> conformity. Instead it holds out technologies of the self, to be adopted
> by willing individuals who take an active part in their own
> "subjectification."[106]

Following this, feminist researchers have demonstrated how a "gendered governmentality" operates through institutions such as schools and the media, which regulate young people against a "neoliberal spreadsheet, a constant benchmarking of the self."[107] Discourses characterize youth of color as dangerous and in need of reform. Yet in a post-racial moment that falsely claims an end to racism (a narrative that hinges in part on the election of an African American man to the nation's highest seat; indeed, Barack Obama's presidency began the year of my research), youth are taught to internalize that success is a matter only of hard work, personal responsibility, and making the right choices.[108] Scholars such as Michael Dumas and Lester Spence have argued that a neoliberal governmentality constructs Black boys "as essentially damaged, as problems in need of technocratic public-private solution."[109] With declining state resources, corporations and other semiprivately owned institutions (such as charter schools) compete for the chance to create programs that will "solve" the problems facing poor Black boys.

This book argues that today's purportedly "innovative" all-male schools revise old notions about Black male reform. In this vein, Roderick Ferguson has suggested that Black actors are "incited" to Du Boisian intellectual and political ideas for the "creation of the self" in concrete moments.[110] In his early work, Du Bois famously argued that formal education, and particularly higher education, should serve as the training ground for a class of exceptional men: a "Talented Tenth" thesis that reverberates throughout today's Black male academies. As Du Bois wrote in 1903, "Men we shall have only as we make manhood the object of the work of the schools."[111] Reflecting on the condition of Black Americans during this period, Du Bois proffered an ideology of racial uplift: that the social advancement of Blacks required their integration into middle-class white society and that this would be achieved by embracing a moral character defined by temperance, chastity, and self-help.[112] Yet a respectability politics proved to be elitist. As historian Martin Summers writes, from the post-Emancipation era to the advent of Jim Crow, demonstrating a "capacity for citizenship" for Blacks "required drawing gender and class lines within the community."[113] Even as Du Bois's thinking evolved and developed a more gender-egalitarian and democratic form of racial uplift, I will show that Black male academies "freeze" specific constructions of Du Boisian thought for their own political ends.[114]

Sociological studies of respectability have typically pursued one of two tracks. In the first, individual Black men assert their moral superiority over less respectable Black men, who are variously characterized as irresponsible, lazy, and hypersexual.[115] Or Black men adjust their behaviors and mannerisms to distance themselves from "controlling images" of deviant Black masculinity.[116] A second line of research examines how academically oriented and law-abiding young Black men ("schoolboys") navigate competing expectations from their peers and from authorities such as police officers and school staff members.[117] *Black Boys Apart,* however, is unique in focusing on how all-male education as a social movement seeks to institutionalize respectability and to lift up and reform Black men. Chapters

3 and 4 hone in on how male academies take part in these practices through their curricula and relationships, respectively.

With its focus on how gender domination is secured through *consent and persuasion,* hegemonic masculinity again proves to be a useful framework.[118] To explain the construction of Black male identity at the start of the twentieth century, Martin Summers stresses that hegemony does not operate through sheer domination. Instead, it normativizes a worldview and seeks to secure the "consent of marginalized communities to that normativization"; therefore, "the relationship between these masculinities is not always one of antagonism," or resistance.[119] As I see it, in seeking what Du Bois called the "advancement of men," Black male academies navigate a dialectic central to Black U.S. political history: that between resistance and accommodation to hegemonic power.[120] Consent, in this instance, is not a matter of people being "duped," but rather clarifies how groups and individuals adopt dominant masculine norms as a means of social advancement.[121] This process has important consequences. Summers continues,

> As hegemonic masculinity relies on negative referents for its construction and contributes to relations of domination and subordination *between* men in dominant and subordinated social groups, so too does the social construction of masculinity contribute to relations of power *within* those marginalized communities. Using a model of hegemony also allows us to think about the influence of marginalized masculinities on the culturally dominant gender conventions—Black masculinity as "counter-hegemonic."[122]

In other words, asserting hegemonic dominance in a local context promotes *intra*-racial division. This book demonstrates that those divisions are aggravated by a respectability politics that intensifies under neoliberalism. Yet because hegemony is always contested, actors can mobilize to challenge its dominance. In the Conclusion I discuss how the seeds of effective counter-hegemonic struggle are found in Du Bois's notion of an abolition democracy.

While governmentality shifts attention to the noncoercive features of power, violence and coercion are not absent under hegemonic regimes. In Antonio Gramsci's original formulation of hegemony, domination is the ability to win the consent of the masses, in conjunction with the state's ability to use coercion to control groups that fail to provide that consent.[123] As several excellent qualitative studies have shown, authorities in and out of schools surveil, harass, and punish young men of color more than their peers.[124] This book is therefore attuned to how coercion and governmentality work together to discipline young Black men.

The Black Feminist Challenge to All-Boys Education

Hegemonic masculinity also subordinates women to men. To round out the historical context of these schools, we need finally to understand the steady resistance to Black male academies. The Detroit and Milwaukee academies never opened as all-male. Alongside charges of racial segregation, the ACLU and the National Organization for Women (NOW) represented families in a case claiming that the academies discriminated against young Black women, who were also struggling in Detroit public schools. In denying similar opportunities to girls, these exclusive all-male schools therefore segregated based on sex. A district court agreed that the proposed all-male academies violated federal statutes mandating sex equality in public education. An unfortunate consequence of these and subsequent battles has been the perception that feminist efforts have sought to thwart interventions for disadvantaged children.[125] According to this view, feminists are elitists who use gender ideology to impede racial progress. Indeed, educators who helped design the Detroit academies described NOW's claims as "an attack from outside the community."[126] More recently, the ACLU's Teach Kids, Not Stereotypes initiative has angered advocates by continuing to call single-sex education a form of segregation.[127] This issue will remain contested given that the judicial scales have slowly started to tip in favor of all-boys proponents. In a 2011 case in which the ACLU challenged the legality of single-sex classes in Kentucky, the presiding judge dismissed the claim of segregation and declared that "no such historically-grounded injury has been recognized as inherent in the separation of students by sex."[128]

Black feminist theory offers a potent challenge to the revival of Black male academies. An intellectual tradition that draws on the collective experiences and knowledges of Black women, Black feminism dates to early Black abolitionist struggles and is today a vibrant scholarly tradition.[129] Black feminist theory casts light on how patriarchy interacts with racism and other systems of oppression. This work unsettles a hegemonic order by focusing on the destructive consequences of domination. A Black feminist perspective is skeptical of initiatives that assume that granting Black men more gender privilege will address the problems facing the Black community.[130] This perspective suggests that all-male education and other well-intentioned programs may reproduce gender inequality even as they press forward under the banner of anti-racism.[131] As Patricia Hill Collins writes, while Black Nationalism and Afrocentrism (traditional pillars of the pro-Black male academy camp) possess oppositional and liberatory potential, they historically have relied on a sexist politics. The emphasis on racial solidarity has tended to rely on a conservative gender ideology in which it is the duty of women to be "good" mothers while a "benevolent male authority ruled."[132] In this way, Black Nationalism has held up the patriarchal and heteronormative family structure as a vehicle to racial liberation.

Black Boys Apart therefore asks how Black all-boys schools reproduce and challenge gender and sexual inequality as part of a larger effort toward the racial uplift of Black communities. Black feminism critiques the view of Black men and boys today as the paradigmatic victims of racial oppression. This view is rooted in historical racial struggles that emphasized "the victimization of Black men through lynching or economic exclusion" while "silencing the particular victimizations of Black women."[133] Following this, Kimberlé Crenshaw argues that federal programs (such as President Obama's My Brother's Keeper initiative) demonstrate how "'fixing' men of color—particularly young Black men—hits a political sweet spot among populations that both love and fear them."[134] Crenshaw implies that those who "fear" young Black men will support programs that will ostensibly groom them to be more respectable.

Moreover, feminist scholars contest the view that intentional race-separate educational spaces are sufficient justification for intentional sex-separate schools. As Juliet Williams argues, Terry and his colleagues (who adopt a Black Nationalist standpoint) make an inappropriate "leap" from Du Bois's defense of all-*Black* schools to an argument for all-*boys* schools targeted to young Black men.[135] This leap suggests that coed schools (and Black girls by association) discriminate against Black boys in a similar way that racially mixed schools have historically discriminated against Black children. Yet according to Williams, this position is untenable as it suggests that Black boys should be provided opportunities at the expense of Black girls, when Black girls themselves are also severely disadvantaged in schools. I agree with Williams that all-boys education can pose harm to women and girls. But to reject all-boys education entirely for this reason overlooks a complex history of Black families seeking greater control in how their schools look and operate.

Researching All-Boys Schools

The next chapter provides a detailed introduction to the city and the schools at the heart of this study: Perry High, a combined middle and high school for boys in grades seven through twelve, and Northside Academy, a college-preparatory charter school for boys in grades nine through eleven. (There was not yet a class of twelfth graders when I conducted my research at Northside.) This section covers how I collected and analyzed my data. I adopted an ethnographic approach in order to gain a "deep social portrait" of the two schools.[136] I observed the two schools during the eleven-month academic year of 2009–10, which included the regular school year and the summer-school period. My observations at each school averaged twenty-five hours per week.

Outside of class, I interacted with the young men in the cafeteria, at practices and games, and at assemblies. I spent additional time with a few different student groups, such as an anime club at Northside Academy and a newly formed gay–straight alliance student group at Perry High. I observed special gatherings, such as back-to-school nights, teacher recruitment events, family information sessions, faculty meetings, and staff professional development sessions. I occasionally accompanied the young men off school grounds to places such as a college fair and the city court. To build trust and to strengthen my presence in the school, I sought out and welcomed opportunities to help.[137] These ranged from serving food at mentoring meetings to leading a résumé workshop for students.

I supplemented my observations with 150 interviews with students, parents, teachers, administrators, and school district officials. (See Table 1 in the Appendix for a breakdown.) The interviews were semi-standardized, with a set of predetermined questions and opportunities for the interviewees to speak on topics of their choosing.[138] The interviews with the young men typically lasted between forty-five and sixty minutes, and those with adults lasted between seventy-five and ninety minutes. I interviewed a small number of parents and students in pairs. Each person received a small gift card for participating in the interview. My goal was to interview a wide range of school community members as well as a large diversity of students ($n = 64$) and teachers ($n = 36$). I intentionally sought out students from each grade and, at Northside Academy, students who had attended a range of middle schools (public, charter, and private/parochial). My sampling was also purposive for the teachers, who taught a range of grade levels and subjects, had varying levels of experience, and were of varied ethnic and racial backgrounds.

My methodological guide for this research was the *extended case method*. This approach to ethnography is not concerned primarily with the "generalizability" of specific cases. Thus, the aim of *Black Boys Apart* is not to assess the "statistical significance" of single-sex education or to offer firm conclusions on what "works" in these schools. This view departs from existing research, which has highlighted similarities among male academies, despite their important variability.[139] Rather, the extended case method seeks "societal significance. The importance of the single case lies in what it tells us about society as a whole rather than about the population of similar cases."[140] It focuses on anomalies and variations among similar cases and uses those to intervene in existing theory. Therefore, despite their institutional differences, my comparison is not to judge the "failures" of one school against the "successes" of the other, but to see how their varied efforts deepen understanding of collective, ongoing efforts to reform Black manhood and of the sociopolitical context in which they occur.

The extended case method involves three "dialogues": (1) between the researcher and those he or she observes in the field, (2) between the local processes of the field site and historical forces, and (3) between theories.[141] First, I was in constant dialogue with people at the schools, who had wide-ranging perspectives on the schools and came from diverse backgrounds. At the outset, people I met were curious about my motivations for the study. I found it helpful to describe how my larger interests in educational inequities grew out of my own experiences as a teacher in a low-income, predominantly Black public school. Many people were also curious about my background, and I found that speaking openly about my identity as the child of Cambodian immigrants helped establish trust. However, I recognized that my experiences of having "been there" could lead to wrong assumptions, so I welcomed conversations with those wishing to tell me what was distinctive about their schools.[142]

The second dialogue behind the extended case method involves a movement between "localized interventions" and "broader structuring external social forces."[143] This dialogue "extends" the micro-level, daily interactions inside Perry High and Northside Academy to a larger urban ecology in which those schools are situated (defined by relationships between and among schools, law enforcement, families, the court system, and churches), and finally to a wider political field, marked by Black political and educational mobilization in the face of failed integration efforts; the enduring embrace of racial uplift ideology; and a current neoliberal conjuncture, years in the making, which has signaled the privatized, punitive, and respectable turns in Black schooling. As I envisioned it, this second dialogue placed the schools on a historical trajectory "to connect the present to the past in anticipation of the future."[144]

Last is the dialogue of theory with itself. One task of theory is to narrate a coherent story out of a diverse set of standpoints and observations. As sociologist Michael Burawoy writes, this means engaging continuously with theory: moving "out" to theories to make sense of observations after a day in the schools, and then moving back "in" to the schools, always with theoretical glasses on, in a recursive process. At a more practical level, I found that theories were never in short supply. People were eager to explain to me why they felt the schools worked or did not work and why the schools even existed in the first place. As feminist researchers have noted, "standpoints" can rise beyond an individual's perspective to the level of group production, or "communal achievement." In other words, they generate theory.[145]

As a first-year graduate student, I read and absorbed Du Bois's *The Philadelphia Negro*, the first systematic study of race in the United States and a model of meticulous urban sociology. Years later, Du Bois spoke regretfully of his relationships with the Black Philadelphians he had met. He had been a "cold and scientific investigator, with microscope and probe," and found that people received him "with no open arms" and "had a natural dislike to being studied like a strange species."[146] These reflections were never far from my mind as I thought of my own positionality at Northside Academy and Perry High. I was fortunate that I generally found it easy to interact with the young men, many of whom wanted to share their thoughts on their school because of its uniqueness. Given Northside's college prep mission, the staff also encouraged students to ask adults (including me) about their college experiences. However, children can distrust unfamiliar authority figures, so it was important for me to build rapport with the boys before requesting interviews.

Following the lead of childhood scholars, I envisioned the young men as both "becomings," or as growing individuals on certain life trajectories, and as independent "beings" in their own right.[147] I used Alford Young Jr.'s interviews with marginalized Black men as a general blueprint for how to organize my interviews with the boys.[148] I asked them to describe their social worlds (the school, their families, their neighborhoods, their peer networks, and larger society) and to situate themselves inside those worlds. I also asked them to imagine how they would fit into these various social worlds as they grew older. I found that the students frequently broached issues about race and disadvantage, especially when I asked them to speak about their communities and to describe why they think their all-male school was founded. Encouraging them to speak about such sensitive issues also helped build trust.[149]

Organization of the Book

The first chapter situates all-boys education in the massive public school reforms that have swept the country since the turn of the century. While Perry High and Northside Academy set out on different trajectories, each was shaped by the transition to market fundamentalism in the public school sector. At Perry, officials—including the school's new for-profit manager—made a hasty decision to convert to an all-boys model. Without a clear mission for innovation, the school fell into disarray. The pressure for accountability within the school district's new neoliberal governance created an unduly punitive environment at Perry. Across town, Northside Academy's founder embraced the city's new market principles and understood that his school needed to gain an edge in an increasingly competitive schooling market. Northside did not so much innovate as imitate the culture, character, and curricula of elite schools.

In chapter 2 I offer a detailed portrait of the young men and how they enacted different forms of masculinity. I then illustrate the myriad and sometimes contradictory ways that members of both school communities understood the separation of boys and girls. These took the form of several discourses, including a discourse of distractions, a discourse of teenage pregnancy, a discourse of competition, and a discourse of motivation. A final discourse crystalized in each school taking on the reputation as "the gay school," a particularly troubling formation shaped by race, sexuality, and gender that refracted different meanings at the two schools.

The focus of chapter 3 is on how these schools teach their boys. I link the curricula of the schools to historical attempts to teach the *head* (to offer a classical, liberal arts education), the *hand* (technical or industrial education), and the *heart* (virtuous character) of Black children. Unlike Perry High, Northside Academy benefited from a clear academic mission intended to prepare the young men for "the race to college." This mission exemplified what Du Bois termed a "college-bred community." The school's curriculum was intended to cultivate the disciplined bodies and minds necessary for a respectable identity. Perry High, on the other hand, lacked a strong standardized curriculum, but the staff made an effort to practice cultural relevance. Key members of the community also challenged the hegemonic utility of a "college for all" ethos and envisioned expanded career and technical education to prepare a greater number of boys for success after high school.

Chapter 4 shows how a religious spirit animated the two schools and considers how they in turn nurtured different kinds of families, or solidarity among fictive kin. To increase the young men's sense of belonging, the "race men" of Perry High—a Black male leadership—articulated a responsibility to provide a care that had eroded in the neighborhood. Drawing on the legacy of the first-wave academies, Perry High implemented a multipronged program to provide boys with male mentors. By contrast, Northside de-emphasized male role-modeling in favor of strong relationships among the boys: a brotherhood of exceptional and upwardly mobile students. This chapter also examines several factors that nurtured or threatened belonging in the school: the presence of influential (white) female teachers, school discipline, and the young men's friends outside the school community.

Chapter 5 links themes from the previous chapters and examines how the schools cultivated different kinds of men. These scripts for manhood and citizenship were shaped and constrained by the very neoliberal context from which the schools emerged. The schools aimed to build different kinds of respectable men. The Northside brotherhood was aimed at protecting young men who would graduate and become successful workers and leaders, whom I call *ambitious entrepreneurs*. The young men looked out for one another in the present (in the form of a brotherhood) so they could one day thrive as individual workers in a global economy. By contrast, Perry High saw divergent tracks for their young men. While school officials hoped that their most accomplished students would go on to stable and successful careers outside the city, they also put forth the vision that their students could become *heroic family men* who care for their children, their partners, and the many fictive kin (especially Black boys) who desperately needed good men to lead the way. The young men also embraced visions of responsible fatherhood. The school, unlike Northside, lacked a brotherhood; instead, the young men at Perry took care of themselves in the present so they could one day take care of their own families and local communities.

In the Conclusion, I take stock of the evidence in these pages to consider the implications of all-boys schooling for the uplift of Black men and Black communities. Evincing neoliberalism's contradictory politics, Black male academies are a strange mix of democratic empowerment and privatization, segregation and separation, strict discipline and love. As a form of schooling given new life by the convergence of neoliberal social policies and a respectability politics, all-boys schools serve ultimately as a cautionary tale for Black activists and school reformers. Rather than asking boys to be resilient and to reform their character, a better path forward aligns with what Du Bois called "abolition democracy," where an alliance of social movements *hopes and hustles together* in a fight against oppression.

CHAPTER ONE

A Tale of Two (Neoliberal) Schools

The Origins of Perry High and Northside Academy

"Morgan is a proud city."

Bill Harris shared these words with me during a visit to his office at the start of my research. He was an administrator with the school district and had earlier led the effort to open the city's first all-boys public school. Mr. Harris offered as evidence of the city's pride a rabid fan base for the city's sports teams. There were also the cultural traditions and quirks that made the city distinctive. "But," he continued, "the problems here are really big." It was common to see empty lots and boarded-up homes. Homicide rates had leveled off but remained disturbingly high. And the school system knew only "the status quo," a phrase he repeated several times that morning. Mr. Harris saw himself as a true entrepreneur, an outsider who came in with the expertise needed to resuscitate a behemoth and severely underperforming schooling bureaucracy. He pointed to a framed article on the wall behind his desk. It was from a popular magazine. The headline read, "DOES THE MORGAN EXPERIMENT MAKE THE GRADE?" The article profiled leaders, like himself, of the privatization movement in the city's schools. "The people here are too set in their ways," Mr. Harris told me. "We needed to show them a different way. And now that experiment is becoming a way of life."

This chapter chronicles the origins of the two schools at the heart of this study. The schools emerged just as the district's experiment was becoming a way of life in the city of Morgan. During a historic public schooling reform effort, key stakeholders came together and grappled with the problem of how to provide their respective schools with a sense of legitimacy. The district's new market fundamentalism shaped the schools' trajectories in dissimilar ways. At Perry High, school officials struggled to offer a rigorous plan for innovation, a key priority of citywide educational reform. With the school's future in doubt, officials relied on punitive measures to meet the city's demands for accountability. With a clear vision laid out by its founder, Northside avoided many of the challenges that dogged Perry High. The school founder recognized the need for Northside to assert a clear, respectable identity in a schooling market that bred intense competition. Rather than truly innovate, Northside found "role models" in other successful schools. Northside envisioned a future by turning to the past, adopting a "dead language," and attempting to emulate elite schools with traditions of excellence. Understanding the respective histories of the schools can help us make sense of developments that would inspire and haunt the schools in the subsequent years.

Schooling in the Neoliberal City

The city of Morgan's demographics were transformed by the influx of African Americans during the Great Migration (ca. 1916–1970).[1] In 2010, the year I completed my fieldwork, African Americans constituted the city's largest racial group at nearly 45 percent of the population, which represented one of the largest native-born Black populations in the United States. The eastern and northern neighborhoods of Morgan that were home to Perry High and Northside Academy, respectively, had for decades faced acute levels of racial segregation. In these neighborhoods, more than 80 percent of residents were Black. The student population of the Morgan Public School District was similarly segregated. In the 2009–10 school year, Blacks represented the largest student racial group at 62 percent, and nearly three-quarters of the student population qualified for free or reduced-price lunch. Deindustrialization had taken hold in Morgan in the decades following World War II, as blue-collar factory jobs dried up stateside and industries moved to other shores. By 2010, Morgan had a poverty rate of 26.7 percent, compared to the national average of 15.1 percent.

At the turn of the twenty-first century, Morgan had emerged as a paradigmatic neoliberal city, determined to use market solutions to address long-standing social ills. Between 1990 and 2010, the city's middle-class core slumped as whites left the city in large numbers for suburbs, enticed by low-interest mortgages and higher-achieving schools.[2] By the early 2000s, many Catholic schools, once vibrant schooling options, had closed for good, which also prompted some middle-class white families to leave the city. In a none-too-veiled attempt to lure these families back, the city entered into the first of several large corporate partnerships. A private organization representing Morgan's largest downtown firms partnered with the school district to create a new downtown school choice area that would give local residents access to some of the city's highest-achieving schools. As part of this larger "urban renaissance," in 2010 Morgan also launched a comprehensive tourism campaign to bring in badly needed revenue.

Black communities have been victimized by the restructuring of space and capital in neoliberal regimes.[3] Neighborhoods on the margins of downtown Morgan grew increasingly white, and by 2000 the metropolis was among the ten most rapidly gentrifying cities in the nation.[4] The city's already-disadvantaged families faced heightened economic insecurity during the year of my fieldwork. As Jordan Camp writes, racial segregation "trapped poor people of color in spaces that have been targeted by finance capital for predatory lending of subprime loans," which helped trigger the decade's Great Recession.[5] As a result of the economic downturn, median net worth of Black households declined by over 50 percent between 2005 and 2009, compared to 16 percent for whites.[6] The recession also wreaked havoc on job market outcomes for African Americans across class backgrounds. The unemployment rate more than doubled for Black college graduates during this period, and for young Black men it had reached 30 percent, a level that surpassed the national average during the Great Depression.[7]

The neoliberalization of Morgan took on a spectacular form in the city's public schools, thus making them ideal sites for my research. In the early 2000s, the city emerged as one of the country's leading laboratories for school privatization. For those who support privatized education, democratic governance deserves the blame for the ineffectiveness of schools. Multiple layers of bureaucracy mean poor oversight, little accountability, and a system ill-equipped to respond to the needs of education's "consumers," or families and children. The embrace of the free market by school systems today is the outcome of a long process going back decades. As Lisa Duggan writes, in the 1970s pro-business interests capitalized on fears wrought by increasing global competition and plunging profit margins. The election of Ronald Reagan as president a decade later marked a vicious backlash against the social redistributive politics characteristic of the earlier periods of the New Deal and the civil rights movement, which had nurtured a welfare state liberalism.[8] This form of counter-insurgency has historical precedent.[9] And as Mr. Harris described it at the start of this chapter, privatization and entrepreneurialism have become a "way of life" in Black communities: a commonsense belief that marks neoliberalism as a "deeply saturating, hegemonic cultural framework."[10] As Lester Spence has argued, "through neoliberal governmentality, a range of problems within Black communities have been taken outside the realm of the political by rendering them *technical* and *actionable.*"[11]

The neoliberal turn in U.S. education can be traced back to the start of Reagan's presidency, as well. In provocative language, a 1983 White House–commissioned report, *A Nation at Risk,* asserted that a "tide of mediocrity" in the U.S. educational system posed harm to "our very future as a Nation and as a people."[12] Neoliberal ideologies began to solidify in national educational policy with Goals 2000, signed into law by President Bill Clinton in 1994, which stressed standards and outcomes. No Child Left Behind (NCLB), however, fully codified neoliberal principles into educational law.[13] Signed into law in 2001, NCLB gave state and local school boards greater flexibility in how they use federal education funds, but it demands greater accountability in return. With an emphasis on experimentation and innovation, charter schools have emerged as popular options for parents. These schools are free to determine their own governance structure, curricula, and hiring practices.[14] While charters predate NCLB, they have thrived under the law. Between 2000 and 2014, the number of charters more than quadrupled, and today they educate more than 2.6 million children nationwide.[15] A bipartisan amendment to NCLB effectively legalized nonvocational single-sex classrooms and schools.[16] In speeches before the Senate, congressional leaders Kay Bailey Hutchison and Hillary Clinton defended single-sex schools on the grounds of increased school choice options.[17] In 2006, the Department of Education (DOE) released additional guidelines for single-sex public education. These regulations specified that, under certain conditions, single-sex education would not violate Title IX.[18] These schools and classrooms must also be voluntary. Eight years later, the DOE offered stricter guidelines for single-sex arrangements.[19] However, the guidelines are intended only for single-sex classrooms, and as of this writing the DOE has yet to release more detailed guidelines for entirely single-sex public schools.

Just as the country was getting to know NCLB, Morgan underwent its own comprehensive school reform. Citing chronic student underachievement and financial struggles, the state capital intervened and assumed control of the school district. The state legislature and the governor viewed the transition as a much-needed opportunity to fix a broken school system. The message was clear: the state had lost faith in the city to manage its own schools. The state created a small committee, the City School Board (CSB), with near total control of school district policies, finances, and major educational goals. Some were worried that the CSB would weaken democratic governance in schools, as power had been consolidated in the hands of the committee's few unelected officials. And in short order, the CSB would wield enormous influence over the school district. The committee's response to critics would become the calling card for privatized schooling efforts all across the country: school reform would empower individual families by letting them make the educational choices they viewed as best for their own children. This also meant that blame fell squarely on individuals, should they fail to make the "right" schooling choices.

In January 2010, near the halfway point of my year of research, Secretary of Education Arne Duncan gave a speech on the occasion of Dr. Martin Luther King Jr.'s eighty-first birthday. "If Dr. King were here today," Duncan remarked, "he would call on a new generation of leaders to build upon his work by doing the most important thing each of you can do: get an education, learn to think, learn to compete, and *learn to win.*" The educational researcher Pauline Lipman disagrees: King would have likely been disappointed by the "self-serving individualism" that animated Duncan's remarks and has become common sense to politicians across the political divide.[20] While other scholars have praised all-boys schools for helping Black boys "win,"[21] we need a deeper understanding of the games that markets produce: who wins, who loses, and what precisely is at stake.

In several ways, the Morgan School District came to bear "the unmistakable imprint of market theory" and of the desire to win.[22] The first way was *standardization*. The CSB required Morgan schools to align their curricula with state math and reading standards. Under the new regime, standards laid out grade-level expectations for children in an attempt to increase transparency. More frequent standardized testing would give families much-needed data about their own children's performance as well as information about school performance that would allow families to be more educated consumers. The school district would hand out "school report cards" that would assess schools on a variety of "measurable" indicators, such as academics and school safety.

Second, the CSB ushered in a new era of *innovation*. With the backing of the governor, the board invited applications for charter schools and educational management organizations (EMOs). The CSB would play a key role in the development of the two schools in this book: Perry High School turned to a single-sex model at the behest of its new EMO, while Northside Academy would open a few years later as a charter school. The state just a few years before had passed legislation that legalized charter schools, and with the new CSB leading the way, charter applications rose sharply. Educational management organizations, meanwhile, are private, generally for-profit organizations that enter into contracts with school districts in order to manage schools.[23] In Morgan, EMOs submitted bids to manage several dozen of the lowest-performing schools. The thinking was that decentralized control of schools would spark innovation and, as

Mr. Harris told me, would "get these schools moving that have been stuck in a rut."

The linking of standards and innovation highlights the third feature of privatization under the new educational regime: *accountability*. Nationwide, public schools began facing the threat of sanctions for falling short of performance targets (particularly AYP, or "adequate yearly progress"). In Morgan, charters and EMOs were under pressure to meet targets in order to have their contracts renewed. As the thinking went, in a competitive marketplace of schools, the high-achieving schools (and presumably the more "innovative" ones) would remain open, and the low-achieving schools would eventually close. For bureaucratic institutions such as schools, increased accountability demands standardization: administrators closely monitor teachers to ensure they are meeting appropriate learning objectives and are using "best practices."

Fourth, public school reform in the city of Morgan had come to embrace an ethos of *competition*. In his masterful 1978–79 lectures, Michel Foucault documented how neoliberal rationality had replaced exchange with competition as the basic principle behind markets.[24] Following the new trend to use report cards to assess, rank, and make quantifiable all facets of schooling, school leaders in Morgan competed with one another for a "passing" score of 3.0, which would win approval for their charter applications. (The CSB used a 4.0 scale to grade charter school proposals along various dimensions, including safety, finances, and school design.) As I argue in this book, an ethic of competition was built into the institutional DNA of Northside Academy, with likely repercussions for equality and the distribution of resources within the Black community.

Last, school privatization has gone hand in hand with expanded *surveillance*. A neoliberal racial capitalism is committed to the strict enforcement of order and has helped spawn the widespread policing of Black bodies.[25] As Victor Rios describes, the seeds of mainstream fears over urban ghettos and threatening Black men were sown during the civil rights movement. Calls for "law and order" set the stage for the now-ubiquitous "tough on crime" measures implemented in the 1980s. The orientation toward maintaining social order rapidly shifted from rehabilitation to exclusion. Aggressive forms of policing, particularly for low-level offenses, are now the norm in urban communities and have "prompted a prison boom," as today the United States incarcerates a far greater percentage of its population than any other country in the world.[26] The spread of neoliberalism has meant that cities have drawn on the language of cost-effectiveness to recruit an array of actors and institutions in their surveillance efforts.[27] In the context of schooling, zero-tolerance policies may push a color-blind rhetoric of equal justice under the law, yet these policies fall unevenly along gender and racial lines.[28] By the end of the 1990s, rising rates of youth incarceration and rates of gun violence in the city of Morgan had prompted changes in youth discipline. The school district began to outfit its high schools with metal detectors. Unarmed police officers became the norm in hallways. Zero-tolerance policies spread across the district. In one of the more vivid examples of the merger of penality and privatization, the school district contracted with a private company to operate its high-security alternative placement schools, which enrolled students who had committed major infractions in their neighborhood schools.

City residents, community groups, and the city's teacher's union organized and protested the city's neoliberal turn in Black politics. To call attention to the mortgage crisis, citizens picketed outside major banks to draw attention to these "subprime predators." Others gathered outside school district headquarters with signs that read, "I AM NOT FOR SALE." They especially targeted the new CSB (a group that had a bad reputation among the people I met), which did not hide its enthusiasm for new charter schools. Still, the entrenchment of market fundamentalism does not cancel out democratic politics completely. Many Black-controlled schools are, in the words of Amy Stuart Wells and her colleagues, "very democratic in a very neoliberal sort of way."[29] Rather than discard corporate and market solutions, Black communities have sometimes used them strategically. In the view of progressive educators, Black families here are not victims of larger forces (such as white flight). Instead, a community control tradition views families as active participants in the school choice process who "tactically navigate a complex educational terrain that is not largely of their own choosing."[30] This tradition protects the right of Black communities to determine where and how their children are educated.[31] The sociologist Lisa Stulberg has shown how privatization and Black democratic empowerment have at times mingled as strange bedfellows. Stulberg identifies several historical forerunners to today's school choice movement for Blacks.[32] In the 1960s, Black families in New York City responded to failed desegregation plans by fighting for "community schools" where they could hire their own principals and teachers and build culturally relevant curricula.

Perry High and Northside Academy emerged from this cauldron of politics and markets. It was a time when Black communities were fighting for shared governance in their local schools and for the right to control where and how their children were educated. It was a moment when public schooling was settling on a bedrock of standardization, innovation, accountability, competition, and surveillance. I next provide an overview of both schools before diving into the schools' respective histories.

Perry High School

The view of Perry High School was striking. Gothic-style architecture and corner spires dwarfed the row homes that lined the surrounding one-way streets. School community members described the school's exterior as intimidating and as resembling a castle or cathedral. Yet it was its resemblance to a prison—with its barred and padlocked windows and metal detectors—that would have the most profound and harmful effect. This reputation had taken on new meanings through the 2000s with the school's focus on crime control, and students felt that community members had stigmatized the school for being criminal and disorderly.[33] The interior of the building, meanwhile, was a study in contrasts. Old pictures of famous alumni hung alongside large laminated posters of the latest state reading and math standards. The hallway's worn-down features alternated with inspirational messages painted in bold strokes: "YOUR OPTIONS ARE ONLY LIMITED BY YOUR FEARS." "EVERY JOB IS A SELF-PORTRAIT OF THE PERSON WHO DID IT. AUTOGRAPH YOUR WORK WITH EXCELLENCE." "A GREAT PLEASURE IN LIFE IS DOING WHAT PEOPLE SAY YOU CANNOT DO."

While other neighborhoods in East Morgan had seen public housing development and moderate business growth, the area around Perry had remained largely untouched, a casualty of entrenched poverty. This neighborhood had a median household income of $22,000, well below the median income of $36,000 for the city. With few funds for redevelopment, abandoned city-owned homes dotted the streets around Perry. Wooden boards were nailed to the windows, and orange signs on the front doors read "In Danger of Collapse."

Perry was a traditional (noncharter) public high school. It had been targeted for additional support after failing in consecutive years to meet benchmarks laid out by No Child Left Behind. After the restructuring of the school district, Perry High saw its student enrollment decline by nearly 50 percent over a five-year period. Many students had left for charters and other public schools. With enrollment down, the school building often felt big for its student body. Even between classes, the hallways rarely filled up. During the 2009–10 school year that I observed there, Perry High School enrolled approximately 450 boys in grades seven through twelve. The school district officially listed the school as 99 percent African American. Neither the school nor the district kept an official tally, but a small number of students were West African immigrants. The large majority of the student body was class disadvantaged, with 89 percent of students qualifying for free or reduced-priced lunch. The school had seven administrators; all were Black, and six were men. These included the principal, Mr. Bradley, and a number of full- and part-time assistant principals who were veteran administrators (some former principals themselves) who took on various responsibilities and served as mentors for the principal. The seventh administrator was a woman who was hired to manage several new initiatives funded by a new federal grant, a proud accomplishment for the school's leadership. Forty-three percent of the faculty was male, and one-third of the teaching staff was Black. Perry High also employed several full- and part-time school police officers.

Northside Academy

Nestled in the northern section of Morgan was Northside Academy, an all-boys charter high school. During my year of observation, Northside served approximately 370 boys in grades nine through eleven. Northside opened in 2007 with one ninth-grade class and added a grade each year. (So there was not yet a class of twelfth graders when I conducted my research at the school during the 2009–10 school year.) Ninety-nine percent of the students were African American. The vast majority came from low-income families, with 86 percent qualifying for free or reduced-priced lunch. While this demographic composition resembled that of Perry High, Northside appeared to have a higher percentage of families who qualified as working poor.[34]

Approximately 60 percent of the students had attended regular public schools for middle school. Most of the remaining students attended a charter middle school, and a small minority came from private and parochial schools. The leadership was much smaller at Northside, with three administrators: the founder/CEO, the principal, and a dean who oversaw discipline. All of these positions were filled by African American men. The makeup of the teaching staff differed markedly from that at Perry. Over three-quarters of the teachers were men (compared to 43 percent of the faculty at Perry), while only 17 percent of the staff was Black (compared to 34 percent at Perry). As a charter, Northside also had a board of trustees. Its members were community leaders who oversaw fund-raising, managed the school's finances, and made sure that the school abided by the terms of its charter. With the help of the trustees, the school had secured resources and programs unavailable at many public schools, from extra technology (e.g., used laptops for each student) to special summer internships.

Northside opened in an old building that had sat vacant for years. After a year of renovations, students and staff found themselves inside a building whose interior contrasted sharply with its old and gray exterior. There were bright lights, wall-to-wall carpeting, and modern finishes. Unlike Perry, a building that was now too large for its student body, Northside sometimes felt cramped inside, with student traffic unavoidable in the hallways between classes. The small building, however, gave the school a daily jolt of energy and a sense of closeness.

Windows in a large third-floor science classroom offered a spectacular view of the city: hundreds of densely packed row homes with colorful awnings in North Morgan and, in the distance, the tall buildings downtown. Unlike the neighborhood that Perry called home, Northside was located on a busy road. Around the corner from Northside was Cole Avenue, the community's designated main street, which teemed with small businesses and street vendors. After school, students from local schools flooded the streets, the schools they attended easily identifiable by the colored shirts the students wore. While Northside drew students from a mostly similar class background as those at Perry High, the neighborhood in which Northside was located had been the site of more economic growth and gentrification. The median household income for the area was $30,000.

In its early years, and during the time of my research, the school admitted students on a first-come-first-served basis. (Since growing in popularity, the school has moved to a lottery system.) To apply, prospective eighth-grade students and their parents first attend an informational session. The students then shadow a current ninth grader in classes and sit for an interview with the school's admissions director, Julia Martinez. As with all charters, a student's academic record did not figure into the admissions decision. As Ms. Martinez said, "We don't ask for grades because we don't want to make it seem like we're being selective." After three years of admitting students, boys representing a wide range of ability levels had donned the Northside blazer. As Mr. Green, the principal, told a room of prospective teachers one day, "Many boys arrive several reading grade levels behind, and some are tenth-graders who are at college level." Still, as I explain later in the chapter, there were strong selection biases, as the school attracted and recruited academically serious students.

Becoming All-Boys at Perry High School

Seeking Innovation

In one of its first bold moves, the new City School Board contracted with a number of different EMOs to manage its chronically lowest-performing schools. Excel, a large EMO, won a bid and was assigned to Perry in 2002, which at that point was still a middle school. Teachers at these schools were given the option of transferring to other schools, and over three-quarters of the staff at Perry departed, citing the change of leadership and an uncertain future as their reasons for leaving.[35] The CSB gave Excel additional per pupil funding and "thin-line" control, which meant that the EMO's purview was limited mainly to academics.

Greater accountability meant a more standardized school. Right away, Excel introduced many academic features: new literacy and writing curricula, lessons that were linked directly to state assessment standards, and more after-school tutoring. The EMO also added more hours of training for staff. The school district assisted Excel in recruiting and hiring a new principal, and the old building received many needed repairs.

However, the most significant change under Excel was the reorganization of the school's coed student body into a new single-sex arrangement. The school was converted into one of the first split academies in the country, with one side of the school designated for the girls and the other side for the boys. The new arrangement, however, was implemented without much consultation with parents, students, teachers, or the community. In 2003, Excel turned to Bill Harris to run the organization's operations in the city. He had led a single-sex schooling effort in another state, and it was Mr. Harris's decision to make Perry an entirely all-male school. Mr. Harris reflected on Excel's mistakes:

> When I got two teachers to pilot the program [in my previous district], I brought all the parents together and I told them about it in a general assembly, and then we brought the kids together and told them what we were doing. We never just carte blanche implemented that program. Excel just carte blanche implemented. They didn't have any parent meetings. The kids didn't know about it. The kids came to school in September and it was a single-sex school. Boys on one side divided by a wall, girls on the other side. I walked the hallways with [Excel officials], and I was appalled. I never would have done it that way.

Seven of the twenty Perry teachers I interviewed had been around during part or all of the school's short period as a split academy. The consensus was that Excel officials felt the split would eliminate distractions and enable the boys and girls to focus more on their work. Beyond that, however, the transition had been so rapid that there was little discussion with the community or staff regarding other important reasons for the sex separation and how exactly the staff was supposed to go about working exclusively with boys. Like Mr. Harris, they criticized Excel for moving forward without a comprehensive plan.

Still, few instructors opposed the idea of all-boys education in theory. The general feeling among the teachers was that, under the right circumstances, splitting up boys and girls could work. It was clear that many of the staff had been invigorated by the possibility of change through experimentation. Deonte Gaines, an African American English teacher, remarked:

> It was kind of a confusing time. None of us had worked with an organization like Excel before. But whether you liked them or not, I think we all understood that Perry had to go in a different direction. Excel and the powers that be made a decision to run the school this way, and I guess we just went with it. I didn't fight it. I just worried about my own classroom. I thought, maybe I'll find out that Excel knows what they're doing after all.

Mr. Gaines balanced feelings of uncertainty with an understanding that change was needed. Perhaps, he thought, the experts who managed the school could deliver on their promise to turn the school around. The dramatic privatized turn marked an "unsettled period" in which a new ideology provides languages, styles, and blueprints for action.[36] During these times, the promise of positive change means that individuals are willing to try different things that may eventually gel into routines.

When Excel took the next step of converting Perry into an entirely all-boys high school for the 2005–6 school year, the plan was to bring in the boys from a nearby coed school, Thompson High, and to make the latter Perry's all-girls "sister" school.[37] It was a big move, as the split academy still felt a bit like a coed school because boys and girls had some time to interact during the day. Yet an entirely all-boys school seemed unprecedented. Excel hired Patricia Henderson, a white woman and longtime educator in the city, to help with the transition. As she saw it, there were two reasons why opening the all-girls school posed less of a challenge than opening an all-boys school. First, Excel had, in her words, a clear "role model" and "inspiration" for Thompson in the Young Women's Leadership School (TYWLS) in East Harlem, New York, which opened in 1996 and serves a similarly nonwhite and poor population.[38] As for Perry, Ms. Henderson admitted, the staff was "pretty much on our own figuring out how to make it work for the boys." Curiously, neither Ms. Henderson nor anyone else cited the first wave of Black male academies as role models. The EMO had pushed immediately to make Perry High all-boys, but without the perspective of history to guide it.

There was also widespread agreement that the girls' side was faring better because it had a more capable principal. Staff members variously described the principal, Lisa Hudson, as a "goddess" and deserving of the Nobel Peace Prize for her leadership. Students gravitated to her for her tough-love approach and empathy, and they respected her because she had also grown up in the neighborhood. As I discuss later in the book, Ms. Hudson and some teachers represented what Antonio Gramsci has called "organic intellectuals," or those leaders who emerge from oppressed classes to help marginalized groups. In a period of major uncertainty and change, what the Perry staff desired was strong leadership. As Charles Turner, an African American man and special education instructor, put it, "I'm thinking if they would have let Ms. Hudson run the whole school, it would have been a functioning school." The feeling, however, was that an urgent task for Excel was to find a capable African American man to lead the boys' side and the future all-boys school. This push for Black male leadership would remain a point of contention as the years passed, an issue I take up further in chapter 4.

Perry's struggles resembled those of a failed single-sex schooling experiment in California in the late 1990s. Amanda Datnow and her colleagues argue that what led to the experiment's ultimate demise was the lack of a "strong ideological commitment": a shared understanding of how the school would address gender inequity and a shared dedication to achieving that goal.[39] Capable school leaders can articulate a clear vision and justify it to others. What the Perry High staff desperately sought was for the school leadership to offer a firm explanation for what made their school innovative. Without it, innovation seemed merely ceremonial. The staff wanted the "myth" of innovation to be true. As schools have increasingly come to resemble technical sectors that demand efficiency and accountability, in order to sustain themselves they require a tight coupling between these myths, or macro-cultural ideals, and their actual day-to-day operations.[40] The Perry teachers wanted their instruction to fit a clear vision and plan of action aimed at helping young Black men.

With no clear "role model" school and no shared commitment to using the new school to address gender inequity, Excel defaulted on a loose set of gender essentialist ideas. At one point, the school turned to Leonard Sax, the director of the National Association for Single-Sex Public Education (since renamed the National Association for Choice in Education), for guidance. Excel officials asked the staff to read Sax's research and invited him to speak at the school. The officials saw Sax's visit to Perry as an important stepping-stone. As he had done at other school visits, Sax instructed staff to change the physical environment—the lighting, room temperature, and wall colors—to make it more inviting for boys.[41] The officials held meetings to prepare parents for the transition, though few families attended.

Ms. Henderson, the Excel staff member tasked with leading the transition to an entirely all-boys school, professed enthusiasm for Sax's work as well as the work of boy-industry authors William Pollack and Michael Gurian. All praise single-sex environments. Gurian has argued that "classroom environments, schedules, and administrative attitudes" favor young women, and has suggested instead that they learn to nurture the "natural essence" in boys.[42] This boy-industry literature has been criticized for relying on conservative notions of gender. According to Marcus Weaver-Hightower, these respond to contemporary gender relations by longing for traditional times. (For example, in *A Fine Young Man*, Gurian traces the basic integrities of young men back to Jacob of the Old Testament, and he extols the virtues of nurturing boys' "honor codes.") Leaving aside their concern with a "natural essence" in boys, these books had an impact on Ms. Henderson because they reinforced what she observed as an educator: that the young men's "hard" masculinity disguised deep emotional pain. Ms. Henderson would continue to lean on this literature (especially William Pollack's best seller *Real Boys* and its accompanying workbook for parents and educators) for guidance when she became the director of Second Chance, an accelerated program for overage students at the school.

Most staff members I interviewed felt these ideas from the experts rested on a rickety foundation. Steven Reagan, a white man and a new eighth-grade teacher during the transition to an all-boys school, recalled being unconvinced by what Excel had to offer the staff:

> They needed to convince people there's a reason we're doing this and here's some strategies that Leonard Sax or somebody else says will work with boys or with all girls. I remember things like they were saying the types of bulbs that were in the lights in the room, the temperature, how you should chunk your instruction and all these other things. I never thought . . . the person who was pitching this was ever fluent enough or had any experience on their own with this to have it be that convincing, but I tried a lot of that stuff—I definitely did—because I was new and I was open to anything. But I wouldn't say the professional development and their reasoning for us doing it was very convincing. They couldn't put anything in front of us saying, "At this school, they've done this, and this was the result." There was just

nothing that concrete. But yeah, I mean we definitely got strategies that said, "This is what works with boys." But I think a lot of times it was generalizations that people were just making up.

Mr. Reagan's comments captured the confusion among staff members: they were hopeful and willing to try new methods but disappointed that the school lacked a strong sense of purpose. Mr. Reagan also found it particularly ironic that there was a lack of convincing data driving the process, given the clarion call across the district about using instructional methods based on proven research.

Liz Channing, a white woman who previously taught at the school, had also been a new teacher during the transition. She was even more critical of Excel. She noted that the building was not even equipped to accommodate some of Sax's recommendations. "We talked about how boys learn better in cooler temperatures, but we had no air conditioning," she said. "Really? You're going to sell me on that point?" As she saw it, the administration and Excel had failed to grasp that the staff was hungry for more guidance:

> We could have had Friday sessions on different topics and had the kids come together and get into groups that were facilitated by someone, and we didn't do any of that. We just pretended like it was an ideal school because it was all-boys. So for me, shame on Excel for having this initiative and not educating people on what to do with it.

Like Mr. Reagan, Ms. Channing was not necessarily opposed to the notion that there were important differences between boys and girls that could aid instruction. She was just disappointed in Excel for not laying out and executing a rigorous plan.

Perry's Punitive Turn

Sensing that the staff distrusted and may have even resented them, Excel officials found themselves on the defensive. To save face, they touted student improvement in reading and math on state standardized exams, though the gains were marginal. But renewing a contract with the school district meant that the school had to show greater improvement. Perry High's all-boys model appeared to be doomed. The administration's response was to meet the goal of accountability by disciplining the students. In fact, the young men of Perry had been punished from the start. First, to avoid a possible legal challenge that the girls were not receiving a "substantially equal" education, Excel decided that the all-girls school would be housed at Thompson, a newer building that had better facilities, including playing fields. But Mr. Harris suspected that school district officials had an ulterior motive: "to lock the boys up." He knew "for a fact that they deliberately did that because they didn't want the boys to tear it up." Others also wondered if the move was intended as a precautionary measure, as if the boys were destined to ruin Thompson if they were given access to that building. The decision to turn Perry into the all-boys school had therefore already criminalized the young men. Interestingly, as some key school leaders saw it, the problem was not simply the fact that the boys had been given a less desirable school; the boys had also been given a less sex-appropriate environment. Mr. Bradley, the principal, felt that the boys needed "more space to move around and do things outside on the field to bridge some of that energy."[43] David Chadwell, the former director of programming for single-sex public schooling in South Carolina, has argued that teachers should harness boys' and girls' energy differently: boys should be encouraged to physically move around the room, while girls should be able to engage with one another while sitting in a circle.[44] Meanwhile, Martin Sherman, a Perry High police officer who had attended an annual conference run by Leonard Sax, observed that Excel had also penalized the boys by not assigning them the building with air conditioning, given that it was "a known fact that boys work better in a cooler climate than the girls do."

Like the school staff, none of the young men from the first cohort I interviewed remembered any official rationale for the sex separation. However, they did recall feeling that they were part of some larger experiment. As twelfth grader Asad described it, "It was some test. Like, we in an urban neighborhood, so they think Black males have problems that need to be fixed. Nothing else worked. They wanted to know if it would be better without the girls." Or as twelfth grader Tyson remembered it, "As I'm going through my first year at Perry, I'm thinking we the lab rats. Like they gonna see how we do as all-male and how they do as all-female and then if it goes good then I guess they start something with the other schools." The young men remembered being singled out as in need of help and believed that the all-male arrangement was a desperate measure to offer that assistance.

As privatization had entered the worldview of the young men, they were left with the uncomfortable feeling that they were left to fend for themselves. The young men were punished in a second way when the school had inadvertently become the site of turf wars between young men from different schools and different neighborhood "blocks" or "squads" (informal street-level gangs). This mixing had been inevitable because Thompson had long been Perry's rival high school. The twelfth graders who had been members of the first all-boys cohort had vivid recollections of feeling uneasy the summer before the transition. As Tyson described it, rumors were flying in the neighborhood that

> it's going to be Thompson versus Perry or Perry versus Thompson, and there's going to be a lot of fights. People are going to be beefing and all this other stuff. . . . Like, you in an all-male school so, you know, you've got your males, they want to be in the group, they want to try to control things or, you know, let people know that they run the school.

As others described it, the first year marked "campaigns for respect" among the young men: jockeying for respect and power, including fighting.[45] The school's rate of assault rose sharply from the previous year. The school had long struggled with a reputation for resembling a prison, and this was reinforced by the new all-male composition and local media coverage that glorified the increased fighting between rival boys and gave the impression that the school housed territorial young men. Susan Wells, a Black woman and a former teacher, hated the school's reputation. "People think Perry is this 'school-behind-bars.' But they're just children." She felt the transition brought unnecessary shame to the school:

> The whole idea was to try to help the boys, and all that happened was we had even more fights. The problem was that it looked like we just wanted the boys to hurt each other more. Imagine if you're one of these young men. You must think, "What did I do to deserve this?" It's shameful, really.

One last development signaled the decisive punitive turn at the school. The school district, with Excel's help, promoted Leonard Mincy, an African American man and former police officer, to be the school's new principal in 2006. Hakeem, a twelfth grader, remembered how the school knew him as "Mr. Military Man." He was "strict, hardcore. I don't know what was wrong with him! Always taking things to the extreme. Always yelling." Mr. Turner, the former special education teacher, likewise described how "people were scared of him because he was the big, bad . . . principal and he handled disciplinary things. His whole thing was, 'Oh, we won't have to worry about that with me around.' " Ms. Wells felt that the turf wars simply fed Mr. Mincy's destructive plan to mete out law and order. Rather than addressing the causes of the strife among the young men (or the school leadership's responsibility in causing it), the fighting gave Mr. Mincy an excuse to discipline as many boys as possible in order to send a strong message to the entire student body. The thinking was that removing the "bad kids" would create a more orderly environment conducive to learning. However, highly punitive schools harm learning for both delinquent *and* rule-abiding students.[46] In addition to identifying the "bad kids" for punishment, teachers also recalled how Mr. Mincy closely patrolled the classrooms and hallways, looking to punish small violations in order to instill fear and to create a sense of order. Criminologists have found that this "broken windows" approach does little to minimize crime. During Mr. Mincy's first year as principal, the rate of suspensions nearly doubled in the school. Thus, four years after adopting the single-sex model, Perry had strayed far from any proposal to empower young men. Instead, the school became an example of what happens when the "punishing state combines with the logic of the market."[47]

While the district had granted Excel some autonomy, the EMO was unable to orchestrate a successful transition to an all-boys model. The frustrated staff felt that their school was a rudderless ship, and they criticized Excel for not taking the goal of innovation and giving it any real substance. Clearly, mere separation was no magic bullet.[48] In this tumultuous period, punishment had emerged as a strategy for meeting the goal of accountability. This process exemplified the "hypertrophied penal state" in the city of Morgan in the early 2000s.[49]

Becoming All-Boys at Northside Academy

Modeling Respectability

Compared to Perry High, Northside Academy's early years were far less chaotic. Still, Thomas Pierce, the school's founder, had his work cut out for him. Mr. Pierce had previously been a teacher and an administrator at other alternative schools in the city and had worked with, in his words, "at-risk kids, kids who'd been truant, dropped out, permanently expelled from the public schools, or kids who were looking for an alternative to those large, impersonal public high schools." So the idea for a very different kind of school—an all-boys school—had been percolating in Mr. Pierce's head for some time. He just needed the right conditions to make it a reality. With the school district's reform efforts well under way, Mr. Pierce submitted an application for an all-boys charter school in 2006, the year that Perry transitioned from being a split academy to an entirely all-boys school. He faced the same opposition that Detroit's Malcolm X Academy had faced fifteen years earlier. Feminist groups cited Detroit as precedent and claimed that an all-boys arrangement remained illegal because it discriminated against girls. Swarmed with applications for other charters and fearing a lawsuit, the school district denied Mr. Pierce's application. When Mr. Pierce reapplied later that year, he came armed with a petition:

> We had nine hundred signatures of people in this neighborhood who wanted the school. We had the support of a lot of elected officials, community activists, religious leaders. People thought this was a good idea. People who didn't know me. This wasn't about me, okay? They looked at the idea and went, "This is a good idea."

Like his counterparts in the first-wave academies, Mr. Pierce wanted to show that Northside Academy had the support of community members, who were angry with the efforts to block the all-boys school. Yet unlike his first-wave counterparts, Mr. Pierce benefited from the support of the law. The same year he reapplied, the Department of Education released guidelines that removed legal obstacles to single-sex education. These helped clarify that Northside would not segregate based on sex. The school founder just needed a clear rationale for an all-boys school. Having once been denied and seeing "all these people coming with applications for their own schools," Mr. Pierce designed a respectable school distinct from other all-male spaces:

> Everybody, when they start thinking about what to do with boys, they approach it from a, "This is where they screw up. Let's get them from here." No. Let's get them *before* they screw up, and let's send them in a different direction. You have to make this school based on academic merit, not just gender or athletic ability or things like that. You've got to shun the whole special ed, boot-camp mentality, disciplinary school mentality.

In designing Northside, Mr. Pierce drew a clear boundary between his legitimate all-male school and schools that have "an immediate, ongoing connection" with prisons.[50] Perry High was just the kind of stigmatized school he had in mind. Northside, by comparison, would be a privileged place that taught the *appropriate* kind of discipline: a strict obedience and work ethic appropriate for young men of high moral character. Mr. Pierce intended for his new school to institutionalize respectability.

The school district was persuaded. In a press release, district officials justified their decision to accept Northside's application because a "crisis" facing young Black boys demanded more "innovative" schooling models. Yet contrary to the school district's claim, Northside was only innovative in the narrow sense that it differed from other local schools. The school founder took advantage of present-day circumstances to reach far into the past. As organizational scholars have stressed, institutions entering competitive markets and facing uncertain futures will tend toward isomorphism. Not necessarily forward-looking, these institutions, like Northside, instead model themselves after schools with a long track record of success.[51] As Chris Lubienski has written, "Curricular conformity and standardization may be encouraged by the very market forces that were unleashed to address those ills."[52]

When I asked school community members what Northside most resembled, I was told that Northside was a blend of elements from prestigious historically Black colleges and universities (HBCUs) and a local elite boarding school. Cam Tomlinson, a science teacher and an HBCU graduate himself, said that Northside "reminds me of a mini-Morehouse. They're both special places with disciplined Black men: Black men who aim for excellence." Students made this connection, too. Speaking of Howard University, Terrell, a ninth-grader, felt that "it's a really good college for Black people, for Black people who will be successful. And that's what Mr. Pierce wants for us." The school also actively linked HBCUs and Northside. Teachers mentioned HBCUs in classroom lessons, and pennants of these various colleges were prominently displayed in the hallways.

Many people in the school community were fond of calling Northside a "free private school." In this respect, Mr. Pierce had drawn inspiration from a few sources. The first was Crane Academy, an elite private all-boys boarding school located a short drive outside the city. Mr. Pierce knew that the school signaled prestige to community members, stakeholders, and district officials. He met personally with the school district superintendent and convinced him that Northside would succeed because it would be modeled after Crane Academy. When those at the school referred to Northside as being "like a private school, but public," the private school they had in mind was Crane Academy. Modeling the school after Crane was appealing to the staff; about one-third of the faculty had attended a private or parochial single-gender school, and several among them had studied Latin while there. Melissa Spring, a Latin teacher and the first teacher hired at Northside, vividly recalls how Mr. Pierce had sold her on the school. "The whole idea for this school is to get it to be like Crane Academy, like a college prep school," she said. "And [Mr. Pierce] believed that these kids deserved a chance. It was the fact that this was like a very much justice-oriented thing that sold me." As Ms. Spring implied, the school founder wanted young Black men to have the "chance" their more privileged peers had. Mr. Tomlinson agreed. "I think it's only fair that we give our young Black men a chance to develop in a boys' school," he said. "I think some people on the outside see this school and they think, 'Splitting up boys and girls is so old-fashioned.' But Crane Academy and other prep schools give them that top-notch education. So why can't we?" By linking North-side to private schools, the community had adopted their own social justice rationale. It was only fair to give poor Black boys the chance to attend "elite" all-boys schools like their more privileged peers. This logic also served as a rejoinder to the claims that all-boys schools are a form of sex segregation.

This social justice rationale, however, had its limits. A politics that symbolically divides "respectable" and "unrespectable" Black boys suggests that these academies may target law-abiding, academically oriented "schoolboys" who are better positioned than their peers to be successful,[53] even as school reform policies purport to reach all young Black men. In fact, while existing scholarship highlights the success of "resilient" young Black men, this work has not fully examined the possible selection effects in these schools.[54] By contrast, Detroit's Malcolm X Academy, the most well-known first-wave academy, developed an "at-risk variables tabulation scale" to identify the most disadvantaged Black boys for admission to the school.[55] This prevented the school from "skimming" for only the highest-achieving Black boys.

To provide their school with legitimacy, Northside Academy officials actively sought the "customers" who could provide it: respectable, high-achieving young men. And unlike the Malcolm X Academy that enrolled disadvantaged young men, Northside lowered the school's risk of closure by targeting the least risky young men in the community. While charters by law must be open to all students, school officials knew that Northside would likely attract studious young men and the families who supported them. As I describe further in chapter 3, two resources signaled prestige and respectability: a demanding Latin curriculum (a mark of disciplined minds) and a professional uniform of blazer and necktie (a mark of disciplined bodies). The school community often referred to the students as "gentlemen." And as Mr. Pierce told me, "We only want serious students." The school made certain that applicants were aware of this. At an informational session for prospective families, Mr. Pierce and Mr. Green, the principal, were firm in that the school required "complete buy-in" from families.

Northside officials felt they had little chance of attracting students who were admitted to the city's few magnet schools. They were therefore competing for the very best students not headed to magnets. As Mr. Pierce said earlier, "Let's get them *before* they screw up." In seeking to attract the most gifted students and to prepare them for college—or those who already stood the best chance of getting to college—Mr. Pierce appropriated

Du Bois's famous thesis demanding the "higher training of the talented few":[56]

> If you could go to one of those [magnet schools], go there, good luck. They're great schools. But if you didn't go there, how well do you believe that the school that you would attend could prepare you for college, and what are the things they're doing that says they're going to prepare you for college?

Jim Chambers was the Black principal of a local middle school that had sent several students to Northside. He echoed Mr. Pierce's sentiments. "If you don't get into" magnet schools, he said, "you end up going to your neighborhood school." He continued:

> I didn't think it boded well for the majority of African American males. If you're lucky, you dodge a bullet. If you're not lucky, I don't know what's going to happen, even though you're a good kid.

Mr. Chambers implied that Northside attempted to siphon off "good kids"—a proxy for studious and obedient young men—who would otherwise be lost to neighborhood schools. Here Mr. Chambers hinted at the boundary work that was central to Northside's institutional identity.

Lessons from Dunbar High School

Crane Academy was not the only secondary school that inspired Mr. Pierce. Two others were elite public schools. While everyone at the school was familiar with Crane Academy, Mr. Pierce's idea for Latin instruction came from the Boston Latin School, a magnet school and the country's oldest public school (established in 1635 by Puritans). Mr. Pierce had been watching a TV segment on Cotton Mather, the early and controversial Puritan leader, when he learned that Mather had attended Boston Latin. Mr. Pierce called it a "eureka moment." He read up on all the prominent graduates of Boston Latin and was convinced that Latin would give Northside an unimpeachable distinction in the community.

Another inspiration was the Paul Laurence Dunbar High School in Washington, D.C. Founded in 1870, Dunbar was one of the country's earliest Black community schools, with Black families seeking control over where and how their children learn. (The school was first known as the Preparatory High School for Colored Youth, but for consistency's sake I will refer to the school here as Dunbar High, as it is most often called.) While the large majority of students came from poor families, the school had a sterling reputation: by the early twentieth century, its graduation rates exceeded those of other public schools in the city (regardless of race), and many of its graduates would attend the nation's top colleges and become influential community leaders.[57] The school boasted a prestigious faculty, many of whom were college-educated Blacks who had faced racial discrimination in the job market and were then hired by the school.

Mr. Pierce's decision to follow in Dunbar's illustrious footsteps positioned Northside Academy alongside a libertarian tradition that resonates strongly with neoliberalism, with its embrace of a free-market education. In fact, libertarian commentators such as Thomas Sowell and Andrew Coulson have championed Dunbar as one of the best examples of what happens when schools are granted the freedom to operate autonomously. Mr. Pierce told me he learned valuable lessons from Coulson's book *Market Education* (1999), which "argues that free educational markets have consistently done a better job of serving the public's needs than state-run school systems have."[58] As Dunbar had operated nearly autonomously from the D.C. school district, so would Northside run autonomously from the Morgan school district. Just as they had done at Dunbar, students and staff would freely choose to be at Northside. Buy-in was needed; Mr. Pierce wanted those who were unhappy with underperforming public schools and who were committed to his school from the start. Northside's mandatory Latin also borrowed from Dunbar's, which had featured an "all-classical pedagogy" and featured a Latin motto.[59]

By keeping the "academic bar astronomically high," Dunbar attracted the very best students and made sure that only the strongest students would graduate.[60] The school tracked by ability group and lost many students who "lacked the courage" to meet the school's high expectations; clearly, the school was "not a democracy but a meritocracy."[61] Mr. Pierce also wanted his school to attract only the most able young men in the city. To emphasize this point, he argued that desegregation had ruined Dunbar:

> In the 1950s with the advent of *Brown v. the Board of Education*, the school district started to pay more attention to it to make sure things were fair, and in making it fair, they screwed up the school. Now it's one of the worst performing schools in D.C. because they don't have the community acceptance that they had before when it was the community idea that this be a high-performing school. What I like is for the community to accept us as a high-performing school, and what that means is that the community will not support parents who have kids in here who don't do their work or don't follow the rules.

As Mr. Pierce noted, the D.C. school district had left Dunbar alone before *Brown*. After the Supreme Court ruling, the school district intervened and made Dunbar a regular neighborhood school. The school lost its elite status.

Mr. Pierce joined with libertarian commentators like Thomas Sowell and Andrew Coulson who saw the loss of an autonomous, high-achieving high school such as Dunbar as tragic. Mr. Pierce discursively linked a community control tradition of Black schooling to Libertarianism, which believes that minimal government involvement results in better and more efficient schools. Writing long before charter schools would become common across the urban public school landscape, Thomas Sowell observed that the goal of desegregation, however noble, should not impede the right of school choice for Black families. He lamented that "the shibboleth of integration is still powerful enough to thwart fundamental educational reform."[62] These complex politics behind Dunbar High and the *Brown* ruling ultimately provided Mr. Pierce with a platform to state his case about racial separation in public schools. For Mr. Pierce, voluntary separation on the basis of gender was in no way comparable to de facto racial segregation in schools. This argument was aimed directly at the ACLU, which has called single-sex schools a form of segregation and has therefore equated sex separation with racial segregation.

Du Bois's Legacy for All-Boys Education

Respectability and Racial Uplift

When Dunbar High was founded in 1870, the South was undergoing a massive rebuild as part of the post–Civil War Reconstruction period. As W. E. B. Du Bois has written, African Americans won important political victories during this time. Blacks thus came to embrace what was later known as racial uplift: with "religious fervor," they viewed education as a vehicle to the full liberation of the masses.[63] By the end of the century, however, Jim Crow policies extinguished many of the real gains under Reconstruction, and Black entrepreneurs and small business owners found themselves falling further and further behind in an expanding capitalist economy. During this moment, a second meaning of racial uplift had crystallized. Black leaders promoted a "politics of respectability" that stressed conformity to middle-class values—such as purity, self-restraint, and moral discipline—that would reject racist discourses of African Americans and win a new Black elite the acceptance of mainstream white society.[64] The focus on reforming Black men's behavior and character, however, would take "the emphasis away from structural forms of oppression."[65]

As a young scholar writing during this period, Du Bois promoted this discourse of uplift and respectability. Enchanted by the Victorian ideals at the heart of this discourse, Du Bois viewed higher education as the necessary training ground for an "exceptional few" men who would go on to be stewards for the Black masses.[66] Today Du Bois has become something of a guiding light for proponents of Black male academies. Northside Academy, in modeling itself after Crane Academy and elite Black institutions such as Dunbar High and Morehouse College, was "incited" to an early Du Boisian discourse of racial uplift and respectability.[67] In fact, as Dunbar High glittered at the dawn of the twentieth century, it not surprisingly bore a resemblance to the country's elite Black colleges. At Fisk University (where Du Bois attended college), the campus culture similarly demanded strict discipline and embodied the late Victorian virtues of chastity and self-restraint.

A respectability politics proved troubling after Reconstruction. The influx of Black migrants into northern cities provoked class anxieties for Black leaders.[68] A respectability politics divided Black communities when upwardly mobile Black men "constructed their own status against that of the Black 'unrespectable' poor."[69] While Black all-male secondary institutions are relatively new, elite Black institutions such as the all-male Morehouse College continue to promote a respectability politics. Saida Grundy writes that Morehouse "embrace[s] conformity to mainstream middle-class gender constructs to produce and sustain normative patriarchal citizenship and 'respectable' Black males," and in doing so draws clear symbolic boundaries against those Black men most in "crisis."[70] As I demonstrate later in the book, Northside would follow the lead of Morehouse College and perform this moral boundary work.

The racial uplift discourse would take a different form at Perry High School. The male administration at Perry High—six of the seven administrators were Black men—came to view themselves in a certain way. These "race men" of Perry High professed an obligation to use their privileged standing to help save marginalized male children, or their students.[71] Half had come from affluent backgrounds and had attended schools like Morehouse College, whose mission has long been to cultivate "exceptional men" who will enter the professional middle class.[72] In fact, the man whose name would grace this college, Dr. Henry Morehouse, is credited with first using the term "Talented Tenth," several years before Du Bois published an essay on the topic.[73] Along with other Black male staff, the Perry High administrators devoted themselves to building a network of professional men who would serve as mentors for the boys.

The discourse of race leadership did not map onto the Northside administration as neatly. Mr. Pierce did not discursively position himself as a race man to the degree that the Perry High administrators did (though many viewed him as a charismatic leader and even a savior of sorts). The school relied much less than Perry on establishing adult male mentoring relationships. The elite status would surface in another way at Northside. The school was determined to train an exclusive group of young men through a classical education. As I explain in subsequent chapters, they would achieve this as a brotherhood.

Women and All-Boys Education

The discourse of racial uplift has had a checkered past. Feminist scholars have critiqued the elitism and chauvinism behind this version of race leadership. Joy James, for example, describes how Du Bois's training in the classics (not much different from the one the Northside boys would receive more than a century later) shaped his thinking on the Talented Tenth. The notion of a Black male vanguard harkened back to a Platonic history in which philosopher kings were chosen to lead their people to salvation.[74] To be sure, Du Bois would later move beyond his original formulation of a Talented Tenth and acknowledge the crucial role that the Black masses can play in political praxis. Yet the strong allure of a Black male elite remains. As James notes, today's discussions of Black male leadership are "frozen in Du Bois's early construction" of the Talented Tenth.[75] As such, it perpetuates a politics of respectability by disparaging both the poorest Blacks and by excluding women from its narrative.

It is a little-known fact that in 1900, Du Bois applied for the position of assistant superintendent of Negro Schools in Washington, D.C. Despite being overqualified for the job, he was turned down. This was because the D.C. school board at the time was an ally of Booker T. Washington and his "Tuskegee Machine," whose educational philosophy differed starkly from Du Bois's. Washington, a former slave, preached a curriculum of industrial and vocational education, while Du Bois, who was born free, argued that higher education would serve as a path to racial uplift. Dunbar High was precisely the kind of school that Du Bois had in mind when he called for schools that could provide "Sympathy, Knowledge, and the Truth," and he was likely thrilled at the prospect of overseeing Dunbar High. Therefore, the school appealed not only to later libertarians who stressed free-market education but also to Black reformers such as Du Bois who saw the college-preparatory school as a necessary alternative, given the dearth of equitable racially integrated schools, and as a training ground for a "better class" of Blacks.

Yet there is a remarkable fact about the history of the crown jewel of the Washington, D.C., school district: its early leaders were Black women. The school shined especially under the leadership of the Black feminist Anna Julia Cooper. Though born to a slave and disadvantaged by her gender and race, Cooper would emerge as one of the leading Black reformers of her era. However, the common view of this historical moment as the "Age of Washington and Du Bois" obscures how women were foundational to early Black reform efforts. In many respects, Cooper was Du Bois's contemporary and ally. She, for example, defended the rights of Blacks to a rigorous college-preparatory education. In other ways, Cooper inspired Du Bois's later work. In 1892, eleven years before Du Bois famously wrote that "the color line" was the defining problem of the twentieth century, Cooper argued that "a race problem" and "a woman question" were co-constructing forces that could not be subsumed under the category of racial oppression alone: the building blocks for the feminist framework of intersectionality.[76]

The discursive removal of Cooper in the history of all-Black schooling, and her erasure more generally behind a history of leading race men, hint at a larger theme in this book: the precarious situation of Black women in today's all-boys schooling movement. Male academies assert men's rightful place as leaders for needy boys, and they teach Black boys that they can assert their worth by embracing patriarchal and heteronormative power. This ideology threatens to exclude or overlook the contributions of Black women within the school community, as parents and as school staff members. Another less examined issue is how Black women in these schools are positioned with respect to white women, who dominate the teaching profession and were strong in numbers and influence at the two schools. I take up this issue in chapter 4.

Conclusion

The seeds of neoliberalism were sown long before the restructuring of the Morgan school district, and the market logics had become "a way of life," as Mr. Harris put it, when Perry High and Northside Academy became all-boys schools. So while Perry High and Northside traveled quite distinctive paths in their early years, they were both caught in the school district's decisive turn to the market in the early 2000s. Mismanagement ensnared Perry from its first days. Without a clear vision or a plan for innovation, accountability assumed "tangible flesh" in the form of punishment.[77] The young men felt they were being "punished rather than privileged" for being there.[78] With its future in doubt, the school would place its fate in the hands of a new Black male leadership.

Northside, meanwhile, fought off early challenges to its charter and took a more deliberate path, drawing inspiration from a number of elite institutions. By defending the right of Black empowerment in schools, the community control tradition has mostly avoided an association with the "ultra-competitive charter schools that have generated the most controversy."[79] Mr. Pierce, however, aligned his institution with Black community control, which dated back to Washington, D.C.'s Dunbar High School, and embraced the ethos of competition wrought by the school district's neoliberal turn. He saw an opportunity to distinguish his new school as respectable, set apart from the stigmatized and punitive all-male institutions. The all-male Northside did not emulate prisons, but other elite all-male schools. The institutionalization of respectability at Northside, however, aggravated divisions between "two fractions of the Black urban proletariat."[80] While male academies purportedly target men of color as if they are a homogenous group, Northside deliberately recruited law-abiding, academically oriented young men. Therefore, while a neoliberal governmentality normally constructs Black boys as an "essentially damaged" problem in need of a solution, Black academies such as Northside recruit the least damaged young men among them: those not marked with the stigma that accompanies all-male institutions such as prisons and disciplinary schools, and those with more of the cultural capital, habits, and sensibilities to be academically successful.[81]

CHAPTER TWO

Contradictory Discourses

Separating Boys and Girls

During Mr. Mincy's tenure as principal, the second full year that the school had been entirely all-boys, Perry High failed to make sufficient academic progress. The school was slapped with the label of "Corrective Action," a probationary category under No Child Left Behind. In 2007, Mr. Mincy—"Mr. Military Man," as Hakeem had memorably called him—was forced to resign, and another administrator, Lavar Bradley, was promoted to principal. Soon after, Excel lost its contract with the district, and Perry High came under full school district management once again. For Peter Jones, who became an assistant principal the first year that Perry was entirely all-boys, these sudden changes showed how the city's new regime of accountability was firmly in place. I caught up with Mr. Jones one day after he had relayed the day's final announcements over the loudspeaker. I asked him what it was like when Excel left.

"The school district wasn't playin' around. Just like that, Excel was out. We had to try something new. And we'll keep trying until something works." I was struck by his message. It reminded me of what Mr. Harris, the school district official and former Excel employee, had shared with me: When something does not work in schools, try something new. Experiment. Keep experimenting.

"And things turned out better?" I asked.

Mr. Jones assured me that Mr. Bradley had steered Perry High School into calmer waters. He asked me if I had seen the movie *Lean on Me*. It was a popular 1989 film about a high school with a troubled history that resembled Perry High's.[1]

"It was like that. Lots of fights going on. It was really, really wild. But today you could walk through the halls and not believe it used to be that way." Like Mr. Pierce, the CEO at Northside Academy, Mr. Jones

understood the need to distance the school from the controlling image of
a prison.

Trying to outrun a troubled history is a tall order. But there was a feeling that the school was turning a corner. Perry High had won a major
federal grant to roll out new programs (the first of its kind, as far as officials knew), including an academic resource center and a parent resource
center. The district helped recruit and hire a number of veteran administrators (some of whom were former principals) who served as assistant
principals and mentors to Mr. Bradley, who was entering his third year as
principal. The school administration was able to interview and hire many
of its own staff, which meant that the school could bring in more people
committed to the single-sex model.

Across town, Northside Academy was entering its third year and now
enrolled students in grades nine through eleven. The school was expanding at a brisk pace and had hired a new principal, Mr. Green. This allowed
Mr. Pierce, the school's founder and first principal, to work with the board
of trustees on fund-raising and on growing the school. With its unique classical curriculum and air of respectability, the school had quickly gained
admirers, including local politicians and community leaders who clamored
for opportunities to help the school. The local media seemed to pay less
and less attention to Perry following the turbulent period under Mr. Mincy's leadership. Northside, on the other hand, had generated considerable
"buzz," as people there described it to me.

Having explored the early days of both schools, this chapter brings us
to the present. Here I turn to the most basic question underlying single-sex
public education: why separate boys and girls? It was one of the first questions I asked in conversations and interviews. As I soon found out, the
answer was so commonsensical that the question answered itself. *Of course*
it's because boys and girls distract one another. The answers came auto-
matically and seemingly without reflection. But as people dug into their
own thinking, I found they at times backtracked, contested, and modified
the otherwise taken-for-granted beliefs surrounding the separation of boys
and girls. They said the "discourse of distractions" was not true in all instances and that the discourse actually did not fit their own past experiences. They even admitted that girls could motivate boys academically. And
while the school communities frequently lumped their boys into a category
opposed to girls, this splitting along gender lines revealed racialized distinctions drawn between deviant and respectable forms of manhood and womanhood. To make sense of this, we need a way of thinking about cultural
expressions of gender identity.

Street and Scholarly: Conceptualizing Culture and Gender

The dominant perspective on male academies views these schools as protective environments that attempt to instill resilience in young men: the sum of qualities such as optimism, self-esteem, and persistence that help people to handle threats to their well-being. A main argument of *Black Boys Apart* is that this focus obscures the forces that have nurtured the logic of resilience and, relatedly, has accepted uncritically that resilience is an incontrovertible asset. In what follows, I examine how the resilience perspective offers a limited view of culture and gender.

In *Schooling for Resilience,* Edward Fergus, Pedro Noguera, and Margary Martin provide an account of seven Black academies. They argue that two "competing discourses" help explain the disadvantages of young men of color and have subsequently shaped the thinking behind schools targeted to this population.[2] On one side of this debate are "structural" accounts that focus primarily on how the political economy and social institutions jointly shape the life outcomes of individuals. According to these structuralists, the disadvantage experienced by poor young men of color can be explained mostly by restricted access to resources and opportunities. On the opposing side of the debate are "cultural" accounts. Unlike the structuralists, the "culturalists . . . tend to downplay the significance of environmental factors and treat human behavior as a product of beliefs, values, norms, and family socialization."[3] The culturalists maintain that specific values and norms promote "criminal and immoral behavior" and other "self-defeating behaviors that reproduce poverty across generations."[4] According to Fergus and colleagues, what has dominated culturalist accounts is a "culture of poverty" argument that maintains that the poor live in a close-circuited space that perpetuates its own harmful cultural norms.[5] While offering distinct accounts for what produces youth disadvantage, what these perspectives share is a poor account of agency, or how young men of color can overcome disadvantage. Structuralist accounts characterize individuals as helpless agents in the face of larger structural disadvantage, whereas cultural accounts tend to see people who have succumbed to poor cultural norms. Due to an enduring "cult of individualism" in the United States, to explain disadvantage Americans are much more likely to blame individual behavior than structural circumstances. In focusing our attention on structural explanations, *Schooling for Resilience* deepens understanding of Black male disadvantage.[6]

The study's conception of culture, however, obscures the complexity of Black male disadvantage. Fergus and colleagues rely on a culturalist framework that begins with a view of culture in strictly deficit terms, and they assert that this framework has dominated understandings of culture in the lives of young Black men over the past half century. Here, the authors ground a cultural perspective in a discredited culture of poverty argument that was once a dominant view. This elides a far more complex view of culture in Black communities. Despite the fact that the schools in their study had little contact with one another—and despite the fact that the schools differed in terms of recruitment and admissions requirements, racial composition, and academic proficiency—the authors found that the schools were "remarkably alike" in their designs.[7] Given these similarities, readers are led to believe that there is a consistent view of culture as a set of deficits that cumulatively deny agency. Urban life, in this view, is nothing more than ghetto culture shut out from the mainstream.[8]

One problem with starting from a deficit view of culture is that culture, as defined, can only be something to be avoided. This unreflexively situates schools as "paragons of morality" and saviors of young men.[9] Culture is reduced to a kind of cultural warfare, or opposing moralities—deviant and "street" on the one side, and respectable and "decent," on the other—where Black male academies fall on the "right" side of the boundary and the "community" falls on the "wrong" side. The schools are seen as being on a noble quest to "undo" and "counter" common stereotypes of Black masculinity. The authors argue that the singular expressed intent of these schools, despite their differences, is to "protect" and "inoculate" their students from the community. The schools are characterized as the only safe harbors in a desolate community. Yet by not examining the social and historical underpinnings of this boundary work, the authors accept uncritically that this mission of protection is virtuous, and largely overlook how this protection may also pose harm. Rather than examining the complex relationships between respectability and deviance, the authors draw clear boundaries, which leaves "no middle ground, little overlap, and faint symbolic interplay between them."[10] Indeed, the dominant culture—in other words, what the schools can provide the boys—falls on the "right" side of boundary and remains an unmarked category in this research.

To address these limitations, in this book I draw on cultural research that assesses the destructive link between macro "diffusion of neoliberal policies and ideologies on the one side" and local "boundary configurations and institutional histories on the other."[11] While this boundary work may indeed help students in these schools, they pose harm by recapitulating a form of respectability politics that may further divide Black communities. I introduced this process in chapter 1. In beginning with a homogeneous view of culture as a set of deficits, the resilience perspective overlooks a long research tradition on urban communities that has emphasized the *heterogeneity* of culture.[12] In this book, I take heterogeneity to mean the presence of competing mainstream and alternative cultural models in the social worlds of young Black men. This framework avoids the victim-blaming implicit in homogeneous culturalist accounts by focusing less on "values" and "norms" (which can quickly collapse into a debate about "good" and "bad" behavior) and instead conceptualizes culture as a set of "frames": outlooks on the social world that structure action, or strategies people use to solve different problems.[13] A focus on strategies emphasizes that people's decisions are enabled and constrained by structural circumstances.

A homogeneous view of culture cannot escape a homogeneous portrait of the boys themselves.[14] Sociologists of youth, however, emphasize that young people adjudicate between "mainstream" and "alternative" cultural repertoires in navigating their social worlds. In Victor Rios's research, "de-linquent" young men, or those who have had contact with the criminal justice system, engage in oppositional behavior and aggressive behavior as a form of resistance. And rather than submitting to unjust systems of surveillance and accepting being rejected by mainstream institutions, young men of color engage in minor criminal acts in order to maintain a sense of dignity. As Prudence Carter observes, for delinquent youth, "cultural presentations of self are better understood as practices of distinction based on a critique of an undiscerning mainstream culture in schools rather than a submission to . . . oppression."[15] These more complex understandings of agency are a welcome alternative to the resilience perspective's narrow definition of agency as the ability to overcome obstacles.[16] This narrow framing implies that Black culture only ever comprises a set of "obstacles" and denies agency to young men who do not overcome obstacles. This definition forecloses any way of explaining why students might disagree with or resist the very school communities of which they are a part.

Young men who ascribe more to a cultural model of "decency" are viewed as respectable and rule-abiding.[17] For instance, Ann Arnett Ferguson and Prudence Carter find that "schoolboys" and "cultural mainstreamers," respectively, seek the approval of authorities and view mainstream values and practices as normative.[18] They are school-oriented and are more receptive to using Standard English than Black English. Researchers caution against dichotomizing these two groups into neat and opposing categories of street and decent, alternative and mainstream. Instead, poor youth juggle a mix of cultural repertoires. For example, many young men feel pressure to some degree to abide by a code of the street. Given how difficult it is to negotiate these competing expectations, decent young men are precariously situated and are constantly in danger of being labeled as "bad." Some young people are especially adept at "code-switching" between their peer cultures and the mainstream norms that animate the world of schooling. Juggling competing repertoires is a strategy for navigating multiple social worlds, but this carries additional burdens as youth risk being alienated from their peers.

A heterogeneous view of culture resonates in this book's view of gender as a "gendered governmentality" and a matter of agency and constraint.[19] Enactments of gender difference are "neither voluntary nor arbitrary in form," but represent a "highly strategic attachment to a social category that has political effects."[20] Actors are not necessarily free to choose how they self-identify; rather, they perform gender acts as a condition of their subjectivities, or political identities. Historical controlling images of Black masculinity mesh today with neoliberal discourses that further constrain and punish young men's expressions of masculine selves. The discourses of choice and personal responsibility view individuals as market actors who are free to choose the solutions that will best address the problems they face.[21] In the context of education, however, researchers note that poverty severely constrains the ability of families to choose and limits access to information about all available schooling options.[22] These families are then criticized for not acting "rationally" and for making the "wrong" decisions. Ann Phoenix observes that a neoliberal governmentality poses harm for Black boys in schools.[23] The idea that they can freely choose to behave as "good students" with a laser-sharp focus on learning—given neoliberalism's mandate that youth work hard to earn the capital and skills to be competitors in a global economy—disguises how a punitive state encourages the very transgressive behaviors in young Black men for which they are punished.

Drawing on these various insights, I examine how young Black men are "recruited to" discourses but "have choices in the 'subject positions' they adopt in these complex locations."[24] I ask how students at Perry High and Northside Academy embrace *and* resist the projects of gender formation in Black male academies. My framework accentuates two cultural repertoires that guide this struggle to achieve masculinity: street and scholarly. Compared to the scholars, the street-oriented young men were more likely to defy authorities and school expectations. This masculine comportment was dominant at Perry High. Street-oriented students believed in standing up for themselves and in not bending to the will of others. These resistant acts ran the gamut from using humor in class to flout school rules to relying on fighting to defend masculine honor. They were the bad boys and the troublemakers. Following the work of Victor Rios, I found that a much larger share of these young men had already had contact with the criminal justice system. (The interview sample of the young men reflects these key distinctions between the student populations. See Table 2 and Table 3 in the Appendix.) As opposed to a street repertoire, a *scholarly* repertoire was embedded in the college-prep mission of Northside Academy. Scholarly oriented young men were more likely to show dedication to schoolwork and school rules and to avoid spaces and situations where they risked getting into trouble with police and other authorities. Unlike Perry High, Northside intentionally adopted the term "gentlemen" to mark its young men as having the high-mindedness, impeccable manners, and elite education that were rare among their peers. Still, the cultural repertoires of street and scholarly circulated at both schools.

The Discourse of Distractions

Single-sex education was preferable to coeducation because girls posed different kinds of hazards in mixed settings. The history of sex-separate schooling reveals variations on a common theme: advocates of all-boys schools turn to these schooling arrangements as strategies to resist gendered threats, such as the progress of women and the feminization of schools. The idea that an all male environment could reduce or eliminate distractions between girls and boys seemed to many people to be common sense. In her important research on single-sex education, Elisabeth Woody termed this a "discourse of distractions."[25]

For those at Perry High and Northside, removing distractions meant greater academic focus and eliminating the need to impress young women. Mr. Jones, the assistant principal at Perry, summarized this general sentiment when he said, "It's better not to have the female presence in the building because the students don't feel like they have to show off." Ella Richardson was the mother of two sons: Danny, who had attended Perry before the transition to all-boys, and Deonte, a current eighth grader at the school. Deonte was doing well in school, and she was convinced that her eldest son would have done better had he also attended an all-male school. She told me that the current students "don't have to focus on the girls, because [Danny] was one of those to chase the girls home and stuff like that. They took that away, and it just makes you want to focus on your homework [as] opposed to having to worry about, 'I'm going to go see this girl.'" Sheila Butler, the mother of eleventh-grade Perry High student Malik, said,

"When you separate the kids like that, you can focus more. If they bring the girls back, the kids are going to be hanging out more in the hallway. You're not going to be able to focus." Brandon, a twelfth grader, had been forced to leave his previous high school, Sellwood High, and ended up at Perry. Like his classmates, Brandon felt he could focus on either school or girls, but not both:

> If I was going to Sellwood, I'd make sure that I brush my hair every
> five seconds. At Perry, you don't even have to worry about nothing
> because . . . who you going to impress? You can focus more on school
> than you would do if girls are there. But I used to focus on a lot of
> things other than my education. That was the main thing: girls.

The discourse of distractions reinforced a commonsense understanding of gender in binary terms. Through repeated acts, individuals reinforce culturally appropriate meanings of manhood and womanhood.[26] As Brandon implied, a lack of educational focus in a coed setting boiled down to performing masculinity appropriately. Brandon's attention to his body is not trivial. For young African American men who lack access to institutional power, the body is an especially important medium through which to earn masculine recognition.[27]

Caleb, an eleventh grader at Northside, told me how the school had removed "the girl element" that would "throw me off my focus." Parents agreed. The Blys were raising their grandson, tenth grader Kahlil. For Mr. Bly, who grew up near Northside, the charter school harkened back to a time when schools were less disruptive and less violent. He recalled his own teenage years when he suggested to Kahlil that his grandson consider Northside: "It's just how you're socialized, you know. We was always trying to impress the girls. But then when you go to an all-boys' school, you can keep your mind on your work." Helena Rodriguez, a Latina woman and the Northside social worker, described how she sometimes heard students (and especially the ninth graders) "complain they don't want to be here because it's all boys or it's corny: 'I need some girls.' But I hate to say it, I think a lot of the success comes from not having that distraction, not having to impress a girl, not being distracted by a pretty girl winking or blinking her eye or whatever." Ms. Rodriguez's comments are also noteworthy because she characterized girls as being more than flirtatious: they seduced young men, who were helpless to control themselves around girls.

Given Northside's college-prep focus, staff members and parents there tended to use language that suggested that the academic stakes were higher for boys who were distracted by girls. As they saw it, their young men needed to learn to compete academically but instead were too caught up in a competition over girls. As Nick Calder, a white man and writing instructor, explained it to me, boys in coed schools "are trying to one-up each other to get some girl's attention." Or as Michelle Rollins, the parent of Northside eleventh grader Rakeem, said:

> I think it's fabulous that there's not any little girl sitting next to [Rakeem] giggling and laughing so it's distracting. [At Northside] they compete, but they compete in different ways. They're not worried about, "Oh, I want Susie to look at me," you know, and it makes it a lot easier for them because they don't have to worry about, "Oh, my God, I ain't brushed my hair today," or whatever. You know, they could just roll out the bed, put their clothes on, come in and learn.

What most people at both schools never fully addressed was the heteronormative character of the discourse of distractions. Yet there were queer- and gay-identifying young men who poked fun at the assumed heteronormativity of the schools.

For Northside Academy officials, sexual distractions posed a threat to the students' identities as gentlemen, or young men with impeccable manners who treated women as "ladies." At an assembly one afternoon in January, the principal, Mr. Green, addressed a recent incident in which several students were caught making offensive comments about a female visitor to the building. The students were now accustomed to the principal opening the weekly assemblies with a "big message," displayed each time in a PowerPoint presentation. But the opening slide that day was mysterious, and it piqued my interest as a researcher. It read: "Theory into Practice."[28]

Mr. Green began:

> So here we have an all-boys school. And there are a couple of theories about why all-boys schools work and why coed schools sometimes have issues that we don't have. And one of those theories is this. You have a male student who by himself is typically strong . . .
> *A stick figure of a boy appeared on the large screen.*
> . . . confident and well-behaved and well-mannered. And he's focused on the task in front of him. But then you interrupt his life with one of these . . .
> *A stick figure girl appeared on the screen next to the stick figure boy.*
> And what happens when females sometimes are around young, adolescent men? This happens. Sometimes they go a little crazy.
> *The stick figure boy does a few backflips.*

The boys laughed. Mr. Green continued:

> For a second I'm not going to blame you for laughing. And now that
> that second's passed, we need to address what that means. For the
> young lady or woman coming to our school, and walks past your
> classroom, and walks into your classroom while Mr. Calder or Ms.
> Larkin is teaching, and you take your eyes off the board, and looking
> at who comes in is a natural reaction. But then you say something, and
> then it goes from a little funny to very disrespectful. It disrupts your
> teacher who's teaching you, it disrupts your neighbor next to you, and
> it's very disrespectful to the female. And I know for a fact that things
> have been said. When people come in here, always show the ultimate
> respect. And if you're going to show more respect for people, it is for
> ladies. All the time. Guys, we have to show respect at all times. Do we
> understand that? (*Yes!* the students respond.) Do we understand that?
> (*"YES!"*) You will very rarely hear the word "boy" in this school. You
> won't hear it from my mouth. How do we call you? Young men.
> Gentlemen. Because that's how I know you're capable of acting. The
> bottom line is, we must always act like gentlemen. *All the time.*

Asking his students to respect women was laudable, but Mr. Green did
not challenge the monolithic discourse of distractions. The humor conveyed this: the stick figures were funny because *of course* boys "go a
little crazy" around girls. What Mr. Green demanded here is something
I will pick up again in later chapters (and was absent in the culture of
Perry High): that scholars, or true gentlemen, practice self-control, or
self-discipline.

The Discourse of Teenage Pregnancy

Female "distractions" could also be perilous. In the absence of a clear rationale for single-sex education at Perry High, over time the community
assembled a patchwork of rumors and conjectures. These portrayed a
student body marked by an uncontrollable sexuality. For Edward Moretti,
a white guidance counselor, the school's job was especially challenging when
it was coed. As he saw it, eliminating girls was welcomed because it removed
sexual tension that the adults were helpless to control. "While the hormones
are flying," he said, "at least they can't have the instant gratification of
screwing someone."

Among the young men, rumors persisted that a major reason for separating the students was to limit opportunities for sex. As the stories went,
school officials were worried that students were having sex in school or

were running off during the day to have sex. "From what I heard from other students," Vince said, "girls in Perry kept getting pregnant, so they wanted to split it up. So there was a lot of sex in bathrooms, stuff like that." The young men were eager to share these rumors with visitors and new staff members. Jennifer Okoye, a new teacher who had been hired to lead the school's program for overage students (called Second Chance), described how she had conducted her own "informal investigation" into how the young men felt about the sex separation: "The students talk about it all the time, how they are missing the girls, so I got that picture very quickly. But they also tell me that horrible things used to happen when they had the girls here. Stuff used to happen in the bathrooms and all that stuff going on between the boys and girls."

In his ethnographic study of marginalized young men in Boston, David Harding found that boys were wary of young women they felt would try to trick them into being fathers.[29] In this way, the girls threatened to derail the young men from a positive path. People at both Northside and Perry felt this was also the case. However, people in the two school communities believed that boys and girls were equally complicit in this behavior. Boys and girls posed mutual sexual threats to one another. This narrative relied on an image of young women who were sexually promiscuous. They were "bad girls." The young men at Perry and Northside called these young women "sluts" and "hoes." A politics of respectability clearly demarcates the "good girls" from the "bad girls." Good girls become Black "ladies" who are nonthreatening and subscribe to the virtues of respectable middle-class womanhood.[30] Sexuality underpins these narratives. Historically, controlling images have framed Black sexuality as pathological, with Black women as sexually rapacious and Black men as sexually predatory.[31] White ladies, meanwhile, hold onto an ideal chastity and purity. At the kickoff for a new mentoring program, Mr. Bradley, Perry High's principal, encouraged the students in the auditorium to find these respectable Black women. "You need to go to college and find a woman with a brain," he said. "Stay away from these hoochie-mamas on the street!"

A discourse of distractions was expressed primarily in terms of gender. By comparison, a discourse of teenage pregnancy was highly racialized. A concern with sexuality has dominated debates over single-sex education for Black girls. While rationales for single-sex education targeted to young men of color have increasingly been concerned with reducing rates of incarceration, the durable rationale for girls' schools is that these spaces help reduce rates of Black teenage pregnancy.[32] This rationale, therefore, assumes a bad Black girl. Moreover, teenage pregnancy "invokes white fears of 'overbreeding' among women of color, as white women are imagined as the only legitimate reproducers of the nation and women of color are imagined as a welfare burden."[33] Rates of teenage pregnancy for young Black women (aged fifteen to nineteen) have declined markedly since 1990—and by nearly 45 percent since 2007—but are today still double the rates for their white peers.[34]

For critics, a focus on sexuality in single-sex education is troublesome because it implies that Black student populations do not need to be empowered so much as contained and disciplined. Perry High sometimes turned to Thompson High, its all-girls sister school, to engage this narrative of containment and discipline. Just as the Perry High staff and students had passed along a sexualized mythology over the years, the boys shared unconfirmed stories about what exactly happened inside the walls of Thompson High. "I think [Thompson] is trying to keep the girls from having babies and ending up in one of those programs for moms," said Tyson, a twelfth grader. "The school is trying to save the girls because when they're moms maybe they can stick it out in a program for moms, but they'll probably end up dropping out of school."

Students at Northside Academy also bemoaned what they saw as the doomed futures of teenage mothers. Ms. Larkin's tenth-grade English class spent a few weeks analyzing the theme of "identity and place." One day, she asked her students to write autobiographical poems that opened with the line, "Where I'm From." Haleem's poem touched on a number of issues, and it swung back and forth between proud feelings and a derision for other things. Like those written by a few of his classmates, Haleem's poem frowned on teenage pregnancy: "I'm from where the plants don't even survive / I'm from where girls get pregnant at a young age / Crying babies who grow up to have no home training." What struck me in this exercise was that the boys seemed to place teenage pregnancy alongside "drugs and jails" (another line from Haleem's poem) as a major problem facing their community. What linked these themes was a belief in the moral erosion of Black families and the limited life prospects for children. Haleem blamed young moms for their children's bad behavior (a result of getting "no home training," or learning basic manners and respect, an especially scathing insult the boys would sometimes toss at one another). This message attached to a larger discourse of personal responsibility: that individual choices determined successes and failures, and so young women failed themselves and their children by "choosing" to have children at a young age. I found that the two schools generally saw young men and women as mutual threats, as the young men were also viewed as sexually aggressive and irresponsible. The focus on teenage pregnancy, of course, also implicated the young men and fatherhood.[35]

The discourse of pregnancy has another twist. A small number of adults invoked the discourse in a manner that implicated "good girls." The feeling among these adults was that certain girls were not at all sexually promiscuous. Instead, they focused on the "right" things (namely, their academic work) and especially needed to be protected from the sexual advances of their male peers. For instance, Kathy Booker, a parent, felt strongly that teenage pregnancy and underage sex derailed the futures of many Black girls. She described years of worrying that her eldest daughter, "who had so much promise," would find a young man who would lead her astray and impregnate her and that her daughter "would end up throwing her life away." As she implied, the cost of teenage pregnancy was especially high for young Black ladies with "so much promise." The father of Ms. Booker's own three children was not an active presence in the family, and so men, in her eyes, could end up being doubly dangerous: by impregnating teenage girls and then "being one of these men who abandon their kids and their kids' moms." As Ms. Booker saw it, then, sex-separate schools would provide an additional buffer to protect young Black *ladies* on their path to college. She felt that Thompson would "help to protect these girls so they can focus on what matters: their studies." She had drawn sharp distinctions between good girls and bad boys, while also suggesting that bad girls were undeserving of protection.

The scholar Farah Jasmine Griffin describes how a "rhetoric of protection" has been central to understandings of Black womanhood.[36] This rhetoric stabilizes a paternalistic gender order by offering protection to women and demanding their obedience in return. As I described in the Introduction, this and similar historical narratives have resonated in efforts to separate boys and girls in schools.[37] These efforts sought to secure white female sexuality as the exclusive property of white men. We can interpret Ms. Booker's comments as engaging a rhetoric of protection. Her comments called to mind stigmatizing portraits of Black women as overly dependent on the state (e.g., as "welfare queens") and therefore as exploiting state assistance. In her rationale for why a separate school for girls was necessary, Ms. Booker felt that state institutions—in this case, a public school—should assume the responsibility (or, in the language of neoliberal education, be held accountable) for protecting good girls "with promise" from the sexual threats posed by the community's young men. Drawing on her own life experiences, Ms. Booker implied that proper institutional support for good girls would delay pregnancies and encourage husbands and fathers to remain present in their children's lives. Restoring the stable, nuclear family was the vehicle for racial uplift.

The topic of teenage pregnancy dominated conversations around sexuality, but the young men were also concerned about sexually transmitted diseases (STDs). I asked Tre, a twelfth grader who had enrolled at Perry a year after it went all-boys, why the school had taken up the single-sex model. He first said that academic issues motivated the switch: "Perry was labeled as a bad school because there wasn't much learnin' taking place." He continued:

> I guess they ain't want to be one of them schools labeled as the highest AIDS level and all that stuff, because around that time, that's when Ferndale [High School], you know, they was labeled as the highest AIDS/HIV and all that, STDs and all that. At that time, they probably was thinking like if we separate them, nine out of ten then it won't happen. That's why I think they did it.

Tre's comments were revealing for a couple of reasons. First, his mention of labels and a ranking of schools revealed the long reach of neoliberal ideologies into the intimate lives and everyday language of the young men. Beyond identifying schools as merely "good" or "bad," students sometimes derided other schools (and their own) in quantitative terms. These widely circulating "normalizing judgments" implied that reform was not possible in certain schools, which instead carried a perpetual stigma and were to be avoided at all costs.[38]

Second, Tre pointed to the vital issue of sexual health for the young men. While narratives of uncontrollable sexuality offered a convenient way to justify separating boys and girls, the students avowed a desire to educate themselves about the dangers of unsafe sex. At Perry High, Lamar Gardner, a Black social worker, spoke often with students about sexually transmitted diseases and contraceptive use, and he organized lessons on the topic for the Second Chance program. Mr. Gardner had also worked with student leaders for the school's new gay–straight alliance to link up with the local chapter of GLSEN (Gay Lesbian Straight Education Network) for resources and workshops on promoting healthier sexual practices. Northside's social worker, Ms. Rodriguez, even described being overwhelmed by how often the young men chose to confide in her. This inspired the school to invite a speaker to facilitate a frank discussion with the young men on STDs. The speaker fielded many questions from the boys and shared a number of statistics and ways to obtain resources and support in the community. There was some snickering and male posturing (for example, when the speaker mentioned gay sex), but Northside, at least, was making efforts, however small, to educate their young men about safe sex.

The Discourse of Competition

Earlier, Ms. Rollins, a parent at Northside, had suggested that girls promote an unhealthy form of competition in young men. There was another form of competition. Girls were to be avoided not because they were a sexual distraction, but because they were stiff *academic* competition.

The young men were bombarded with the message that their female peers were better students. "You need good grades to get good jobs! And those jobs are going to the girls!" "I bet all the students at Thompson are on track to graduating!" And as far as parents and school officials were concerned, the data were there for all to see. During a period when school districts felt pressured to be as transparent as possible with performance data, the Morgan school district was fine with comparing boys and girls in district materials. (Perhaps because there were so few non-Black students in the district, these materials much less often shared performance data broken down by race.) According to Morgan school district records, in 2011 45 percent of Black male students dropped out of high school, compared to 29 percent of Black female students; and only 27 percent of eligible Black male students had enrolled in college, compared to 41 percent of their female counterparts.

School community members who had previously characterized young women as flirtatious and sexually promiscuous now offered a starkly different picture of female subjectivity. They again invoked the "good girl," one who was disciplined, rule-following, and mature.[39] In his comparative study of two public schools, Edward Morris explains how the performance of masculinity for young Black men inhibits their academic achievement.[40] These young men's quotidian masculine practices involved a carefree attitude with respect to school rules and academic effort (what Morris terms a "contrived carelessness"). These practices were grounded in a desire to resist submission to authorities. Meanwhile, as a group the young women took their schoolwork more seriously, worked harder, and were more apt to follow school rules. Collectively, these different behaviors help explain the gender gap in academic performance.

My findings were consistent with Morris's. People at both schools— students and adults—overwhelmingly felt that boys were not as invested in their schoolwork as their female peers. I was told that young men "fooled around too much," "don't care enough," are "too immature." Mr. Bradley, Perry High's principal, summarized a consensus opinion at the school when he said, "I think boys are not mature enough to understand the importance and the significance of education at this present time, and girls tend to do better in these years."

As Maurice Riles, a Black eighth-grade English teacher at Perry High, put it, "The all-boys model works . . . primarily because it gives young men an opportunity to be smart in the classroom. It's not necessarily cool to be smart." Or recall Mr. Reagan, the first-time teacher at Perry we met in chapter 1. Mr. Reagan thought back to a few professional development sessions (when the school was still under the direct supervision of the Excel educational management organization) where it was stressed that "when boys raise their hands and want to answer, you're kind of a nerd, you're a dork, you shouldn't do that. But then when you took girls out of the classroom, then all of a sudden it was okay to be smart."

The feeling was that the "too cool for school" mentality behind masculinity inadvertently had become a kind of coping mechanism. "I see a lot of young men puff their chests and say they don't need to put in the time, the work, to be successful," Mr. Tomlinson, a science teacher at Northside, explained. "That they'll be just fine without digging in and doing the work. But I think for a lot of our young men, they're afraid they'll just fail, and so they learn to brush it off." As Mr. Tomlinson suggested, a contrived carelessness may have enabled the young men to flout authority, but it also concealed the young men's deeper feelings of insecurity. And in a deepening, destructive cycle, young men would then come to dislike school altogether. All-boys schools, therefore, could build up the young men's damaged self-esteem and confidence. Reflecting again on his early training at Perry, Mr. Reagan remembered hearing that few young men would admit to low self-esteem. It was therefore incumbent on school officials to interpret other outward signs—such as embarrassment and frustration—as signaling low self-esteem. Mr. Reagan recalled being told that, in an all-boys environment, "boys are more likely to take a chance and answer a question that maybe they're not sure of the answer to if girls aren't in the room, because they won't feel as embarrassed if they get it wrong." While the two schools taught young men in distinct ways, their academic missions were both driven in part by a desire to raise young men's self-esteem and to address the related concerns over disengagement and low levels of motivation.

One day, the Perry High administration organized an assembly after a rash of student violations. "We are fed up with this crap!" Mr. Bradley screamed at the start, and it only got worse from there. The administrators announced that they would be coming down hard on violations of basic school rules, such as not wearing the uniform or showing up to school late. This seemingly spontaneous change of plan was, in fact, a legacy of Mr. Mincy's "broken windows" disciplinary approach from earlier, where administrators penalized low-level violations harshly in the hopes of deterring more serious violations. At one point, William Sharp, an administrator, told the boys that they should save the energy they "wasted" on "messing with one another" and apply it to their schoolwork. He then compared the boys to the girls at Thompson High: "I was shocked to hear that Thompson made AYP and we didn't," he screamed at the boys, referencing "adequate yearly progress," a measure of academic and school climate measures under No Child Left Behind. He continued: "You saying the girls are smarter? I don't think so. They just follow the rules!"

Mr. Sharp's proclamation highlighted some important themes. First, he followed the script that the girls' academic success was a product of hard work. This message was especially ironic given that, as I described in the last chapter, staff members attributed Thompson's early success to the school's strong leadership and not necessarily to the school's gender composition. Now that the girls were physically absent, the school wanted the boys to act like them. In this way, school officials had gendered the image of an ideal student who was obedient and rule-abiding. Indeed, especially at Perry, school officials were far more likely to compare their boys to girls (who were always seen as higher achieving), rather than compare their own students to one another. This also demonstrated how Thompson High served as a flexible and available resource for Perry High to "do gender."[41] Adults could variously describe Thompson girls as "bad girls" to be avoided, or "good," sexually responsible girls who required protection from the young men of Perry.

Second, Mr. Sharp pitted the girls' school, which had achieved AYP, against the boys' school, which had not. Mr. Sharp, like Mr. Bradley before him, implied that the boys and girls were in competition with one another. Instead of encouraging partnerships between the sibling schools, the administration relied on a discourse of competition (wrapped up in a larger obsession with data and standardized assessment) that reflected a neoliberal agenda. This hinted at a core belief behind support for single-sex education: that the success of girls was coming at the expense of success for young men. And while Mr. Bradley's and Mr. Sharp's comments shared the sentiment that the boys needed to work as hard as girls, Mr. Sharp's comments were obvious attempts to shame the young men as well. By merely summoning test scores, Mr. Sharp dishonored the young men and questioned their collective masculine pride. Instead of offering positive encouragement, the administration counterposed their "bad boys" to Thompson's "good girls" and reinforced a troublesome ideology of "weak men, strong women" in Black communities.[42]

The Discourse of Motivation

For some, the proof was in the pudding. If it was true that boys could focus more and perform better in an all-boys school, than why had the school consistently underperformed under Excel's management? Vince was especially interested in sharing his thoughts on this issue. Since he had transferred from another middle school as a seventh grader, he had no stake in the turf wars that consumed Perry High in its first year as an all-boys school. Over the years, he had cultivated an identity as a scholar. He was one of the top students in his class. While many of his peers had embraced hip-hop, Vince had intentionally cultivated an identity as a poet. He was eager to recite lines from his favorite poems, as well as his own poetry, to anyone who would listen. Some of Vince's poems, in fact, dealt with masculinity and identity. A history teacher, James Brennan, was fond of using a line from one of Vince's poems (entitled "The Test of a Man") in his classes. He asked his students "to be a torch in dimly lit places." Mr. Brennan interpreted it to mean that his students should be a source of strength in the community. Vince preferred an interpretation of the torch as an inner strength. As he explained, it was a counterweight to the displays of physical or outward aggression that were important to his peers.

School officials, Vince said, "told us that we'll learn better with the girls out of the school. They figure, you know, if girls are out, you'll be more focused on what you're supposed to do. But it hasn't progressed since girls left. It's pretty much been the same." According to Vince, the main takeaway, leaving aside other factors, was that the school's overall lack of success had cast doubt on the claim that girls impede young men's achievement. Vince was also certain that the transition had occurred too quickly. Referring once more to a word he used in one of his own poems, Vince told me that a change of that magnitude is not "microwavable": the school needed to fight the urge for quick results when the situation demanded patience and planning.

While Vince reasoned that the discourse of distractions was faulty, elsewhere in our interview he suggested, to the contrary, that the discourse was not untrue so much as it only applied to certain boys. A different discourse operated for the young men who most embodied a scholar identity. These school-oriented young men were "recruited to" what I call a "discourse of motivation": girls and boys motivated one another to be mature and, above all, disciplined and studious students.[43] As Vince explained:

> If you got a girl in the classroom most likely she's not going to want to hang around with you if your grades are not doing too well. So basically that's kind of motivation. Because if you fail a math test, she's not going to talk to you. You think, like, "I've got to get my grades up." Your grades get better, you know?

I asked Vince why he believed that. He told me that it was a message that had been drilled into his head by his two aunts, the only members of his immediate family to attend college. Being a real man, Vince continued, meant showing that you were headed somewhere in life, and that meant "taking care of your business in school."

His classmate, Tyson, agreed. As forcefully as anyone, Tyson believed that all-boys schools were appropriate for some students, and coed schools for others. Boys who fooled around, he thought, should all be placed together in school "where they can get straight," or become more disciplined students. Other young men cared about their schoolwork and wanted to impress young women by looking smart, he said:

> When you in a coed school, especially when you in front of a girl . . . you want to be smart. I mean, you don't want to be the guy in the classroom that says something dumb once in a while because I seen girls got a certain attention for, you know, if you say something dumb or if you a smart guy. [They say], "Why you saying that stupid stuff?" Obviously it's just a joker or a clown saying that stuff.

While Vince and Tyson best embodied the scholar identities, the discourse of motivation was not exclusive to them. Tre (interviewed earlier) was a twelfth grader at Perry. He had been kicked out of several schools and had most recently spent time at an all-boys high-security high school for a weapons violation. For most of his schooling life, then, Tre had embraced a street identity. Because he was almost nineteen years old and had been identified as especially "at-risk" by the district, he enrolled in Second Chance, the special program for overage young men at Perry. He was making enormous strides with the extra support, and he shared with me that he had given much thought to how his masculine identity might hurt or help him with getting his high school degree, which seemed like a distant prospect years earlier. Based on his experiences in all-male spaces, he concluded that young men "don't care about looking smart. You let things slip, just do corny stuff. Stupid shit." He was now certain that "if it was girls in here . . . everybody going to try to be on point, try to keep their grades up and everything."

Northside Academy actively recruited and cultivated students who drew on scholarly repertoires, and so the discourse of motivation circulated even more widely at that school. Jeremiah and Terrell were two ninth graders who had attended different middle schools and had quickly become friends at Northside. During lunch one day early in the school year, they pleaded with me to interview them together so that they could share their initial impressions of the school.

> TERRELL: I truly need—to sit in class to pay attention sometimes—girls around . . . because at my other school I used to have competitions with girls, like because you know how they say girls are smarter than guys? I used to test them, like, "I want to see [how you did] on this test," and all that. Here, you can't really do that because you would just see how smart a guy is.
>
> JEREMIAH: To add on to what he says, he might be right about being focused more because, you know, when our teachers brought two girls into the class and as soon as they came in and sat there, the whole class, everybody had their hand raised, trying to answer questions.
>
> TERRELL: Yeah, trying to look smart in front . . .
>
> JEREMIAH: Trying to impress the girls, wanting to look smart.

Like their counterpart Vince at Perry High, Terrell and Jeremiah came in thinking that a discourse of distractions was common sense. But what they found in the switch to an all-boys environment surprised them. They had flipped the discourse of competition—which maintained that girls pose a serious academic threat to boys—on its head, maintaining that competition between boys and girls was healthy and a way for boys to prove their academic prowess to girls they were out to impress. This discourse challenges the notion that the performance of masculinity harms educational attainment for young men of color.

"The Gay School"

Perry High and Prison Rape

A final discourse crystallized in the separation of girls and boys. Perry High and Northside Academy each took on a reputation as "the gay school." De jure sex separation, in a community that had long experienced de facto race and class segregation, was shot through with deeply sexualized meanings.

The Perry High students felt that their peers in the community believed that boys who attended Perry were gay and that the school attracted gay-identified students. Tyrell, a tenth grader who had transferred to Perry High in the past year, seemed to resent the school before he ever stepped foot inside it. He had heard "the school was full of all these gay boys. Like, you come here if you into gays." The school's reputation provoked something even more fearful. As Tyrell also pointed out, "You become gay if you stick around." The students believed the reputation in the community was that Perry High students would "go gay" from attending an all-male school.[44]

To understand what "the gay school" meant to the young men, we need to see how it intersected with the school's stubborn reputation as "like jail." The school physically resembled one with its intimidating exterior and metal detectors, and the students perceived that outsiders stigmatized the school for being disorderly. "It looks like an institution," Lamont, a twelfth grader, told me. "I've been locked up. I know what it looks like when you get locked up. There's gates on the windows, all boys in the schools." As I described in chapter 1, this reputation was further reinforced in the school's penal turn under Excel's management. The local media had portrayed the turf wars between Perry students and (the former) Thompson students as evidence of a school overrun by territorial and criminally inclined boys. Mr. Mincy, himself a former police officer, responded forcefully with calls for law and order in the school.

The transition to an all-male setting, which had cemented the school's resemblance to a prison, had provoked anxieties around a strict prison hierarchy. This highlighted a second meaning behind "the gay school." Most troubling for the boys was the threat of sexual assault inside prisons, which they learned about from friends and family members who had been incarcerated.[45] Researchers believe that a culture of inmates sexually assaulting and prostituting more vulnerable men is typical inside prisons.[46] Keith, a twelfth grader, told me:

> Some of the boys in this neighborhood think they're tough. They're not tough. My brother tells me, "Men get locked up and they learn real fast they're nothin'. They meet some real goons and soon they be someone's bitch. And no one can save you then."

The topic sometimes came up in school. One day, some friends were chatting about the recent episode of the television show *The Boondocks*. They enjoyed it especially for its lead character, Huey, a politically conscious young Black teenager. Eddie brought up an episode where one character, a Black man named Tom, is arrested and fears he will be sexually assaulted in jail. The boys discussed how often people make jokes about prison rape, before Eddie said, "Real talk: that episode was messed up. That man was scared." His comment effectively ended the conversation, suggesting that prison rape was an especially difficult and taboo topic.[47] In the United States, the rise in a hyperaggressive prison masculinity coincided with a steep rise in incarceration rates during the 1980s.[48] With more street gang members incarcerated, prison culture itself came to adopt an organized gang structure. Therefore, as the criminal justice system has come to be identified with Black masculinity, sexual domination has become a defining feature of the prison experience. The association of Blackness with prisons has likely augmented public perceptions of prisons as sexually predatory institutions. And there is evidence of sexual assault in juvenile facilities. The Bureau of Justice Statistics found that in 2012, 10 percent of youth in these facilities reported at least one incident of sexual victimization.[49] The threat of victimization is likely greater for juveniles sentenced to adult facilities, which compounds the already severe consequences of "adultification" for Black male youth.[50]

Sexual hazing and antigay sentiments are present at elite, white-dominated all-boys schools, but their students' privileged identities—by race and class—help protect their masculinity.[51] For the young men of Perry, however, sexuality was linked to punishment and was therefore an especially tenuous identity, one that had to be actively defended. As Carissa Froyum has written, a vigorous assertion of being heterosexual is an "especially important identity for kids made vulnerable by racist images that stigmatize their sexuality and families."[52] The Perry High students were especially concerned about the cruelty of sexual victimization and about what it represented more generally: a debased identity where one is completely stripped of one's manhood. To perform appropriate masculinity and to earn respect, the young men frequently denounced sex between men, as well as an emasculated "fag identity."[53] One day, a student stood near the doorway and "dry humped" students as they came to class. Jared walked right by him and said, "I think it's gay having all these boys here. We need some girls, not 'sword fights,' " which refers to sex between men.

Joking, however, was the main currency for shoring up heterosexuality. In an eighth-grade math class one day, a group of boys discussed their weekend plans. Kenny adopted a "fag act," where he impersonated an effeminate identity in order to mock it.[54] In a high-pitched voice, he said, "Larry, I need new jeans that make my butt look good. Take me shopping!" Larry, who risked being emasculated, shot back, "All your butt's getting is a good workout in jail!" The boys called this *bussin'*: putting down others in ways that ranged from playful teasing to hurtful insults. (Much of the boys' interactions involved *boastin'*, or bragging, often about girls and sports, as well as bussin'.) In some cases, the students' joking rejected the school's own reputation. One day in the lunchroom, Doug surprised some friends and pretended to be a cop. He yelled, "What are you Perry boys up to?" The boys laughed and someone yelled, "We gettin' booked!" Xavier shouted, "Officer, let me go! These Perry boys been in this school too long. Take them: they like being on their knees now!" If Perry High "was known" (or had a reputation) for being "the gay school," then Xavier knew to "be known" for (or to stake his reputation on) rejecting a powerless identity linked to incarceration. The other boys howled and did not seem particularly offended, perhaps because—by joining in on the joke—they also benefited from the way Xavier denounced both meanings behind "the gay school": that boys turned gay at the school and that they would likely be dominated once incarcerated.

The young men's joking interactions are more comprehensible when viewed in the serious context in which they emerged. Linking to the African American tradition of verbal sparring, the joking both earned young men respect and served as a veiled critique of the deep inequalities of punishment. As in the example above, the boys at times impersonated officers, using a harsh and mocking tone. Indeed, Black humor has historically been used to circumvent the threat of castigation that accompanied more direct and serious critiques of injustice. As Richard Majors and Janet Billson have observed, these interactions allow Blacks to engage "deadly serious issues" and "express deeper truths with impunity."[55] Although the serious issue of prison sexual assault was only ever addressed obliquely through the jokes, the threat of it appeared to produce some level of anxiety among the young men. As Keith shared earlier, a fag identity suggested not simply emasculation, but total incapacitation, a permanent imprint of shame and stigma ("No one can save you then"). This identity signaled that the potential to live one's life as fully human had been lost. These fears are amplified for young men who are already denied opportunities to grow and mature.

As I discuss in chapter 4, some Black male leaders demonstrated care by speaking honestly with their students about imprisonment. Yet the officials failed in this instance to see how the young men themselves expressed fears of incarceration. I observed few instances of serious dialogue between adults and students on the topic of sexuality, outside of the examples I shared earlier in the chapter. These conversations may have offered the young men a language to talk productively about feelings of fear and shame, which were so taboo that they were virtually unspeakable outside the context of joking.[56] Without these interventions, their struggles to be known—to earn respect—spoke "of masculinity in a grammar of power," using language that suggested they could be victims of harm, and language that posed harm to others.[57]

Northside Nerds

While the language of "choice" assumes that families decide which schools the children will attend, parents normally have the final say. The large majority of the students I interviewed (thirty-two of the thirty-nine) made it a point to tell me that their parents had chosen Northside for them. (They liked to say that their parents "forced" them to attend.) And the source of opposition was no surprise: as at Perry, the boys felt that the school attracted gay students. I asked Marlon, a tenth grader, what went through his mind when he learned that Northside was all-boys. He responded, "I instantly said 'no' because I was used to a coed school, and I ain't wanna come here. I thought everybody was going to be gay and stuff. People tease us walking down the streets." The staff members were well aware that this was a general feeling among the ninth graders. As Anish Gupta, a former teacher, told me, "I think the biggest social challenge that they face is . . . people's perceptions of what Northside is. So guys thinking that Northside students are freaks because they only go to school with boys and they must, therefore, be homo."

A common fear I heard was that the school would make the students "go gay." This came across loud and clear when I asked students what they thought of Mr. Pierce's proposal to add an elementary school and a middle school. Terrell and Jeremiah, the two ninth graders we met earlier in the chapter, responded in this way:[58]

> TERRELL: Whoa, no, that cannot happen. That's gonna be like their whole school years. And then they have to wait until college. Like from kindergarten, preschool, whatever. . . . No, kindergarten to twelfth grade, that's too many days without seeing girls every day. And then they have to wait 'til college, like that's only going to be four years.
>
> JEREMIAH: I really don't think that he should do that. If he did . . . I think that if something like that will happen, and [boys] will have to go through all-boys in school all that time, then that would not stay the same. That would *spark something.*
>
> FREEDEN: Spark what?
>
> JEREMIAH: I mean, say that I'm staying with all boys from first grade all the way to twelfth grade in school, all boys, 24/7, all school, all day, all boys, no girls, all boys. Being by yourself with all those boys all the time, from being a little boy when you don't know better, from like first grade, I don't know what might happen to you.

FREEDEN: Like what?

JEREMIAH: How do you think somebody just comes out and says, "I'm gay"? How do you think somebody comes gay, becomes gay? Like it can't just happen out of nowhere; it has to be something that leads up for that to happen. So I'm saying if you're in school with all dudes, 24/7 from when you just a little kid, five, six years old, all those years added up with all those dudes, you're not going to feel the same way about girls.

For many marginalized young men of color, the embrace of heterosexual power is central to a legitimate masculine identity. As Terrell and Jeremiah and a handful of other students shared with me, a lower school posed a grave threat to that identity by nurturing sexual attraction among young men. This was a fearful prospect because it emasculated boys. As C. J. Pascoe has shown, young white men do not necessarily reject an abject "fag" identity that is equated with same-sex desire; rather, they renounce the assumption of weakness behind a fag identity.[59] However, this rejection is racialized differently for poor young Black men. As Carissa Froyum notes, these marginalized youth conflate gender nonconformity—in this case, an emasculated identity—with homosexuality.[60]

Therefore, especially among the ninth graders, who experienced these anxieties most acutely, there was a strong need to prove to others that they were not, in fact, gay. Here again are Terrell and Jeremiah.

TERRELL: Some boy, he was like, "What school you go to?" I was like, "Northside Academy." He was like, "Oh, the new gay school?" I'm like, "What?" I was like, "Yo, you can look at my phone, I've got all these girls' numbers in there."

JEREMIAH: My girlfriend, she just asked me, "You know gay people around school?" I said, "No." She was like, "Are you sure? Because that's what I heard." And I was like, "Well, you know, you're probably wrong because whoever said that is probably spreading rumors." She's like, "All right." But with my friends, the guys, they just say the same thing: "Yo, they gay, that's Northside." They say, "You go to Northside, you shouldn't go there because people gonna think you gay, and people are gonna lose respect for you."

To defend himself against what he saw as an insult, Terrell had to prove that he was, in fact, straight, by showing the other young man that his phone was full of girls' phone numbers.

While Northside also had a reputation as "the gay school," this carried profoundly different meanings than those at Perry High. Mr. Pierce had intentionally created a respectable institution, and so a prison discourse was absent at Northside. The school also did not carry the baggage of being "the hood school," as Perry did. Instead, as the Northside students perceived it, the "gay school" reputation was doubly emasculating: the perception was not only that they were attracted to other boys, but that they were physically weak. The students conflated sexual orientation with gender nonconformity: being gay meant being unable to defend oneself. This was especially emasculating because being able to fight was such a valuable form of masculine currency in their communities.

The Northside students were certain that this was why young men from other schools harassed them on the streets and sometimes "jumped" them, or tried to start fights. They were viewed as easy targets. Richard, an eleventh grader, said he had grown accustomed to boys making fun of him when he walked home after school (because of Northside's extended school day, throngs of other high school students were often already hanging out on the streets). "If I see a group of people," he said, "I go the other direction because I know they're going to try to say something because I go to an all-boys school and they think I'm not going to do nothing. They think we're a bunch of homos and nerds."

The prison discourse at Perry High, I argued, had entered the young men's verbal play. Without a sense of school pride, the young men had turned the insults on themselves. At Northside, students coped with feelings of emasculation in a different fashion. When I followed up with Jeremiah later in the year, his tone had changed:

> I'm like, how is this a "gay school" if girls coming up here trying to talk to us because we go to a smart school? And then I was like, "That's not a gay school, it's a really smart and strict school. We got other stuff that schools don't even have." . . . A new building that's not really trashed, and we have good teachers and some good students in here." So I'm like, "Yo, I bet my school could probably do better on the [state exam], better than your school."

Jeremiah had learned to deflect insults that he attended "the gay school." He was proud to attend a "smart and strict school." He implied that he and his classmates were being "cared for."[61] The school's strong academics and strict disciplinary culture meant the school was serious about learning. Being called gay could no longer emasculate the respectable scholars of Northside Academy. Or as the school community members liked to say, Northside had generated positive "buzz": their students were *exceptional* and on the path to success. As I demonstrate in the next two chapters, this status—the school's brotherhood—had to be protected at all costs.

The Perry High administration never addressed the entire student body about antigay language and behaviors. In part due to Northside's strict Code of Conduct, the school took more deliberate steps to curb this behavior. One of the most powerful moments from the school year was a speech that Nate, an eleventh grader, gave at a weekly assembly. Nate was the captain of the school's Mock Trial team and wanted to be a lawyer. He asked the administration if he could read a prepared speech about needing to respect not merely the cultural identities of gays and lesbians, but their political rights as well. Nate spent a good portion of his speech arguing that marriage equality be extended to same-sex couples. I followed up with Nate after the assembly. He told me he was trying to take a stand against antigay sentiments among his peers. He felt he had the support of adults, too:

> Everyone should have that right. I think that it's something that should have never been tampered with, and personally I understand that some people who [are] Christians and things like that don't believe it, but we're in a country that's not really based on Christian liberties. We're based on pursuit of happiness and giving everyone the right to a free will, and I think that when they took that away from people, I think they're taking away their civil rights, something that was given to them at birth. In the Declaration of Independence it says that you're endowed to certain inalienable rights, and I think by them taking that right away from them, they're alienating them as citizens.

Nate received loud applause at the assembly. Several teachers hugged him. In an especially symbolic display, Mr. Green shook Nate's hand and held his grip, which affirmed Nate's message. While heteronormativity undergirds all-male schools, the collective work of students and staff during pivotal moments such as large gatherings can go a long way toward creating more inclusive environments.

Conclusion

This chapter took up the ostensibly straightforward question of why to separate boys and girls in schools. The commonsense "discourse of distractions" proved, in fact, to be one of several competing discourses that refracted complex meanings around teenage pregnancy, girls as competition and motivation, and a reputation as "the gay school." The assumptions of deviant and respectable subjects, bad girls and gentlemen, emasculated fags and victims of prison rape, revealed how these discourses produced not "static identities," but represented "social formations that produce protean and historically temporal subjects."[62] "The gay school" discourse helps especially with articulating the troubling ways that the sociosexual binary between deviance and respectability organizes Black male subjectivity.

What these discourses shared was an assumption of heteronormativity. In one context, Northside officials could implore their students to control their masculine impulses and to treat women as true gentlemen would. In another context, young women were cast as sexual deviants who threatened the young men's own positive futures. Through it all, stakeholders from parents to school officials drew on these discourses strategically to enforce the notion of the much needed separation of young Black men from their female peers. Having laid out the history of Perry High and Northside Academy, I turn in the coming chapters to how the two schools diverged sharply in terms of how they taught their boys, promoted a sense of belonging, and groomed their students to become men.

CHAPTER THREE

Teaching Black Boys

From Cultural Relevance to Culturally Irrelevant Latin

Ms. Spring greeted her ninth graders warmly at the start of class.
"*Salvēte, discipuli.*"
"Salvē, magistra," the young men respond.[1]
When students walked through Northside's doors for the first time, Latin was the great unknown. A few were familiar with dramatic films set in Roman times, such as *Spartacus* and especially *Gladiator,* the blockbuster featuring Russell Crowe. (The school mascot happened also to be a gladiator.) Others had encountered Latin in the spells cast in the hugely popular *Harry Potter* novels. Ms. Spring wanted nothing less than for her students to share her love of Latin and to understand that it was the language of true scholars. But Latin was strange and hard, full of rules and images of white gods.[2] Fully aware of Latin's steep learning curve, Ms. Spring created an immersive classroom dedicated to the subject. To increase their vocabulary, the students created comic strips using Latin words. Students flocked to the Latin Club Ms. Spring hosted for boisterous games of Scrabble. Others would boast of winning awards in national Latin competitions. The language marked them all as exceptional.

Educational researchers have long observed that schools rely on two forms of curricula: a formal academic curriculum and an informal or "hidden" curriculum that encapsulates the unstated beliefs and values that reproduce inequalities along lines of race, gender, class, and sexuality.[3] In this chapter, I expand on this idea by drawing on Martin Summers's helpful framework for how Black-controlled schools historically have sought to (and debated how to) educate their students. This includes teaching the *head,* or providing a classic, liberal arts education; teaching the *hand,* or offering an industrial education; and educating the *heart,* or teaching character, a set of characteristics that renders one "a virtuous member of the community."[4] As a mode of governmentality, Black academies teach appropriate conduct: a proper way of being a student and being a man.

Northside Academy taught the head in order to reach the heart; the school modeled its Latin curriculum after the classics curricula of elite institutions, which marked students as having the disciplined minds required of men of high moral character. A second resource—the school's second most visible resource alongside its Latin curriculum—helped mark the young men as "good students." Uniforms conveyed to the outside world that the young men had disciplined bodies that set them apart from the undisciplined bodies of dangerous boys in the neighborhood.

With the aid of a new federal grant, Perry High had made strides. While Perry lacked many of the advantages of Northside, the school felt much of the same pressure to test well and to increase its graduation rate. The thrust of the school's efforts was aimed at providing culturally relevant teaching. The school challenged the "college for all" philosophy that has dominated public education in the past several decades and envisioned a school that would prepare students for multiple career paths after graduation, including vocational education that cultivated the hand.

Northside Academy

Disciplined Minds

The hundreds who attended Detroit's "Saving the Black Male" conference in 1990 demanded that city officials take intentional steps to help their struggling young Black men. The educator Clifford Watson worked with various city task forces (one with the memorable name of "The Hope Team") to create a school that would eventually become the Malcolm X Academy. While the term "charter" was not yet common then in the educational world, the school closely resembled one, as it was free to determine its own curriculum while still bound to district guidelines. Watson's proposed curriculum for the school was, among other things, "futuristic" (aimed at preparing the students for future jobs in high-demand areas such as engineering) and "linguistic" (aimed at teaching strong foreign language skills).

Afrocentrism was the centerpiece of the curricula of the first-wave academies. W. E. B. Du Bois was a lodestar for the schools in this respect. Through the 1920s, Du Bois became heavily involved in the work to highlight the shared experiences of oppression among African peoples around the world. This work crystallized into Pan-African education, a key principle of a Du Boisian philosophy of education.[5] In its design, Detroit's Malcolm X Academy identified Du Bois as an "elder . . . who advocated the necessity for Black Americans to uncover the truths about our African origins and to correct the distortions of our history, before, during, and after enslavement in the U.S."[6] Both Detroit and Milwaukee sought to establish "African American Immersion Schools" that included the "concepts, content, themes, perspectives, and pedagogy reflective of the African/African American ontology."[7] These public schools would be the first all-male *and* African-immersion schools in the country. For these educators, Afrocentrism was an innovation long in the making. Proponents of Afrocentrism and other culturally relevant curricula have wanted, in part, to address what Du Bois famously termed a "double consciousness" in which Blacks are forced to view themselves through the eyes of a white majority.[8]

Afrocentrism squares with larger efforts to integrate a culturally relevant pedagogy in classrooms serving youth of color.[9] In "Does the Negro Need Separate Schools?" Du Bois argued that Black-controlled institutions could provide Black children with "Sympathy, Knowledge, and the Truth." For Du Bois, Black children should be taught with dignity ("where children are treated like human beings"[10]) and taught their history ("Negroes must know the history of the Negro race in America, and this they will seldom get in white institutions"[11]). Educational researchers have built on these two Du Boisian insights. First, cultural relevance is a matter of *pedagogy*, or how teachers relate to and teach their students. Among other things, teachers view their students as knowledgeable agents who should play a central role in their own schooling. Second, cultural relevance is a matter of *content*, or the forms of knowledge and curricula that are rooted in the lived experiences and cultural lives of youth.[12]

The faculty at Northside were an eclectic mix of young and old teachers, some with years of teaching experience and others who had come straight from college. There were Teach For America recruits, teachers who had taught for decades and had even taught with Mr. Pierce before coming to Northside, and a new Latin teacher with a doctorate and previous experience as a college instructor. In hiring teachers, Mr. Pierce prioritized fit with the school community and expertise in a content area. Prospective teachers visited the school for a day, where they observed classes, gave a mock lesson, and sat for a group interview with current staff members and students. Interviewers were provided with a rubric to assess teaching candidates on a 1 ("Not for us!") to 5 ("Hire him/her now!") scale. Candidates who earned a score of 5 were seen as "outstanding teammates," had a history of "doing whatever it takes to move students academically," and had "beliefs and values" that were "fully in line with our mission." One day I shadowed a teaching candidate and was told this woman was among the stronger teaching candidates Northside had hosted. She had taught for several years at another charter school. During her interview, she described having "the highest expectations" for her students. She preached "tough love." And above all, she had a strong preference for teaching boys over girls.[13]

Understandably, staff with more teaching experience were more likely to practice a culturally relevant pedagogy. Rachel Holden was a white woman in her thirties with over a decade of experience teaching middle school social studies, in both traditional public schools and charters serving low-income children, in several cities. She was widely adored by her students. Her lessons were organized and engaging, and she often gave her students opportunities to act as teachers themselves. During a lesson on the Revolutionary War, she set up a debate where students defended the side of the Loyalists or the Patriots. After students answered questions, she asked students to "roll it": to check for involvement and to give students a chance to affirm their classmates' answers. The students told me they appreciated that she offered clear directions, was organized, challenged them, and was always there when they needed help.

Yet the school's identity, success, and fate were bound to content and curricula that were culturally irrelevant. Northside's fateful decision to embrace the ancient language of Latin evoked a Du Bois different than the man who had spearheaded the Pan-African movement. This was a younger Du Bois who viewed a classical education as the necessary enculturation into elite society and as the language of future race leaders. It was a Du Bois who had excelled in this curriculum in grade school in his predominantly white town of Great Barrington, Massachusetts, and who would go on to be a professor of Latin at Wilberforce University after earning his doctorate at Harvard.[14] It was a man who believed strongly in a challenging, liberal arts education.

For some boys, Latin was light years apart from their own cultural histories. Several young men came from middle school charters with a focus on African history and culture. This included Marlon, a tenth grader. I asked him to describe his transition from middle school. He responded:

> Bizarre. I never really learned Roman history and had a history class
> about Christopher Columbus and all that because the middle school I
> went to, they just talk about Black history, like Martin Luther King,
> Malcolm X, and all those kind of people. And so we never talked about
> Christopher Columbus. We never talked about world history. We just
> talked about Black history.

Indeed, compared to Perry High, Northside placed less of an emphasis on both African and African-American history in its social studies curriculum. Instead, the school hitched its fortunes to Latin, which was impossible to avoid across the school. Extended school hours and occasional Saturday classes meant extra time dedicated to Latin. Directions near the stairs were written in Latin. While the language was the focus, the school also taught Greek and Roman culture. Some teachers adorned their classrooms with popular images of Roman culture. In one classroom, "What we do in life echoes in eternity" graced the wall, a line from the movie *The Gladiator*. It was followed by the question, "What will your echo be?" In another room, a banner read, "HONOR THE GODS. LOVE YOUR WOMAN. DEFEND YOUR COUNTRY." I came to think of this as the school's unofficial slogan. It conveyed a sense of pride and tradition. It anticipated competition and asked the young men to protect one another. It was heteronormative.

And above all, Latin was hard. This was drilled into the students' minds long before they enrolled, which was part of the school's plan to mentally prepare the students and to weed out those who were not serious. I observed this at an interview with a prospective student, Khyri, and his mother. The interviews provided an overview of the school and gave prospective students a chance to share their interests and to ask questions. Above all, it was a chance for Julia Martinez, the school's admissions director, to make sure the prospective students and their families were serious about attending.

At the end of the interview, Ms. Martinez asked Khyri if he had any questions.

"How hard is Latin?" Khryi asked. "I heard it's hard." His mom's eyes widened. She seemed embarrassed by the question and was likely worried that Khyri came across as incapable of handling the school's workload.

Ms. Martinez smiled. She had gotten the question before. "It's the hardest you'll ever work, that's for sure. But you have to. Our goal is to prepare you for college."

Before Khryi could speak again, his mom interjected. "Well, Khryi is willing to do whatever it takes, Ms. Martinez." Ms. Martinez was accustomed to being reassured by parents that their sons would live up to the school's high standards. The school may have wanted complete buy-in from students, but the truth was that many were apprehensive and even strongly rejected the idea. The uniforms made them look nerdy. There were no girls. The hours were long. They wouldn't attend the same school as their friends. And what *was* Latin anyway?

Latin weighed especially heavy on the boys because many came in at a disadvantage, having underperformed in their English classes and having never taken a foreign language. (Those who had language experience typically had taken some Spanish and French in middle school.) Fortunately, their gateway into the language was Ms. Spring, a white teacher who was widely regarded as the best instructor at the school. Ms. Spring had attended an all-girls Catholic high school. There she learned Latin from a "little old nun who terrified" her but who was "the best Latin teacher in the world." Ms. Spring aspired to similar heights and earned a college scholarship to study Latin. With her culturally responsive pedagogy, she helped bridge the gap between her students and a culturally irrelevant curriculum.[15] The school founder was wise enough to know that he needed his best teacher to work with incoming Latin novices. Ms. Spring demonstrated deep care and empathy: she stayed as long as needed after school, forged strong connections with families, and went out of her way to get to know her students outside of class. The students were effusive with their praise; Ms. Spring was "always there for you," "passionate about teaching," and "the one and only." (In the next chapter, I address the racial and gender politics behind white female teachers working with Black male students.)

Still, Latin was a shock to the system. Early headmasters borrowed the classical curriculum from the British, and the language was once common in secondary and post secondary education in the United States.[16] However, Latin grew less popular in the early part of the twentieth century. Why Latin rebounded in the 1970s is important for this story. Verbal scores on the SAT, the ubiquitous standardized exam used in college admissions, had dropped markedly, and worried educators turned to Latin for help. While the research is mixed, some studies show that Latin improves English grammar skills, and especially vocabulary, given that nearly two-thirds of all English words are derived from Latin.[17] Northside officials told prospective families and students that Latin would give the young men a substantial leg up with the SAT and state standards-based exams. They would see progress each month when they took practice exams. In the era of "No Child Left Untested," where exam scores rank and sort and breed competition among families and schools, this message resonated powerfully.

Beyond the functional utility of improving language skills, Latin was a form of elite cultural capital, a set of knowledge, skills, and preferences that are valued by dominant institutions.[18] Staff members frequently told students that earning medals on the National Latin Exam and their experience giving mandatory "declamations"—Latin recitations of famous texts— would shine on college applications. In recalling the school CEO's recruiting pitch to her, Ms. Spring said:

> He told me that every kid was going to have four years of Latin and
> that it was mandatory for all of them, that it was the most important

thing that they could be studying because it was going to set them apart from everybody else in the other city schools. That he was looking for something that was going to be hard for them, that would impress college admissions people. It will *set them apart*. It will make them special.

While the ninth graders were getting accustomed to the language, the tenth and eleventh graders sang Latin's praises. Latin had become a point of pride. Charles, a tenth grader, told me that "lots of people don't know a language like that. That's a great thing to know. And then a lot of colleges might accept you in there because you took up to four years of Latin." From Tamar, an eleventh grader: Latin "looks pretty good on a college application because people think, 'He can speak a dead language.' " Northside had embraced the language just as other major cities were turning to it to give their students an advantage in the race to college.

On the website for an expensive tutoring company, representatives of elite universities gush over applicants who take a rigorous course of study in the "dead language." An official at the University of Chicago offered that when he sees Latin on a high school transcript, he thinks, "This student is likely to be *disciplined*, have a strong basis for further learning, [and] be a little more creative toward intellectual pursuits than most."[19] Indeed, in selecting Latin, Northside Academy had adopted the "major objective" of elite boarding schools: to cultivate a "disciplined and trained mind."[20] As I learned during one of my first visits to the school, the Latin word for "student" is *discipulus*. As Peter Cookson and Caroline Hodges Persell have written, classical languages have always aimed to police the behavior of youth; they "were to the mind what cold showers were to the body: tonics against waywardness."[21] Clark Holmes, an assistant principal (and who, coincidentally, oversaw student discipline), was fond of telling the boys that in its third year, the school was entering a pivotal moment in its history. "The first two years were all about setting a tone," he announced at an assembly. "But year three is about establishing a *culture*." What he meant partly was the absolute discipline of mind and body. And discipline was empowering. As Mr. Pierce told me:

> If we teach these guys Latin, first of all, we're insisting that they take on something that we know is very complex, okay, and that will have to challenge them. What it will do in taking on that challenge and overcoming that challenge, it will empower the boys.

Ronald Davidson, a white math teacher, had attended a private all-boys school and had taken Latin himself in school. He likened Latin to a complex form of math:

I struggled through four years of Latin. I look back and I'm kind of glad I had it and I tell the kids that, that even though I had a very difficult time with it, I'm glad that I went through those four years because it did teach me things. I also think that it does teach exactness. The five declensions and everything else. So that, I think, teaches you to be more particular. And I was a scientist for a long time so obviously having that trait is not a bad trait if you're going to be a scientist. To understand and to be very careful and particular the way you put things together.

A disciplined mind required absolute dedication and hard work. (A strict disciplinary culture, based on a demerit system, also helped with keeping the students on task. I examine this topic in the next chapter.) The student handbook clearly spelled out "classroom concentration" as a characteristic of appropriate student conduct. One of the first assemblies of the year was devoted to the topic of "always doing your best." Ms. Holden opened by telling the students: "You bring your game. You bring it hard. You bring it every single day." Or as Jeremiah described it, "I just gotta keep hustlin'."

The zeal with which the school preached hard work and discipline was matched by an obsession for testing. The young men took monthly exams in reading and math, and the faculty pored over the test results with Mr. Green, who insisted that the teachers adjust their lessons based on the data. This was all to maximize the school's performance on the state exams at the end of the school year. For the eleventh graders especially, testing was a way of life. They were so accustomed to it that they took to making fun of the testing culture. During an assembly that doubled as a pep rally for the upcoming benchmark exams, Mr. Green told the students, "You've all worked hard. And you're ready for these tests." In a robotic-sounding voice audible to just those sitting near him, Jack said, "Testing! Testing! 1–2–3! Is this thing working?"[22] For Mr. Green, however, testing was a gravely serious matter. At a faculty meeting before the start of the school year, Mr. Green told the teachers that the new culture of the school (Mr. Green was starting his first year as principal) would require a total commitment to collecting, measuring, and analyzing student data. Mr. Green would struggle on an interpersonal level that year with his teachers, in part because he was committed to not putting his teachers ahead of his students. In other words, he would hold his teachers as accountable as he did the students. (This approach may have been grounded in what he took to be "best practices," but it did not ingratiate him to the teachers who had been with the school before he arrived.) Or as he told his faculty at that meeting, "We're going to ask our young men to work very hard. We have to expect the same of ourselves."[23] At all levels of the school, absolute discipline and commitment were expected. As the teaching candidate rubric revealed, the school wanted resilient teachers.

Hope on the Race to College

Hard work was not enough. The young men needed hope. Henri Desroche describes hope as an "exuberant" expectation, a powerful and emotional "peak" that nourishes individuals in the face of disadvantage.[24] This understanding of hope has been a pillar of African American cultural traditions and politics.[25] Throughout the African Diaspora, the Black church's "philosophy of hope" has laid the foundation for a "culture of resistance in the anti-colonial struggle."[26] From this perspective, hope is not irrational or a sign of "false consciousness"—of a mistaken belief that equality is possible—but instead fuels the long march toward social justice and racial uplift.[27] I find it helpful to think of hope as a resource, one that motivates transformative action and positions individuals as morally worthy.[28] Barack Obama had run his campaign on a message of hope, and his election victory had a profound impact on the students at both schools. When I asked Marquise, a tenth grader, about the President Obama sticker he had on one of his binders, he responded, "Hope: that's gonna be our new four-letter word on the streets!"

The school's primary hope was for what Mr. Green called Northside's "guiding star": that all the students would attend college. Or to borrow Du Bois's term, Northside aimed for its young men to join the "college-bred community."[29] At an induction ceremony for the incoming class of ninth graders, Mr. Green told the audience: "I don't want 2014 to be the year [the students] associate with graduating from high school. I want 2014 to be the year they enroll in college." The families erupted in applause. At a weekly assembly, Mr. Pierce described the glowing media coverage around the all-male Urban Prep Academies in Chicago, which had recently earned a 100 percent college acceptance rate. Referring to the school's eleventh graders, Mr. Pierce yelled enthusiastically, "That'll be us with our first graduating class of 2011!" The eleventh graders roared. Across the school, the college focus was impossible to miss. Pennants of different historically black colleges and universities lined the hallway in a "wall of flags." Each homeroom was named after the teacher's alma mater. At weekly assemblies, the homerooms took turns reciting their teacher's college cheer.

Tapping into the larger ethos of competition, the Northside community framed the path to college as a high-stakes race. This language, in fact, is common under No Child Left Behind. In 2009, the year I began my research, the Obama administration introduced "Race to the Top," a program in which states compete for a share of a $4.35 billion grant that rewards educational innovation.[30] The race to college was not a sprint, but a test of endurance. This framing—that the students were in it for the long haul—reinforced the need for strict discipline and the best educational training available.

Imagining the path to college as a race stoked the school's competitive drive. In fact, the school community believed that boys were predisposed to competition. At a meeting for prospective families, Mr. Pierce first expressed shock at how far the school's new Mock Trial team had advanced in a recent competition. Then he said he should not have been so surprised at the result. "At an all-boys school," he asserted, "competition is your friend." The parents laughed. Sam, a tenth grader, described the path to college as "like you gotta run all these laps to get there. It's not fun at first, and you feel like you want to drop out. But you get better and faster and you want to just keep running and running." As Sam implied, a sense of forward momentum and improvement motivated him to keep running, and he was gaining a sense of control over the race.[31] Khalil, a tenth grader, recalled the "buzz" in the building when he matriculated the previous year. The experience had felt "like the static in the air just before a football game." He later added that the path to college was "the most important game of my life."

Protecting Status and Hope

This mix of hope and hard work squares with the notion that an aim of all-boys education is to build resilience. As Peter Hall and Michèle Lamont write, nurturing resilience is especially vital under neoliberal regimes that deny safety nets for the most marginalized citizens.[32] Yet the focus on hard work elides the fact that the Gladiators of Northside Academy were given a form of status that set them apart from their peers in the community. As Saida Grundy has written, "In the ideological pressure cooker that has been built up around black male advancement in a time of widespread crisis, aggressively policed codes of class and gender emerge and are vividly apparent in men's experiences."[33]

Continuing the boundary work present in the design of the school, the Northside community continually enacted symbolic boundaries to mark its young men as exceptional. The respectable character of Latin was coded by race and social class: at the country's elite boarding schools, for a long time only men from the country's well-to-do white Protestant families had access to the "dead language." "As an intellectual status symbol," Cookson and Persell have written, "the classical curriculum helped distinguish gentlemen from virtually everyone else."[34] The Northside community participated in its own local boundary work. The school set the disciplined minds and work ethic of their students apart from young men who were viewed as undisciplined and lazy.

Chris Madsen was a white, first-year Latin teacher at the school. He attended an all-boys Catholic high school, where he learned Latin, and he went on to study Classics in college, which included a deep immersion in Latin, mythology, and archaeology. Mr. Madsen faced tall hurdles his first year. He was coming straight from college and had little experience working with poor Black youth. But he was accustomed to disciplined environments, with his Catholic school background and his experiences as a college football player. (These qualities clearly made him an attractive teaching candidate for the school.) To his credit, Mr. Madsen remained enthusiastic and was eager to improve, and he adapted to feedback from colleagues.[35] But he still struggled with classroom management, and some students were exasperated to not have a more experienced teacher for such a difficult subject.

Like other teachers, he asked his students to work as hard as they could. And while he was still improving as a teacher, he had already learned that being a member of the Northside community required drawing boundaries to elevate the status of their own students. "Other kids just don't work hard enough," Mr. Madsen declared. "It becomes a bad habit you can't break. Our students are different because Latin demands so much of them, and so we're helping them build a habit that really sets them apart from other kids." Given how much work was expected of them, the students also came to draw these boundaries between themselves and their peers. One day, Jeremiah was honored at an assembly as the "Top Gladiator" for the week, awarded to boys for their effort, achievements in and out of the classroom, and assistance to classmates. A few boys complimented Jeremiah for the golden tie he received with the honor. He told his friends he earned the award because he had committed "24/7 to working hard on my Latin." Referring to other non-Northside students, he continued: "All these other kids ain't got their minds right and don't grind as hard as we do. They can't never get this tie. That's just for us." Even as Northside had offered their own young men a highly desired resource in Latin, laziness was always viewed as a personal failing. In this context, then, success was a matter of making the right character choices, a guiding principle of both neoliberalism and a respectability politics.

Northside also occasionally counterposed its respectable "dead language" against urban slang or Black English. The school officials did not actively suppress the young men's slang (their "living language," as I came to think of it) because it was so ubiquitous, but in certain moments staff members clearly marked Black English as illegitimate compared to Latin. For example, one day in class, Mr. Madsen asked a few boys to stop talking and to return to their work. When they continued to talk, he said, "You know, that language won't get you into college." Pointing to the Latin vocabulary on the board, he said, "But knowing this will."

Northside Academy also needed to protect hope. While hope normally implies exuberance, it is always "on intimate terms with despair."[36] If hope is a cultural resource that positions actors as virtuous and capable of enacting transformative change, then despair is its opposite: it marks actors as morally unworthy and incapable of positive change. Following this, the Northside community actively drew symbolic boundaries between their own young men's genuine hope and the despair they saw as pervasive throughout the community. Despair was to be avoided at all costs because it could "anesthetize" hope.[37]

The Northside community mentioned gangs, drugs, and violence as persistent threats. But they also frequently invoked actual persons as threats, those dangerous young men who were "lost to the streets," as Mr. Bly, a grandparent, described it. Or as Yolanda Bridges, a parent, explained, young men "have lost hope and you see it from the younger generation looking at the older guys that stand on the corner, sell drugs, who might just stand on the corner and do nothing all day." From Jerome, a tenth grader: "You look around and all you see is African American youth on the corner . . . doing drugs, selling them or just pretty much on the streets wasting all of their lives." As Jerome implied, these young men had resigned themselves to a hopeless future. While the Northside students had a sense of control over their participation in the long race to college, the school community members often described deviant young men as stuck in place. They were taking "passive, receptive stances toward an approaching future over which [they had] little control."[38] While hope has forward momentum, despair lacks it or has a downward momentum. As Erica Hassell, the mother of tenth grader Deandre, told me:

> Some boys, they have no future. They'll get shot, locked up, stuck on a corner selling drugs. You might see them, but then they're banished. Maybe their name show up in the obituaries. I just don't want them to take Deandre down with them.

In her eyes, these maligned young men were not merely passive, but were active and aggressive threats to her son. Their downward momentum was dangerously contagious. By constantly invoking these shameful and abject identities, Ms. Hassell and others reinforced the virtue of the boys' own aspirational identities. Northside was characterized symbolically and quite literally as a protective space inside the community.

School officials participated in this boundary work as well. At one assembly, Mr. Holmes recommended that the students hurry home after school to avoid confrontations with boys from other schools. "You have everything to lose, and they have nothing to lose," he asserted. "[Those boys] see you as having opportunities." As the administrator implied, these other boys could easily derail the Northside students off the path to educational success. In other words, the *symbolic* distinctions Mr. Holmes had drawn carried important *socioeconomic* consequences for the students.[39] At a later assembly, Mr. Holmes again addressed the issue of confrontations with other students: "Those other fools feel nothing but misery. And it's like a disease they want to spread to you. Don't forget you're above all that and that you have more to live for!" Here, the administrator warned of the despair that haunted other young men and suggested, like Ms. Hassel before him, it was a contagion that could afflict the Northside students. He implored the Northside students to remember that they instead possessed a hope that was "above" the misery of others.

At another assembly, Mr. Green highlighted starkly the costs of losing out on the "opportunities" that Mr. Holmes had mentioned:

> We started school with 382 students, and sixteen young Black men are no longer wearing the Northside logo. And that breaks my heart because I know the kinds of schools where they're at now. And some are going to ask to come back, and I have to say "no." And I'm afraid to see where they'll be in six months, or two years, or five years.

Here, the boys who had left school had been redirected toward a dreaded future and now regretted losing out on the opportunity of a Northside education. Like Mr. Holmes before him, Mr. Green believed that other boys were jealous of the hopeful futures of the Northside students. This message encouraged the Northside students to think more highly of their education, and it increased a sense of unity among the students. The message was also a fearful reminder that if a Northside education was lost, it would be lost forever. And their lives could plunge into despair. As Bobby, a tenth grader, told me: "Can't slip, not even once. Who knows where I might end up."

Disciplined Bodies

Many charter schools have strict uniform policies to maintain a semblance of order in their schools.[40] But these are rarely viewed as points of pride for students. The Northside uniform, however, was a mark of high status.

As the school's student handbook proclaimed, "The apparel oft proclaims the man": a line from Shakespeare's *Hamlet*. The students wore blazers with gold buttons and the school's emblem on the left breast pocket, striped ties in the school colors, black belts, and black dress shoes. As I described in the last chapter, some students—and most of these students were the newest ninth graders—were torn over the uniforms because they felt their peers in the community derided them for "looking gay." Yet they largely overcame these feelings of emasculation by viewing the uniform as a source of status and empowerment.

While Latin signaled that the Northside young men were destined for college, the community associated the uniform with a professional career and therefore a secure, middle-class future. In this instance, the school community likened Northside to elite boarding schools, given that these institutions have uniforms and that universities do not.[41] "Fittingly," Cookson and Persell have written, "the uniform of choice for American elites is the business suit, and the prep uniform of choice has generally been jackets and ties."[42] Charles, a tenth grader, felt that the uniform helped classify him as someone who was destined for a financially secure future. His father, who worked for a mail carrier service, had told Charles with great pride that his son would be the first man in the family to wear a suit to work. Like other students, Charles invoked Barack Obama (who had just started his first year as president) in projecting a successful future for himself:

> The uniforms make you feel like you're a professional, like you're
> going to an everyday job. Makes you feel kind of good about yourself.
> It makes you feel like a person like Barack Obama, makes you feel like
> you're up there and that you're somebody.

The uniforms also required and taught discipline. Four pages of the school's "Code of Conduct" handbook were dedicated to the school's uniform policy, which spelled out when and how students were to wear the uniform. School officials carefully inspected each student's uniform each morning to emphasize how important it was that the students presented themselves respectably in public. The idea here was that if the students took special care in their dress, then each morning they would be "warming up," as Richard, an eleventh grader, put it, for the hard work needed in school. Above all, the uniform was a visible marker of the young men's commitment to the discipline required for a successful future. Richard wanted to be the first lawyer in his family. A member of the school's football team, he used a sports analogy to explain what the school uniform meant to him:

No one likes practice. But I feel when I'm a grown man I'll be in a law office somewhere. And I feel like lawyers have to get their fancy degrees first. And they wear their fancy suits, too, and so I see our school uniform as like a practice jersey for that job.

For Richard, the uniform was a "practice jersey" for the *real* uniform he desired: a lawyer's suit. In the same way that a practice jersey represented the hard work needed to be competitive in a game, Northside's uniform represented the disciplined self that Richard was training.

According to Charles's mother, Yolanda Bridges, when community members see the Northside students, "they look up to them. You know, even older women you find complimenting all the boys and how well-dressed they look and all that, and that makes a person feel good." One poignant example reinforced Ms. Bridges's observation. During a fire drill one day, the boys stood in perfect lines along the perimeter of the school. A woman pulled her car up next to the boys and shouted out, "My, what school is this? All these young men heading to college!" Pleased with the compliment, several of the boys stood taller, fixing their blazers and ties.

The uniforms had made such an impression on the students that a group lobbied Mr. Green to adopt an "alternate" third uniform they could wear. (This term was taken from the popular "alternate third" uniforms that professional sports teams now regularly adopt, to supplement standard home and away jerseys.) They recommended a cardigan, which "looked like" a blazer and which they believed would command the same respect. The proposal conveyed to the staff that the boys were involved and had bought into the school culture. Sharif Khan, a math teacher, told me that several of his students were

> obsessed with this idea of cardigans. I was really just interested to see how they didn't want to get rid of the uniforms. They didn't want to say, "Look, we should be able to wear whatever we want." They didn't even say that. They've bought into uniforms. They just wanted to have a different style.

That "different style" was hip-hop. Tenth graders Ricky and John eagerly described the cardigans that the multimillionaire hip-hop artist Kanye West wore, part of a preppier style that had taken over mainstream hip-hop fashion styles around the time of my research.[43] Along with Sean "P. Diddy" Combs and Jay-Z, West was a "hip-hop mogul" and a trendsetter for fashion, music, and culture.[44] Above all, hip-hop moguls were entrepreneurs: innovators and leaders of industry. As I describe in chapter 5, the entrepreneur was the vision of desired manhood at the school.

A respectability politics disciplines bodies by reforming individual "manners and morals."[45] To prepare for the school's annual mother-son luncheon, Ms. Spring taught the young men fine dining etiquette, complete with plates and silverware. The young men were advised to surprise their mothers by opening the doors for them. The luncheon, Ms. Spring observed, is "all about behaving like a gentleman for ninety minutes." At the event, the president of a local nonprofit, Imani Coleman, told the families she had taken Latin herself and that the boys were "the cream of the crop" for doing the same. She gushed at "all the gentlemen in the room" and how they had such "impeccable manners" that "you just don't see with many boys anymore." While the expressed intent of the annual ritual was to celebrate mothers, it also served to fortify the brotherhood's privileged standing in the community. (I revisit the significance of this mother-son luncheon in the next chapter.)

Northside set its own students apart from the unrespectable bodies of other young men. In two ways, the Northside community repudiated other young men in the community. The first was to distinguish between the respectable dress of their students and the self-presentation of other boys. Enyo Agyeman, the mother of Johnny, a ninth grader, believed that the uniform set her son and his "intelligent" classmates apart from the community's "worst boys":

> They look very intelligent. I love to see them when they all come out
> with their suit jackets, their blazers and their ties and everything. I
> really like that because it just seems like they're going somewhere in
> life, you know? And you don't see them with the pants hanging down
> or the shirts out of their pants or anything.

According to Ann Arnett Ferguson, "schoolboys are under enormous pressure to 'exorcise' . . . forms of Blackness and learn to comport their bodies in a more 'respectable' manner."[46] Parents of Black "schoolboys" will "through a careful selection of clothing, mode of self-deportment and style" attempt to "derace" their sons from the "prevailing image of Black males as poor, lawless, and dangerous."[47] The young men participated in this boundary work as well. Tracy Bly recalled the initial visit her grandson, Khalil, took to the school:

> When he saw how well Northside was with the neckties and the dress
> pants and the shirt and how well, first thing he said, he said, "You
> know, Grandma, their pants is not hanging down." And then he said,
> "This is where I want to go."

In his early writings, Du Bois famously promoted an elite group of Black men—a "Talented Tenth"—who were tasked with uplifting the Black masses. Yet the notion of a Black male leadership has long been problematic for engaging a politics of respectability. As Kevin Gaines has written, "Amidst legal and extralegal repression many black elites sought status, moral authority, and recognition of their humanity by distinguishing themselves, as bourgeois agents of civilization, from the presumably undeveloped black majority."[48] This elitism comes more fully into view when we see that Du Bois (in *The Philadelphia Negro*) identified "the lowest class" of Blacks as a largely unsalvageable "submerged tenth."[49] The Northside community participated in a similar kind of boundary work. The school drew on a legacy of Black elites using the criteria of self-discipline to draw moral and social boundaries against disreputable outsiders, a stigmatized group of young Black men most in trouble with the law and thought to occupy illegitimate all-male spaces. The school's newfound status therefore promoted intra-racial divisions within the Black community. Northside experienced success by imitating other successful schools. By drawing symbolic boundaries against those young men most in crisis, the school could deride those boys (and by extension, their schools and their families) who failed to imitate Northside. Yet this ignored how presumed cultural and moral differences fell along structural lines, as Northside had the privilege of recruiting law-abiding young men and provided them with resources unavailable at most schools. The next chapter discusses how a school brotherhood worked aggressively to protect that status and those resources.

Perry High School

Cultural Relevance

Mr. Reagan, whom we met in chapter 1, had been a popular math teacher at Perry High during the transition to an all-boys arrangement. At the time of my research, he was a principal at another high-achieving charter school in the city.[50] He summarized Perry High's academic struggles in the years immediately after the transition to an all-male model, when they were operated by Excel, the educational management organization (EMO):

> So students who were high-achieving students, who could get into like a magnet high school or another high school: I was encouraging them to leave. I used to make the analogy: I'd say, "You can't be a good salesman if you don't believe in what you're selling." And I didn't believe in what I was selling.

With Excel out of the picture, the school regrouped under its new leadership and won a large federal grant to start several new initiatives, including a male mentoring program, a full-time tutoring center, and a resource room for parents. For a school labeled as in need of "Corrective Action" under No Child Left Behind (NCLB), the grant brought a jolt of positive energy. The school district hired a Black woman, Nellie Snyder, to oversee the initiatives as an assistant principal. She was the school's only female administrator. Despite the grant and a renewed commitment from the school district to help guide the school out of NCLB probation, the school was not able to develop a cohesive academic curriculum. Rather, the school officials focused their energy on male mentoring, the topic I take up in the next chapter.

Northside's charter granted the school complete oversight over the recruitment and hiring of teachers. As a district school, Perry did not have that luxury, though the school district did help with finding potential candidates, who were then interviewed by Mr. Bradley and his staff. The staff was larger and more racially diverse than Northside's. Like at Northside, the levels of experience among the teaching staff varied widely.

Consistent with previous research, staff members at Northside and Perry felt that a major structural challenge facing young Black men was low expectations.[51] This was especially damaging at Perry High, which ranked among the city's lowest-achieving schools based on standardized test performance. A poster in Hannah Allison's math classroom was intended to motivate the boys, but it was also a reminder of the school's painful academic underperformance. It featured a table with the percentage of Perry High eleventh graders who scored at or below grade level on the previous year's state standardized math exam. Below the table was the question, "Will you be the first ABOVE GRADE LEVEL eleventh-grader in Perry's history?"

Like at Northside, I observed that culturally relevant pedagogy was practiced unevenly among the staff. Where the school did differ was in content. Latin provided Northside with a distinctive academic identity, and given that it was a charter, the teachers were beholden to the school's clear standards and expectations (many of which were geared toward preparing their students for the standardized exams). Mr. Bradley's administration at Perry High did not demand this strict uniformity; the teachers' perceptions of why this was ranged from the administration being crushed by responsibilities, to unprofessionalism and laziness. This meant that the expectations that teachers had of students varied quite a bit across classes, and students were challenged at different rates.

Despite this, the school curricula—across multiple subjects—bent toward offering culturally relevant knowledge, a wide-ranging category that includes the content of curricula, as well as the knowledge cultivated through the young men's own experiences.[52] There were two main ways that Perry teachers engaged knowledge: by teaching African American culture and history and by making lessons applicable to real life.[53] With respect to culture, many teachers (of all backgrounds) embraced or at least attempted to bring in examples of the student's favorite TV shows and hip-hop artists. Carrie Swanson, a young white math teacher, was fond of creating word problems using names of people and places from the local neighborhood. Victoria Rivers, a middle-aged white history teacher, discussed with her students how prisons that were built after Emancipation represented a different form of slavery and asked them to consider how Morgan might be experiencing the effects of that today.

A few teachers practiced culturally relevant pedagogy in ways that formed strong connections with their students. Yet in an all-boys setting, this practice was rife with contradictions. Omar Youseff was a science and math teacher and a leader in the local Muslim community. His pedagogical approach was to help his students build a "self-knowledge" that he cultivated in his own personal, political, and religious life as a devout Muslim. As he said:

> I think this is a major failing of the education system. I always give this
> example. If there was a crowd of people, I took a picture, and I gave
> you that picture, if you knew you was in that crowd, the first person
> you'd look for in that picture would be yourself. I always use this
> analogy. Now, in the case of education, when the picture's taken of
> education, they don't find themselves in the picture. So, as a result, they
> have no connection there. So that's part of the disconnect too. The
> education's got to be relevant to the circumstance that the person is
> involved in. It's got to address those human issues that a person
> is undergoing, and the person's got to be able to see that there's a
> relevancy of what I'm learning to my situation.

Mr. Youseff had earned the respect of his students because he was deeply familiar with their personal lives: their favorite stores at the shopping mall downtown, the price of a bag of chips at the corner store down the street, the ins and outs of the drug economy that gripped East Morgan. Having earned this respect, he felt that as a Black man he should, as he described it, "keep it as real as possible" with the young men, in a manner that was foreign to the classrooms I observed at Northside Academy.

Mr. Youseff actively rejected a respectability politics in his pedagogy. Instead, he wanted to meet the boys on their own life terms, contradictions and all, and therefore used a street cultural orientation—predicated on an aggressive masculinity that was openly skeptical of the law—as a way of engaging his students. He seamlessly adopted slang when he spoke with students. He was unafraid to broach racial issues, from calling for the need to understand the "psychology" of whites in positions of authority to discussing the "human warehouse system," or mass imprisonment, that ensnared Black men. He told the boys to "ditch the excuses" because a Black man was now president, while also asking the young men to consider how Obama was forced to "sell out" and "abandon the ghetto" to ascend to the Highest Office "built on white power." He frequently asked the boys to "man up." Since the young men could not afford to be "little bitches out on the streets," then he would not expect them to be "little bitches in the classroom either." Keeping it real also meant adopting what others might consider questionable methods, but which Mr. Youseff thought were not only reasonable, but necessary. For instance, in a lesson on conversion factors, he told the boys that their lives depended on being accurate, just like "the money gotta be right when you sell a kilo [of cocaine]." The students found Mr. Youseff's classes to be alternately exhilarating and painful, empowering and emasculating. But most seemed to appreciate his authenticity.

To a lesser degree, the other two Black male teachers I observed wanted to meet the young men on their own cultural terms. None of these teachers were able to escape the achievement ideology that dictates that success is a matter of personal will and hard work. Yet to a greater degree than teachers at Northside, these teachers were explicitly distrustful of laws and even outside authority figures (like the police and politicians), grounded the students' lives in systems of oppression, and tried to harness rather than reject the young men's street mannerisms and experiences.

Challenging "College for All"

Helena Peters was an African American woman and a social services liaison at Perry High. She grew up in Morgan and attended an all-girls Catholic high school. Ms. Peters began our interview by giving me an aerial view of the school. She described a complex network of administrators, guidance counselors, teachers, and families tasked with working together to "educate healthy children," a phrase she repeated several times. "And my job," she said, "is to understand what our neediest kids need, and to go from there." Nearly a decade after the massive shake-up of Morgan's public schooling system, Ms. Peters saw two options for Black boys. The focus on raising achievement and standardized testing carried with it the assumption that "college is the ultimate destination," she said. "But what happens to all the children who don't go to college? They face the real possibility of going to jail. But where are the other options for them? College isn't for everyone."

I was surprised to hear this, but I discovered that hers was a widely shared sentiment. As the sociologist James Rosenbaum writes, historical developments such as an expansion of higher education since World War II and the increasing skill demands of the labor market have helped solidify a mantra of "college for all" in the United States.[54] Public school reform has further elevated college as the "ultimate destination" for poor children, as Ms. Peters described it, even if not all schools are equipped to prepare their students for that goal. "College for all" has had other unintended consequences. For instance, an open admissions policy in community colleges has brought in many more students without the sufficient means to support their transition into four-year colleges. These various developments have further pushed the country's "forgotten half" out of the labor market.[55]

Darrell Westbrook, an assistant principal, agreed with Ms. Peters. According to him, what interfered with stronger vocational training was the district's single-minded devotion to college, a result of the state takeover of the school district. He found it disheartening:

> What I would like to see for those kids who have the ability or want to go to college: that's a great aspiration. But at the same we have to prepare young men for the real working world, so we need to find out . . . what their interests are, and then sort of create some type of curriculum where they get job-skill counseling and information on different types of jobs and how these jobs are and what the requirements are for these jobs, because every kid's not going to go to college. I seen a lot of kids head out to the college fair. But are they prepared for college? No. We're just setting them up for failure if we don't give them more options.

Some parents felt the same way. Sofía Valenzuela was a well-loved staff member in the building. Years before, she was called up to the school one day because her son, Jay, had gotten into trouble. She said the moment changed her; she was a recovering drug addict, and she did not want Jay to be "taken by the streets." And so, she said, "I told myself I wouldn't leave the school until he graduated." She took a part-time job at Perry as a school assistant, a do-it-all position with responsibilities including monitoring the halls and the school grounds. Within a few years, she had taken on several leadership positions in the school, including serving as the school's Title I representative, tasked with meeting with school district officials to ensure that the school was receiving necessary funds and was using them appropriately.[56] Ms. Valenzuela embodied what Antonio Gramsci called an "organic intellectual": someone who comes from disadvantage and works closely with similarly oppressed individuals to articulate their struggle (a process that Gramsci calls "good sense") and to help them work toward positive change.[57] I asked her to describe what, if given the chance, she would change about the school:

> No more tests. All you're doing is testing them. And they're bored. And they're tired. Our boys need that barbershop and woodshop and auto mechanics and stuff that we had when we was kids! The boys need that hands-on training. Maybe they'll find something if we just gave them some options.[58]

Northside Academy viewed testing as the practice necessary for completing the long race to college, its "guiding star." But their students were groomed to be exceptional and were motivated by the very sense of competition on which the school had been founded. Ms. Valenzuela, however, felt that the city's testing culture had dealt her students a bad hand. It was misguided to prioritize testing and college above all else. So Mr. Westbrook and Ms. Valenzuela had embraced a particular meaning of "options." Ms. Peters's comments from earlier in this section are also telling. The mantra of "college for all" conveyed to the young men that college was the way to avoid prison. She and others wondered if the school could prepare young men for productive lives even if college was not in their futures.

Indeed, the share of Perry High students who matriculated to college was low, at around 15 percent, which was about half the citywide average. Despite these figures, a majority of students still saw college in their future; fifteen of the twenty-five students I interviewed (60 percent) mentioned college as part of their future plans. (See Table 3 in the Appendix.) Educational researchers have found that poor youth hold unrealistically high academic expectations for themselves: many believe that they will earn a bachelor's degree when in fact the odds against that are very high.[59] High educational expectations are driven, in part, by an enduring meritocracy discourse in the United States, which maintains that success is primarily driven by individual work ethic. This narrative—what many call a myth—has taken on new life in a neoliberal era that further reduces achievement to a matter of individual choice. This has had an especially devastating impact on poor Blacks. As Lisa Duggan has written, through the middle of the twentieth century, as New Deal welfare programs were eroding, conservatives held up "personal responsibility" as a moral barometer against controlling images of irresponsible Black families.[60] "The specific neoliberal spin on this cultural project," Duggan continues, "was the removal of explicitly racist, misogynistic language and images, and the substitution of the language and values of . . . *personal responsibility*."[61] Going even further back, even as he promoted the Talented Tenth, Du Bois recognized that a "self-help" politics stood little chance of lifting up an entire race in the face of an expanding, discriminatory economy.[62] In schools today, the language of collective self-help is foreign; poor young men of color are told they alone are responsible for their uplift. For a school that lacked many of the advantages of Northside, it seems too convenient and unfair to blame Perry students for not being resilient enough.

Promoting a track to college is not itself a problem. Rather, the hegemonic mission of "college for all" has created additional pressures that many high schools have been unable to tackle, and have blinded schools from promoting noncollege pathways that may in fact benefit more youth in the long run. "The interesting sociological issue," Rosenbaum writes, "is why schools and colleges focus on raising students' plans . . . while so thoroughly failing to provide clear information about realistic probabilities and incentives for school effort."[63] He found that many high school students are both uninformed and misinformed by their schools. Students do not always understand what is expected of them in college (such as placement exams), while guidance counselors feel they are under pressure from administrators and parents to promote college.

Indeed, it was distressing to find out that among the fifteen young men I interviewed who aspired to college, there was a poor understanding of what it took to get there. My interview with Larry, an eleventh grader, is telling. I had spent a couple of weeks in class with Larry before our interview. He was doing well, if not spectacularly, in his classes. I asked him what his plans were for after high school.

> LARRY: Go to college. That's my dream. Just need to get my grades right.
> FREEDEN: Did you take the Practice SAT last month?
> LARRY: Nah. I didn't hear about it. I figure I can take the real one next year? And I think there's some class that you take to help you apply for college?

Larry may have been one of the stronger candidates for college in his class, but he was already well behind, having missed out on the PSAT and being unaware that the class he had in mind did not exist at the school.[64] Contrast this with the young men of Northside Academy, who acquired the requisite cultural capital by being on a college-prep track and having access to a full-time college counselor.

The divergent paths envisioned by Northside Academy and Perry High evoked memories of a monumental debate in Black politics at the start of the twentieth century in which Du Bois played a leading role. Booker T. Washington, the influential and highly visible Black American educator, had advocated a politics of accommodation. As director of Alabama's

Tuskegee Institute, Washington laid a comprehensive plan for Black social and economic development in the South. Washington believed that Black advancement rested on a foundation of industrial education in carpentry, agricultural economics, and related fields. While Washington emphasized the need to teach the *hand*, Du Bois famously disagreed and defended the need to teach the *head*, or a rigorous liberal arts education, for "the higher training of the talented few."[65] Meanwhile, Washington told his Tuskegee students in no uncertain terms that "we are not a college," and he even forbade the teaching of Latin.[66] Yet Washington's policies failed because they acquiesced to the demands of white capitalists and made it easier for the South to roll out repressive laws that would help to usher in Jim Crow.

A century later, public schools have largely failed to meet the vision laid out by Du Bois, while technical training has been overshadowed by "college for all." My intention here is not to adjudicate an old debate. Indeed, in an era of "college for all," it may even seem offensive to suggest that schools should do anything but promote a college pathway for their students. Yet if it was true, as the Northside community felt, that the "race" to college was a competitive test of endurance, then Perry High officials were left to wonder if they could opt out of the unfair race altogether, while still charting a separate path to dignified and successful futures for their young men. It seemed patently unfair to the Perry High staff that schools would promote "college for all" without providing the structures to make this possible and for students to thrive when they get to college. In this respect, the Perry High staff drew on the spirit of the community control tradition, which gives Black communities the power to determine where and how their children learn. In a more just society, college would be a viable path for larger numbers of Black boys. Du Bois himself understood that "things seldom are equal" and that local Black communities should therefore have the power to take the steps they deem necessary to lift up as many of the children in their care as possible.[67]

In fact, strengthening local communities is a primary goal of technical education. Recently, policies for expanded career and technical education (CTE) have received bipartisan support in Congress. According to Tim Kaine, the Democratic senator from Virginia who has spearheaded this effort, "A high school education should prepare students for any pathway they choose, whether that's attending a four-year university, earning credentials from a community college program or getting a high-skilled job after graduation."[68] Indeed, what CTE stresses is lacking entirely from the Northside's "race to college": a commitment to building stronger relationships with local communities. (And as I describe in the next chapter, the

Northside students felt they were receiving the implicit message that they should leave their communities in order to maximize their chances of success in life.) As James Rosenbaum notes, vocational and technical teachers provide important employer contacts and help link graduates to local jobs. Tim Kaine's CTE caucus has promoted the virtues of technical skills that are in demand by local communities.[69]

Conclusion

Black male academies in particular, and charter schools in general, have embraced the language of resilience. As Marlon James has argued in his research at one Black male academy, even when a culturally relevant curriculum is "not enough," staff and students are able to dig deeper and draw on the "power to persevere and to never quit."[70] Surely it is worthwhile to view young people as change agents in their own schooling. I found that Northside Academy blended an absolute dedication to schoolwork with a critical hope nurtured by Barack Obama's inauguration as president. It was a captivating formula. But the danger with teaching students to "never quit" is that it misses the broader dynamics that produce success for schools like Northside, while perpetuating an intoxicating achievement ideology that success and failure are largely a matter of trying hard enough. In recent years, "grit," a close cousin of resilience, has taken public education by storm. Grit is a measure of noncognitive ability, or the appropriate character needed to succeed in school against all odds.[71] Some famous charter school organizations have even taken to grading their students using a "grittiness" report card. Yet, "grit and resilience frame individual and social problems in ways compatible with a politics of austerity that eviscerates the care-giving roles of the state."[72] When children fail, the state can shrug off that failure as a lack of individual resilience.

The young men of Northside were in fact developing character (or heart), but this included much more than resilience. In the phrasing of the social theorist Max Weber, Northside Academy emerged as a unique status group during a period of profound change in the Morgan school district. It is a "social estimation of honor" that delimits the boundaries of those within the status group and those excluded from it.[73] Respectability allowed the school to reconfigure educational attainment as a criterion for virtuous masculinity, rather than an impediment to it. And the school was getting results. While many boys in the school's first entering class left Northside, a high percentage of students in subsequent cohorts made it to graduation. And the results earned the school widespread acclaim. Nearly 85 percent of students in the second cohort enrolled in college, a percentage that placed the school in the top three of all high schools in the city.[74]

Perry High lacked the standardized curriculum of Northside, but many teachers still worked hard to connect lessons to the young men's history and culture. A group of Black men practiced a culturally relevant pedagogy that refused to engage a respectability politics, but this still presented something of a paradox. Mr. Youseff, for example, was widely respected, but he embraced the young men's own street mannerisms and practices, which could be emasculating and violent. Finally, school officials challenged the hegemonic "college for all" philosophy and dared to ask if more young Black men would be better served with exposure to career and technical education. In the end, only 49 percent of Perry ninth graders in the fall of 2006 would graduate on time (within four years) by the end of the 2009–10 school year, the year I completed my fieldwork. The average school district on-time graduation rate was 58 percent. Only 8 percent of those graduating Perry High seniors would go on to college, which was slightly lower than the district average of 10 percent for Black male students.

CHAPTER FOUR

Black Male Belonging

Race Leadership, Role-Modeling, and Brotherhood

With a grueling week of standardized exams behind them, the staff and students at Perry High turned their attention to the school's first-ever father-son breakfast. It was taking place in the grand ballroom of a hotel in downtown Morgan.

To help realize his goal of making Perry High a respectable school, Mr. Bradley envisioned a day when his students wore blazers and ties. He was therefore overjoyed to see his students arrive that morning in formal attire, some in full suits. And there were lots of smiles and laughter as the boys waited outside to board charter buses to take them to the event. It was the happiest I had seen the students all year.

"That's corny!" I heard Tyson yell. He was making fun of other boys for wearing clip-on ties.

He walked over to me. "Check out my kicks!"

I glanced down at his spotless, white, alligator-skin dress shoes. "They're *fresh,*" he continued. He pointed at my shoes. "Not like them raggedy wheels!"

"Just playin', Mr. Oeur." Fashion and self-comportment were incredibly important to the boys, and so clothes were common ammunition for bussin' and boastin'.[1]

"Yours *are* nicer," I conceded, though I thought my dress shoes didn't look all that bad.

"Just got 'em," Tyson said. "Needed new ones for church."

As the historian Manning Marable writes, W. E. B. Du Bois was himself not a religious man. But as a *radical prophet,* he recognized the central role that the Black church played in communities following Emancipation: how it rested at the nexus of the religious and the secular, anchoring political, social, and spiritual life for African Americans.[2] In *The Philadelphia Negro*

(1899), Du Bois observed that "the Negro church has become a center of social intercourse to a degree unknown in white churches."[3] Black congregations have created schools and banks, groomed community leaders, and lent support to civil rights organizations such as the NAACP. [4] In Du Bois's memorable words, these churches have been marked by their "frenzy": their energy and persistent hope for the salvation of the historically disenfranchised.[5] Morgan was home to some of the nation's oldest Black congregations, including the African Methodist Episcopal Church and the Black Baptist Church. The Black church remains a well of community strength in Morgan, linking families in a collective struggle for a measure of salvation in this world.[6] Approximately one-third of parents and grandparents I interviewed were self-identified people of faith. How they came to understand the education of their sons and grandsons was profoundly shaped by their sacred worldviews. A smaller percentage identified with the Nation of Islam. This religious and political organization has endorsed a Black Nationalist ideology that inspired the community control tradition of which Black male academies are a part.

While Perry High and Northside were not religious institutions, a religious spirit animated the daily life of the schools. Adults were not afraid to say they were praying for the boys. At Perry, a favorite line of several young men was, "if the Good Lord allows," which they had adopted from their parents. Boys shared stories of men they knew who had "discovered God" while incarcerated; others were even junior deacons in their church and professed a desire to be preachers when they were older. Staff members cited their religious commitments as inspiring them to teach young Black men. In this particular context, "saving" young Black men took on profound meaning. I met a parent volunteer who was a reverend himself, and two teachers who were former prison ministers.

Above all, the goal of the Black church has been to bring together and strengthen the family, which C. Eric Lincoln and Lawrence Mamiya have called the "primary unit" of the church.[7] Perry High's first-ever father-son breakfast was shot through with the "frenzy" that Du Bois had observed himself. The students were greeted at the hotel by their fathers and other men: uncles, grandfathers, family friends, pastors, and a few school staff members. John Peters, a representative from a local congressman's office, welcomed everyone to the breakfast. His opening statement set the tone for the event. "Sons are the seeds that their fathers planted," he said. "It's the responsibility of our fathers to water and nurture their seeds." (I return at the end of the book to the significance of the seed imagery.) Regina Gann, a local politician, picked up where Mr. Peters left off and asked the guests to look around and see how few of the men were actually the boys' biological fathers: "The fathers: if they're not in this room, then where are they?" she asked. The guests responded emphatically, "In jail!"[8] Together, Mr. Peters and Ms. Gann highlighted a grave concern for the community: men needed to take responsibility as fathers, and incarceration greatly harmed a man's chance to be a good one.

The students at both schools professed a deep love for their brothers (blood relation or not), their boys, their homies. Mr. Bradley wanted his students to see how much he loved his own brother. So he invited his brother to say a few words. Speaking directly to the young men, Mr. Bradley's brother said, "My father didn't hug and kiss me. Because back in the day that's not what brothers did. But I'm here to tell you boys: We love you. We care about you." Then turning his attention to the mentors, he continued, "You don't need to go to Afghanistan. There's a war being waged in our own community. Parts of our community look like the third world. You can be a homeland defender!" Mr. Bradley's brother wanted the boys to know that there were men who loved and cared for them. He used the word "war" several times, by which he meant a fight to save a community that had been terrorized (by crime and drugs). As "homeland defenders," the mentor-fathers would be the "first line of defense," or those working in the trenches to support young men in need.

Leroy Downing, a community leader who supported the work of historically Black colleges and universities, spoke last. He described how the Reverend Martin Luther King Jr.'s teachings had shaped how his own mother had raised her family. (She had been an acquaintance of King's.) Mr. Downing punctuated the messages of the speakers before him—to mobilize men to be more active fathers and male mentors—with hope. "A new day is coming," he declared before quoting Romans 8:24–25:

> For in this hope we were saved.
> But hope that is seen is no hope at all.
> For who hopes for what they already have?
> But if we hope for what we do not yet have, we wait for it
> patiently.

Just weeks before, Northside Academy had held its own event for parents, also in a hotel ballroom. This luncheon was distinct from Perry's gathering in one important respect. The event celebrated the young men's relationships with their mothers. At the luncheon, the young men doted on their moms—who came dressed in fancy evening wear—and proudly showed off the fine dining etiquette skills they had learned in school that week. A small choir serenaded the mothers with a rendition of "A Song for Mama" by the R&B group Boyz II Men. The students surprised their mothers with roses. They were gifts, as I overheard Jeremiah say, for "moms, the most important people in our lives." The luncheon opened with remarks from Imani Coleman, a local community leader. Ms. Coleman assured the mothers that their sons were in good hands at the school. "There's a special bond between mothers and sons," she said. "You can hear something different in mom's voices when they talk about their sons." Ms. Coleman never mentioned fathers. Instead, she called on the school community to support the school's brotherhood: "God has blessed these young men. But they still need all of our support. And they need one another. I look out and I see a very special school, a very special family." "Amen!" the moms responded.

Why did Perry High host an event for fathers while Northside Academy hosted one that honored mothers? Both schools drew on the religious "frenzy" that Du Bois observed to call for the nurturing of certain kinds of families, of nonblood relations bound by shared struggle, in order to increase the young men's sense of belonging. As Allison Pugh writes, belonging is primarily a matter of dignity, or the "right" of people "to speak in their own community's conversation."[9] Poor Black communities have historically relied on strong nonblood "fictive kin" networks for support, care, and the exchange of resources.[10] The two school communities lamented the erosion of "strong families" and care networks and envisioned new school-family arrangements, or ways of being at home among fictive kin. Like its first-wave counterparts, Perry High sought to establish stronger relationships between older men and boys. At Northside, caring took on a much different form. The school largely dismissed the role-modeling thesis in favor of another form of collective care: peer camaraderie, a tight-knit brotherhood. School officials envisioned their students as continuing on to college and to being leaders and entrepreneurs. But they could not get there alone. This chapter also examines challenges to care and belonging in these academies. At Perry High, the Black male leadership lamented the popularity of a group of (mostly white) female teachers; while at Northside, some boys navigated the volatile terrain of being forced to choose between the school's brotherhood and friends who did not attend the school.

Perry High School

The Loveless Generation

In *The Philadelphia Negro*, Du Bois mapped out the lifestyles and living conditions of Black residents in the city's "Seventh Ward." While Du Bois argued that it was primarily environmental and social factors, and not cultural values, that determine disadvantage, even in his early writing he was clear that the "submerged tenth"—the most destitute portion of the city's Black community—was defined in part by moral weakness. Even as Du Bois convincingly mapped out the structural explanations for disadvantage, he could never fully escape the trappings of a Victorian respectability that demanded strict adherence to certain moral virtues. This played out most vividly, as Kevin Gaines has argued, in Du Bois's description of Black family disorganization. For early Black activists, nothing provided a clearer path to middle-class respectability than devotion to the patriarchal family and Black men assuming their rightful place as the "patriarch, the master of one's family."[11] Early Black reformers stressed that slavery had denied Blacks the opportunity to cultivate the morals and traits necessary for respectable selves before the public. To fend off urban pathology, Black reformers stressed the need to teach a devotion to families, a strong work ethic, and a respect for the law.

The topic of family disorganization in Black communities revealed itself most clearly decades later in Oscar Lewis's "culture of poverty" thesis, which maintained that the poor values of disadvantaged communities helped explain their disadvantage and dependence.[12] Soon after, in 1965, the controversial Moynihan Report argued that the "matriarchal family structure" was primarily responsible for the Black community's disadvantage. As blame also fell on absent Black fathers and male role models, conservative commentators accused Black families of having women who are "too strong" and men who are "too weak."[13] The rise of a carceral state has further amplified in the popular imagination controlling images of Black men as criminals and failed fathers.

Research on urban schools is rife with stories of school officials who place the blame for failure squarely on the shoulders of poor children and their families. This logic remains pervasive, given an entrenched neoliberal ideology that overlooks structural explanations of disadvantage and that promotes the idea that success is contingent alone on personal responsibility, behaving correctly, and making the right choices. The Perry High staff was not immune to this. Younger teachers and those who had not grown up in Morgan were more likely to take part in a "blame game" with parents. Mr. Gaines, a Black English teacher, said that "if the parents value education, they wouldn't put their child in a situation where they couldn't sleep. Some parents party all night. How can you as a thirteen- or fourteen-year-old kid be focused and learn something?" Very few staff members targeted only the moral failings of individuals. Rather, most staff members acknowledged structural causes of disadvantage—a weak and discriminatory labor market, increased policing and incarceration, a drug economy, the prevalence of violence, and a general lack of resources in the community—alongside stubborn beliefs in poor family values. This section highlights a common way the school viewed the interplay between structural and cultural factors: structural conditions impacted how people in the community could care for one another.

Martin Sherman had been a city police officer for twenty years before transitioning into schools. He had entered the force during a period of expanded policing and a national rise in incarceration rates, which have eroded trust between law enforcement and residents of poor communities. I found this generally to be true among the boys at both schools, who expressed feelings of frustration and disdain for police officers. The students, however, widely respected Officer Sherman, who had grown up in the neighborhood. In his previous job, he had gotten to know many of the students' parents. In his work in the community and in the school, he came to be something of a middleman who mediated conflicts between the law, on the one side, and community residents, on the other.

Officer Sherman's unique structural position helped articulate the tensions and contradictions of Black boys coming of age in communities burdened by gangs, drugs, and violence. He sympathized with the challenges of being raised in poverty and racial segregation, but he felt that "the grip" of drugs and the underground economy meant that many Black boys were beyond saving. He defended the work of the city police but acknowledged that officers could have done more to build trust. Having gotten to know every public school in the neighborhood, he was discouraged by perpetual structural problems such as understaffing and high turnover among school leadership, but he also wanted students to know that they could buck the odds if they just worked hard enough.

More than anything else, Officer Sherman distilled problems and solutions down into individual families:

> Morgan has a vibrant Black community. Black folks helped to make this city. But city hall long abandoned us, and so we've basically had to fend for ourselves. From the city's perspective, East Morgan is just one big scary stereotype. Life ain't easy, but around here it's just mostly folks who mind their own business and who just want a fair chance in life.

Officer Sherman portrayed East Morgan as home to modest, law-abiding "decent families."[14] Given the chance to recommend a first step toward positive change, Officer Sherman, like many others, brought it back to families. In particular, he felt that weak parental involvement was the biggest challenge the school faced. "We need to get a parent in here," he sighed. "Or just a general interest in what their child is doing. It seems to be nonexistent. You know, when you have almost four hundred boys and you have a parent/teacher's meeting and you're feeding them dinner, and you're lucky to get twenty-five [parents]."[15] He paused for a second, appearing conflicted over his own thoughts. "I understand parents have a lot on their plate. But I guess we're just asking them to make more of an effort to care more."

During my first week of fieldwork, I struck up a conversation with Lee Jeffries, who was a school assistant. I was blessed to have had Mr. Jeffries as a generous confidant during my year of fieldwork.[16] Few adults in the building were as well respected as Mr. Jeffries, and the school viewed him as an unofficial administrator. He grew up near the school, a "product," he said, of "the housing projects," or government-subsidized low-income housing. Mr. Jeffries truly embodied the notion of an organic intellectual. People admired Mr. Jeffries for his dedication to school after a childhood defined by, in his words, "a lot of heartache, a lot of false starts." Having been on the front lines of the drug economy and incarcerated as a young man for a drug charge, he had gained a unique perspective on how drugs had crippled the community:

> The evolution of drugs in our society is causing what's going on now in this society. Okay. Now my generation dropped the ball. The people before me was strong, in my mother and them generation, they were stronger, less affiliated with drugs. The drugs not only took your ambition and your focus in doing it the legitimate way, it also took your time. And that time brought on a loveless generation. We didn't have time for the kids because we was always out hustling and partying and everything like that.

Having witnessed firsthand the deterioration of caregiving in the community, Mr. Jeffries felt he "owed it to these kids" to work in the school. Officer Sherman, meanwhile, reflected longingly on a past when parents looked out for one another's children.

> When growing up, if an adult said you did something, you did it; there was no question. If you did something wrong, they were going to tell because we didn't want that kind of a neighborhood. We wanted everybody to feel safe. We looked out for each other. But these days, everyone looks out for themselves.

Officer Sherman's vision of his old neighborhood resembles the community described vividly by Carol Stack in her classic book, *All Our Kin*. Stack shows how families in a poor Black community survived and even thrived by participating in the reciprocal exchange of resources, time, and care. Following the work of feminist scholars, I take "caring" to refer to acts that nurture the basic dignity of dependent others: of meeting their needs and helping them flourish, especially when the care recipients cannot fully meet their needs on their own.[17] Black feminists have long documented "othermothering" practices in Black communities, where Black women are entrusted with caring for other children, or fictive kin.[18] Schools join families and other community organizations as extended care networks for Black children. As Lisa Bass has written, school officials acknowledge unjust situations in their schools, take corrective action, and show deep empathy for students.[19] Yet the kind of community that Stack and Officer Sherman described seemed harder to come by. Intensifying poverty, the increased presence of law enforcement, and other structural factors have nurtured greater distrust among poor Black residents, leading people to look out for themselves, as Officer Sherman put it.

Race Men and Caring

Along with Afrocentrism, the major innovation of the first-wave academies was to recruit Black men to be role models for students. The principal spokesperson for the role-modeling thesis (and a leading proponent of the first-wave academies) was the psychologist Spencer Holland. He suggested that young Black boys, and especially those raised by single mothers, would benefit from "positive" Black male role models.[20] Like other districts, the public schools in Morgan struggled to recruit and hire Black men. Nationwide, the teacher workforce is predominantly white (83 percent) and female (75 percent).[21] Less than 2 percent of all teachers are Black men. About one-third of the instructional staff at Perry was Black; half of this population included Black men. As Perry High and the other city schools struggled to hire Black men as teachers (even if their numbers were far better than dismal national percentages), the district focused its efforts on establishing a strong Black male leadership. Black men with extensive teaching and administrative experience were hired to work alongside Mr. Bradley and serve as his mentors. Six of the seven administrators at the school were Black men.

A "father figure thesis" maintains that Black men are more capable than women of handling Black boys and that Black men are needed to provide strict discipline and tough love.[22] The Perry High leadership was somewhat wary of this approach, in part because of the memory of Mr. Mincy, or Mr. "Military Man." Yet they felt it was appropriate for men—and especially Black men—to care for Black boys. They saw themselves as surrogate fathers. Caring is strongly gendered, as practices of nurturing have long been thought to be "women's work." Meanwhile, the enduring image of the stoic father reveals how men are normally given a "pass" for intimate caring; instead, they are expected to contribute to their families by protecting and producing (or laboring).[23] Black men are precariously situated within this framework. The complementary narratives of the "absent father" and "single mother" suggest that poor Black men make few contributions to their families. These discourses strongly echo in *The Philadelphia Negro*. Even as Du Bois emphasized the negative impact of environmental factors, the message in the book's pages was that the "construction of class differences among Blacks was predicated on cultural and moral distinctions measured by the degree of conformity to patriarchal family norms."[24]

A core group of ten Black men at Perry High—the six administrators, Officer Sherman, Mr. Jeffries, and two of the teachers—held enormous influence in the school, and collectively they shaped the vision for how caring looked inside the building. While the research on the first-wave academies emphasizes how individual Black men could serve as mentors for Black boys, here I want to stress how these Black men, as a group, viewed themselves as needing to lead the way. In their pioneering book *Black Metropolis*, St. Clair Drake and Horace Cayton offer a typology of leadership in Black communities. Two categories are relevant here. *Race leaders* promote a politics of respectability and approximate Du Bois's "Talented Tenth." As Drake and Cayton write, race leaders lead through "appeals for discipline within the Black belt" and "needle, cajole, and denounce" the masses into action.[25] Crucially, race leaders speak on behalf of Blacks before mainstream white communities. The next group are the *race men*, who work diligently to advance the cause of marginalized Blacks. One defining feature of a race man tends to be overlooked, however. Communities may respect race men for their leadership, but they remain suspicious about the motivations behind their decision to lead; specifically, that race men may lead the masses out of a selfish desire for adoration and self-advancement.[26] The Perry High leadership did not fall entirely into either of these two ideal types, but they seemed to embody both. I refer to the Black male leadership as race men, as others have widely adopted the label to refer to Black leaders and activists. The race men of Perry High appeared to be driven by a genuine concern for helping young men, and they took pride in the fact that *they* were the ones leading the way. They saw their work as an obligation, but they professed love for their students. They acknowledged structural causes of disadvantage and poverty, but they sometimes lapsed into blaming the students for their moral failings and therefore imposed a politics of respectability. And while the father figure thesis tends to assume uncritically that appropriate male role models are needed to be disciplinarians for boys, the Perry High race men mixed in empathy and tenderness with tough love.

As Patricia Hill Collins has written, Black feminist praxis is grounded in an "ethic of caring."[27] More recently, Joan Tronto has written that neoliberalism undermines caring in democratic societies by valorizing "personal responsibility" and "individual choices" at the expense of vital dependent relationships among people. Tronto articulates five principles of caring in the face of a threatening neoliberal order.[28] First, there is attentiveness, or "caring about" others. People, such as school officials, acknowledge that others have unmet needs, and they put those needs ahead of their own self-interests. Next, there is responsibility, or "caring for" others. School officials take ownership of meeting the needs of others. Competence, or "care giving," represents the third principle. Here, school officials provide that care. The fourth principle is responsiveness, or "care receiving." The care recipients respond to the care they are given, and care-givers adjust the additional care they offer accordingly. Last, is plurality, or "caring with" others. School officials work together to provide care, and they see their work as nurturing young people who can go on to be good care providers themselves. The Perry High race men were attentive to some of their students' needs, took responsibility for them, at times offered care competently, and approached this task collectively. Where they fell short the most was in being responsive. The staff only rarely considered what the boys themselves desired.

The Black male leadership drew on a discourse of racial uplift to justify their claim to leading the school and, by extension, to lifting up as many young Black men as they could. The Black male leadership saw it as their duty or calling to save their students, and they approached the task of being respectable role models for their students with the utmost gravity. And it was imperative that it was Black men who led the way. Mr. Jeffries said, "Right now, the principal has been trying to find the right way to reach them because as a Black man, as a person, as a man, you know, it's my job to reach my child. And they are our children. They're not Oriental. They're not Caucasian. They're not Italian. They're *ours*." While Mr. Jeffries himself never went to college, the race men understood themselves to be exceptional. Nine of the ten were college graduates, and all the administrators held multiple degrees. Five of the ten had parents who were also educators. William Sharp grew up in an upper-middle-class family and had gone on to be a principal himself for nearly twenty years before he was hired to help out at Perry and to serve as a mentor for Mr. Bradley. Darrell

Westbrook, whom we met in the last chapter, grew up in the neighborhood and served in the military before becoming a teacher and principal. (In fact, he had been a teacher at a local high school when Mr. Bradley was just a student there.) Borrowing from the language of his military background, he described his responsibilities to "serve" and "protect" young men. Meanwhile, Mark Richards had a promising career as a cancer researcher before he transitioned into work in the public schools. His parents, he told me, "were in the trenches of the civil rights movement," as he pointed to a picture of them standing next to Martin Luther King Jr. For Mr. Richards, being in the "trenches" of an urban school was his way of building on his parents' legacy.

I opened this chapter with a quotation from a congressman who described sons as "the seeds their fathers planted." The male staff drew on this imagery often to describe their responsibilities as race men. Mr. Youseff, whom we also met in the last chapter, had been a child of the civil rights era: a time of "moral awakening" and "social unrest," as he described it. After graduating from an Ivy League institution and after a stint overseas in the Middle East, he returned to the United States as a devout Muslim and a follower of the teachings of Malcolm X. He found his calling in work with troubled Black men, turning to both prison ministry and public schools. Mr. Youseff saw himself as a teacher and spiritual guide for men in prison and for boys who were being tracked in that direction. So when he discovered the all-male Perry High School, he felt he was destined to work there. For Mr. Youseff, there were clear links between prisons and schools. Beyond the tired refrain of a "school-to-prison pipeline" where punitive schools channel young men of color into jail, Mr. Youseff offered other distressing details of connections between schools and prisons. For example, he once shared with me how the incarcerated men he met regretted being absent in their own sons' lives.[29] And these men had a request for Mr. Youseff, a self-identified "prison messenger":

> I used to go up to the prison to talk to the prisoners—the inmates—and a lot of them are the fathers of some of the young men from this neighborhood. And almost to a man, they always ask . . . they always request of me in my other role as the Muslim leader. They say, "Brother Imam . . . make sure my seed"—meaning their sons—"don't end up in the same place."

By positioning themselves as surrogate fathers, the male leadership adopted a paternalistic stance. Families and incarcerated men depended on the race men for help, and the young men collectively needed those race men to lead the way.

Role-Modeling

"More male role models" has become the axiomatic response to the question of how to lift up marginalized young men of color. As the race men of Perry High saw it, their students experienced "father hunger," in the words of bell hooks.[30] Mr. Westbrook described it this way:

> I see a lot of kids, especially the younger kids, who really cling on to certain adults for attention, and you become that surrogate father that so many of them are looking for and need. And one of the travesties that I find is, just like this morning when I was dealing with a young man, first thing comes out of his mouth is, "Shit, my father's locked up." You understand? So you have a lot of kids who are missing a positive male image in their home, and you have a lot of kids who are angry because of their individual circumstances and the environment that they live every day, and they don't know how to come to someone and ask for help. They know how to strike out, and this is what happens a lot of times.

Perry High undertook role-modeling in three ways and with varying degrees of success. The first was through a "Male Speaker Series" that exposed boys to successful Black men, who served as "aspirational benchmarks," as Mr. Bradley memorably put it (one of many examples of how the language of measurable standards had become common sense at the two schools), as well as failed men, or "negative role models," who were reminders of the consequences of failure.

Many speakers gave what I came to think of as "just like you"/"just like me" lectures. They asserted that they were "just like" the boys—were Black men and come from similar neighborhoods—and had bucked the odds. The moral of the story was that the boys could be "just like" the successful men one day. These messages were sometimes given respectfully and with a sincere attempt to engage with the boys' own lives. But they did not resonate strongly with the young men, who seemed to distrust men who visited for a few hours, often lectured at great length, and then would leave and never return. (I overheard a student refer to these visits disparagingly as "flybys.") One event captured this perfectly. Just before the Thanksgiving break, three Black men—two of whom stressed that they were Morehouse College graduates and saw Perry High one day ascending to the heights of their alma mater—spoke about coming from poor backgrounds and later becoming engineers. Their lecture was peppered with phrases that the boys had had grown numb to: "broken families," "Dad ain't around," "Avoid the streets," "Choose college over prison." One guest said, "I see a lot of my younger self in you. And I want you to see your future self in us." Students bristled. Asad, a twelfth grader, was offended, and said loudly, "You don't know me." During the Q&A, Reese, a twelfth grader, stood up to mock the event and the speakers, saying in a formal voice while carefully enunciating each syllable, "I am a poor Black male in need of a mentor. Will one of you gentlemen be my mentor?" The students cracked up. The speakers looked baffled.[31]

Too often, visitors came across as disciplinarians or judgmental, which led to confrontations that torpedoed the lectures completely. There was the community leader who started out by saying he was disappointed with how long it took the students to get quiet. The banker who pointed to two attentive students sitting up front and shouted, "I guess these are the only young men who care about their future!" Another visit was widely anticipated by the school leadership. J. T. Thomas was an assistant admissions director at an HBCU. Whether it was a performance or not, Mr. Thomas was aggressive from the start, his presentation an odd mix of observations on the structural causes of Black male disadvantage ("The capitalist system is set up for you to fail! It has always exploited the labor of Black people!") and caricatures of U.S. meritocracy ("Want to be successful? Then you have to be the last person to go to bed and the first person to rise in the morning!") At one point he yelled, "You're no different than I am! Don't let the suit fool you. We're all the same!" For young men who distrusted older men, this came across as an assault. Dashaun, a twelfth grader, yelled back, "I don't need this shit," and walked out. His friends applauded, and Mr. Bradley had to step in to restore order.

Another tactic was to invite in speakers who were "negative role models," or the "reminder[s] of the costs of failure."[32] These speakers laid bare the repercussions for getting involved with gangs and violence as a way of motivating the students to "choose" a more hopeful path. An especially poignant moment was a daylong event called Education over Incarceration. The assembly was hosted by a local radio station, which broadcasted the program live over the air. The boys were given T-shirts that read, "Use your brain to break the chains," and were told to chant, "Yale over jail!" Inmates from the state's largest penitentiary called in and implored the boys to avoid criminal behaviors and expressed deep regret for their own actions. One inmate told the boys that under state law they could be charged as adults for certain crimes. The event was heartbreaking. Boys cried when a speaker asked who among them had lost loved ones to gun violence. Two students had the chance to speak with inmates over the phone and asked about their fathers, who were incarcerated at the prison. The program stressed the overrepresentation of Black men in prisons and hinted at the failures of mass incarceration, but the data and statistics took a back seat that day to the visceral impact of being confronted with the horrors of prison, which represented "wasted lives" and a "point of no return," as the speakers explained. As David Harding has shown in his work on violence in poor neighborhoods, the presence of these negative role models levels expectations: so long as boys "avoid trouble," then they judge their lives to be partially successful.[33] The boys of Perry High were then asked to "choose" a much higher standard of success—not simply education, but college—to direct them off the path to prison.

A second kind of role-modeling took place in the form of lessons. The thinking here was that Black male staff members would facilitate productive and difficult conversations on the topics of men and masculinity. The least effective lessons focused on the boys' relationships with their fathers. Some staff members wanted the young men to be vulnerable about not having a father present in their lives, but this provoked a lot of anger. One day, the boys in the Second Chance program for overage students got together for an activity led by Laron Buckley, a school district aide who visited a few days each week. Mr. Buckley passed out sheets that read "WHO IS YOUR DADDY?" and "SO HOW DO YOU KNOW WHO YOU ARE?" across the top. He told the boys that "it may hurt to have to fill this out." The boys were asked to think about questions such as "What is your birth father's name?" "When was the last time you spoke to your father?" and "Has your father ever told you he LOVES YOU?" Xavier pushed the sheet aside, said "I don't want to do this shit," and got up and left. Other boys shouted out: "We already know this." "My mom is my pop." "Where's my pop? He where he at."

The most helpful lessons provided what Clarence Terry and his colleagues (who draw on a Black Nationalist tradition in support of all-male education) call "counterspaces," which enable boys to "debrief" on structural oppression.[34] The beginning of Barack Obama's presidency marked a period of social transformation for the young men of Perry High, just as it did for their counterparts at Northside. On the day of President Obama's first State of the Union address, Mr. Gaines had his students read excerpts from the president's celebrated 2008 "A More Perfect Union" speech. Mr. Gaines asked his students what resonated most with them. Reggie pointed to passages in which Obama described "young men . . . languishing in our prisons" as a form of discrimination and supported "enforcing our civil rights laws and ensuring fairness in our criminal justice system."[35] "Obama's a real leader. He knows it's a big problem for the whole country," Reggie observed. "He's saying this is us needing to fight for our rights, like we're the new civil rights [generation]." The other boys cheered. Mr. Gaines beamed with pride.

The school's flagship program was a new mentoring program for ninth graders the school had identified as especially needy. Led by Mr. Jeffries and Mr. Gaines, it had the support of several local organizations.[36] The program recruited Black men but welcomed any man who wished to serve as a mentor. A team of organizers (including a member of the organization 100 Black Men) had done research to find the "best practices" for mentoring. The mentors visited once a week for events scheduled for the entire program and were also free to meet with their mentees on their own time. At the program's kick-off event in December, Mr. Gaines told the room full of ninth graders that "the majority of dropouts are in ninth grade." Research backs his claim. Ninth graders fare worse than their classmates in the upper grades on a range of academic and social measures. Ninth grade has therefore become a "make or break year for many 14- and 15-year olds."[37]

The program benefited tremendously from the efforts of the school's resident organic intellectual, Mr. Jeffries. He told me he was excited to have many professionally successful men participate. But he wanted them "to be humble" and, as I came to see it, not to be condescending or demeaning as the guest speakers could be. At a meeting for some of the mentors, he announced:

> You can't just be a role model. Yeah, our students need to see positive men and what positive men do. They need to try to see what it's like to walk in a successful man's shoes. But the hardest thing is for a man to walk a mile in their shoes. That's the thing: as a man, you can act your age by imagining what it's like to live the hard life of a Black child.

The program was effective because it honored the principles of caring laid out by Joan Tronto. The mentors demonstrated *competence* by investing in the lives of the boys. Many showed up each week, hung out long after the weekly meetings ended, and arranged separate times to meet with the boys. The boys collectively demonstrated *responsiveness* by affirming the care they received and taking obvious pride in the mentoring program. And the program embraced a final principle: *plurality*. Some mentor-mentee pairs were meeting with others in small groups. It was the closest Perry got to forming a brotherhood, which was a defining characteristic of Northside. Two months into the program, the mentors and mentees would hold hands in a circle and share words of appreciation for one another. While individual experiences varied, the program's "approval rating," as Mr. Jeffries called it, seemed to be high by the end of the year.[38]

I sensed that the program had potential because the boys together not only responded to care but were holding the program and their mentors accountable for that care. Young men offered suggestions on how to improve the program, and Mr. Jeffries encouraged students to help with organizing the meetings. A few students broached the topic of expanding the program to the entire school. At the end of the school year, Mr. Jeffries gave the mentees a chance to reflect on the program's inaugural year. Raymond, who had a quiet confidence to him, had emerged as a leader among the mentees. Given this opportunity to reflect on the program, his request was that the mentors continue to see them as children in need of care:

> We're still learning how to be men, and we need your help. We learn lessons every day, and after a few years we'll be more mature because of all the lessons we've learned. Eighth grade was only last year. *Give us some time to bloom.*

School Discipline

If caring involves taking responsibility for meeting the needs of marginalized young men, then the issue of discipline poses a particular challenge for all-boys schools. Unjust school discipline has gone hand in hand with the rising rate of Black male incarceration nationwide. In this respect, the reputation of Perry High weighed on the administrators, who were aware of the recent "law and order" approach taken by their predecessor, Mr. Mincy.

Morgan public schools had implemented zero-tolerance policies during the district restructuring. One of the Perry High administration's most consequential acts of care was to try to curb rates of punishment in the school. In their position as administrators, they had a better sense of overall, cumulative patterns of punishment and criminalization in the boys' lives. The administrators shared with me that they found it hard to placate their teachers, who were often quick to fill out "blue slips," violation records that could quickly accumulate and lead to a formal punishment. The administrators understood the challenges of teaching in a low-income school, and therefore they sometimes gave in to teachers who felt that removing particular students from class would allow everyone else to learn without being disturbed.[39] Mr. Gardner, a social worker at Perry High, was working with the administration to try and reduce rates of punishment in the building. He described his experience:

> There is an intense fear for a lot of our young men here. And so any time that a student shows any level of frustration . . . we automatically either just suspend them or write them up. And I think that there is a great deal of fear that the staff have. And the kids, they sense that.

Mr. Gardner had good insight into the disciplinary culture at the school because he stepped in to assist many boys who suffered from mental and other health issues, several of whom found themselves in trouble more often than not. He suggested that teachers mistook frustration for aggression.

On five occasions, I tracked the "blue slips" that teachers had filled out for boys who had violated a school rule. Only two led to the commensurate punishment mandated by school regulations. In three instances, the administrators intervened because the boys in question were "repeat offenders." The administrators used a variety of tactics to resolve the issues in a way that would avoid harsh punishment. In one instance, Mr. Westbrook convinced the principal not to "twenty" Percy, an eighth grader, for fighting between classes. "Twenty" was code for punishment that required a guardian to escort her child to school before the student could be reinstated. Some believed this was more effective than a suspension because it held parents more accountable, requiring them to come in when they might otherwise be at work (and as a few teachers confessed, they hoped this would anger parents enough that they would discipline their children at home). Mr. Westbrook, however, feared that this hurt both children and families: students might not return for days, which would set them back in their classes. As for parents, they were positioned so precariously in the labor market that missing any time at work might harm their status on the job. Mr. Westbrook practiced what Kathleen Nolan has called a "culturally relevant disciplinary style," which "necessitates a deep knowledge and respect for students' home cultures and requires educators to engage students in ways that are not divorced from the larger context of their lives."[40] In one instance, Mr. Westbrook sat down with the child and his teacher, and they agreed that the student would complete extra schoolwork. Later, he explained to the teacher that he had overheard that Percy's older sister was having personal problems that were weighing heavily on the entire family. Mr. Westbrook intentionally did not follow a school law he knew to be unfair. Instead he demonstrated care for Percy and his family, all of whom could have been punished more than the offense necessitated.[41] The hope was that Percy would recognize the care he received by avoiding trouble in the hallways and heading straight for class.

The Gay–Straight Alliance

As part of the school's caregiving efforts, Mr. Bradley felt it was important to start the school's first gay–straight alliance (GSA).[42] These are extracurricular student groups that support lesbian, gay, bisexual, transgender, and queer (LGBTQ) youth. Mr. Gardner, who was tapped to help direct the new group, had previously been at a school that had been hostile to the idea of a GSA. Mr. Gardner assumed "that being in an all-male environment . . . there probably are some students who would like to have some level of support," and so he was encouraged that the administration wanted to launch a GSA that year in conjunction with the new mentoring program.

The GSA took its lumps its first year but began to thrive, not unlike the mentoring program, because of the involvement of committed adults and a tight-knit group of students. The weekly meetings were a mix of structured activities and discussions on whatever was on the students' minds. At one meeting, the group watched the film *The Laramie Project* based on the brutal murder of Matthew Shepard, and discussed new federal legislation passed that year that broadened hate crimes to include those motivated by a victim's gender or sexual identity.[43] During open discussions, the students—a core group of four young men, with a few others who attended less frequently—chatted about topics including relationships and student safety. These discussions sometimes led the group to take action. Jabari scheduled a time for the group members to visit a clinic to get tested for STDs. At another meeting, everyone made and laminated "Safe Zone" posters to remind students and staff about the importance of creating inclusive environments for gay and gender nonconforming students.

By the middle of the year, the GSA occasionally met with the members of the GSA at Thompson High, Perry's sister school. These were especially empowering meetings. Mr. Gardner reflected on one joint meeting where the participants shared their experiences coming out to loved ones:

> It was very touching because a lot of people were actually crying. And it wasn't out of sadness, but it was out of joy and appreciation, and I felt like we really connected as a group, you know? And for people to express that level of vulnerability, I thought, was really important. And it showed me that they were actually able to trust one another within the group because they were able to share details and levels of intimacy that were very important to their hearts.

Core members Randy, Jabari, and Malik praised Mr. Bradley for encouraging staff members to take part in the GSA and for providing the boys with resources so they could put on events like a dance and fashion show. The students had two wishes, however. First, they wanted the administration to encourage more adults to participate as allies. That year, Mr. Bradley was the only member of the school leadership who attended meetings. The lack of involvement by the school's race men was particularly flagrant because of their outspoken support for and pride in the mentoring program. This further highlighted the heteronormative character of the mentoring program.[44]

The GSA members also wanted the administration to do more to address the use of antigay language and verbal assaults against gay and gender nonconforming students. As Jabari said:

> An assembly could be good for the students. I think they would get it a little more if it came from the principal. I think maybe hearing it coming from such a successful man, I think it would give them more guidance and stop them from saying so many ignorant comments.

Northside Academy

Building the Brotherhood

The Northside administration resembled Perry High's in one way: all three administrators (the CEO and founder, the principal, and the assistant principal) were all Black men. The similarities largely ended there. As a model second-wave academy, Northside de-emphasized Black male role-modeling in favor of building stronger bonds among the boys: a brotherhood. The school hosted events featuring local Black male leaders, but the school did not promote the idea that the young men should learn primarily from Black men for their success. As Northside officials saw it, they needed to learn from the smartest and most capable teachers, regardless of race or gender.

As Patrick Finn has written about elite private schools, "The hard work demanded of students furthers their sense of shared struggle, solidarity, and entitlement to status and power."[45] The shared struggle to master Latin united the young men of Northside Academy. The students were told that they would be successful if they supported one another. The school stressed that each student could achieve great things with the help of his fellow scholars and that individual achievements were everyone's achievements. Mr. Davidson told me:

> [The principal] talks about Gladiators and he talks about family at the same time. And I think he's trying to get the idea that this is a community. You're all in this together. If one succeeds you all succeed, and if you all succeed the individual succeeds.

The fraternal culture was a defining feature of the school.[46] Richard, an eleventh grader, had been skeptical of the all-boys model at first but came to value a brotherhood that he did not think was possible in larger schools.

When I asked him about the school's challenging curriculum, Richard appealed to the importance of brotherhood:

> If we see one person struggling, we'll try to pick him up and help him.
> Just like how we do in the football field, we all work as one team. And
> if we all work as one team, we all can go to the next level together. And
> that's why everybody got to push somebody to get to that next level.
> And some people don't want to be pushed. You just try to tell them,
> "I'm trying to help you to get better," and nobody can get mad
> because you're trying to help them or they're trying to help you. That's
> why I try to just help everybody that I can, and I take some help from
> other people too. Because I know I don't know everything.

As Ann Arnett Ferguson writes, academically oriented Black boys experience a "psychic strain" as they attempt to navigate the competing expectations from schools and from their peers.[47] This frequently results in feelings of isolation. Northside Academy sought to overcome this alienation by bringing together like-minded students who were bound by a sense of relative privilege and shared academic struggle. Knowing that their exceptional education oriented them to college would motivate them to work hard together. It also gave them hope. "Hope is a rope" that individuals toss into the sky, Henri Desroche writes; individuals have faith the rope will hold, and they pull themselves up to heaven.[48] Yet "climbers sometimes climb in teams."[49]

The burgeoning brotherhood and its message of hope gained strength as part of larger collective efforts in the Black community. For instance, several parents drew on the collectivist maxim "It takes a village to raise a child" to describe how Northside was supporting the mission of caring for fictive kin. Some of the most vivid descriptions identified Northside as a place of spiritual nourishment. The Black church has long been an "anchoring institution" in the city of Morgan.[50] Ms. Bridges remarked that it was "God's grace" that led her son Charles to Northside. She invoked the Holy Trinity and explicitly identified her church, her immediate family, and Northside as forming Charles's "true" family. As she said, "It's a team effort. Everybody has to come together collectively in the family in order to make him the strong young man that he is today." Other parents described how the school's fraternal mission mirrored the church's mission of service to others, which imbued the school with a "biblical second language."[51] Sylvia Page's son, Jay, was a tenth grader at school and a junior deacon at his church. Reflecting on the similar missions of the two institutions, Ms. Page said, "if these children can learn to put others ahead of themselves, then the community as a whole will improve."

Protecting the Brotherhood

The Northside brotherhood had disciplined bodies, set against the undisciplined bodies of their peers. The school community drew boundaries between its respectable young men and the undisciplined boys who were prone to fighting. As the Northside community viewed it, public schools were environments full of young men who had chosen fighting over schoolwork. At an induction ceremony, Mr. Green told the school's newest students:

> You are all here right now because either you or your parents want
> better for you. Whether "better" means not having to pay for a private
> school tuition—for a good education—or whether "better" means
> avoiding your neighborhood school, where fighting and failure are
> more prevalent than love and learning.

The failure of these schools could be explained by their lack of discipline. David, a tenth grader, shook his head when I asked him what he thought about the middle school he had attended. "It's like a juvenile school mostly," he said. "It was fights every day, people bringing weapons." Here David likened his middle school to the very disciplinary schools that Mr. Pierce had rejected when designing Northside.

The Northside community was constantly worried about potential fights between their students and other boys in the community. Earlier I described how some students felt the uniforms emasculated them, which made them the target of antigay taunting. The school rationalized these behaviors by concluding that other boys were envious of Northside students and that jealousy prompted them to be aggressive toward their more respectable peers. I asked Charles why other boys initiated fights with Northside students.

> They think we're bettering our education. We're wearing blazers and
> ties and all that. Maybe they wish that they still had the chance to
> come to Northside so that they can get a good education like we do.

As I mentioned in the last chapter, at one assembly, Mr. Holmes recommended that the students hurry home after school to avoid confrontations with boys from other schools. "You have everything to lose, and they have nothing to lose," he shared. "[Those boys] see you as having opportunities. You've got to have discipline. It's that discipline that's going to make the difference between you and all the other boys." While fighting is a valuable form of masculine currency in poor communities, the school officials emphasized that the boys stood to gain far more by being disciplined and by avoiding fights with neighborhood boys.[52]

Nate, an eleventh grader, described himself and his classmates as "roses in concrete": persons that needed to be nurtured and cared for in order to grow in an environment that otherwise offered little hope.[53] And those roses require protection. Symbolic boundaries are not simply moral appraisals; they also justify the creation of social boundaries, or "differences manifested in unequal access to and unequal distribution of resources . . . and social opportunities."[54] The Northside community constructed boundaries to protect the valuable opportunities their students possessed. One boundary was physical. Before and after school, staff members literally lined the streets so the boys could walk safely to their buses. The school's "safety zone," which no other local schools organized, gave the impression that the boys were law-abiding and therefore worthy of protection. This "safety zone" extended beyond this physical border to include other adults and authorities in the community. The school boasted that strangers not only respected the young men but were "looking out for our boys," as Ms. Bridges, a parent, put it. Ms. Holden, a teacher, described how the school sometimes received calls from strangers complimenting the boys, and she noted that some community members had gotten into the habit of telling other boys they should "act more like Northside students." An esteemed school had propped up a respectability politics and had been used by the institution's many admirers to judge the failures of delinquent boys in this city. This supports findings that authorities criminalize delinquent young men of color, in part, by pitting them against academically oriented and law-abiding boys.[55] Over time, the respectable identities of the Northside students had likely granted them advantages in the community. Compared to other maligned young men, it appears that community members gave Northside students the assumption of innocence and therefore more protection of the law. This was confirmed to me by a mother of two sons, one a ninth grader at Northside and the other a twelfth grader at Perry High. The school had therefore institutionalized a cultural practice that Victor Rios has called "acting lawful," where "individuals who experience punitive social control attempt to avoid becoming victims of criminalization and punishment."[56] By relying on authorities to help keep watch over their students, and by winning over many others in the community who viewed their boys as exceptional, the Northside community had in its own way participated in the larger forms of surveillance in the neighborhood.

While the school asked its young men to stand together in solidarity, this was not easily secured. Some young men critiqued the very brotherhood that claimed to offer them protection. At one assembly, the administration honored Lenny, an eleventh grader, with an award for helping "to prevent," as Mr. Green said, "something potentially tragic from happening."

Lenny had overheard a boy from another school threaten some Northside students, and he reported the incident to Mr. Green. Later, school officials allegedly found a weapon on the boy in question (rumored to be a knife). There was usually plentiful applause for award winners each week, but this award drew suspicion, with many boys refraining from clapping. As tenth grader Stephan said incredulously, "they really just gave the boy a certificate for being a *rat!*" A "rat" or a "snitch," someone who cooperates with the police or other authorities, has long been an object of scorn in marginalized communities.[57] In a later interview, David recalled the incident: "What happened with Lenny: that gives us a rep. Everyone already knows we different. We look different, we dress different. And now people know us for snitching."

Viewed from one angle, Lenny was protecting his brothers. The administration used Lenny as evidence of the strength of brotherhood. Yet Lenny had violated the snitching code in the community. Therefore, being told to choose school solidarity over a manhood that demanded other ways of resolving conflicts was not a simple choice at all. While parents and school officials were deeply concerned about removing their young men from a path that led to the criminal justice system, the young men themselves experienced anxiety about being asked to cooperate with the law. The divergent interpretations of masculinity alienated some of the community's members and threatened solidarity. Jack told me that the school may have thought the boys were growing closer, but he and his friends at school were still close with peers outside of school:

> JACK: See, this school, they don't know what goes on outside of here.
> They may put that mentality on you that "there's some stuff you
> don't gotta do," but there's some stuff you *gotta* do. Like you can
> come here, like I'm a whole different person when I'm in this
> building. I let my guard down, I ain't worried about nothin' in here.
> But once I leave I'm back on point.
> FREEDEN: Back on point?
> JACK: Take care of myself. Take care of my boys. People I had before I
> stepped through [Northside's] doors.

Jack had learned to be a "code switcher," or someone "who could navigate the streets and mainstream institutions."[58] Or to draw on the conceptual language I laid out in chapter 2, Jack was adjudicating "street" and "scholarly" cultural orientations. Seventeen of the thirty-nine students I interviewed (44 percent) described trying to actively hone this skill. They envisioned themselves at the boundary between the school and the streets, which they still identified with and which the school largely vilified. The school officials made it clear that their old friends were holding them back. Their best option was to embrace their new brothers. The school may have articulated a conveniently bifurcated world separating Northside from the streets, but many boys still struggled to navigate the school's demands and the expectations of their outside peers.

School Discipline

The Northside leaders may not have viewed themselves as surrogate fathers, but as an institution, the school operated in loco parentis.[59] Even if Jack and his classmates were not fully committed to the school's brotherhood, the school was able to secure obedience through a strict culture of discipline to a greater degree than at Perry. This discipline, however, was not merely an issue of meting out punishment, though there was plenty of that. Rather, discipline was a matter of governing conduct and character. Discipline was the foundation of what Émile Durkheim termed a "moral education."[60] As Durkheim argued, schools use discipline to inculcate important values and to "regularize conduct" in children. But in order for schools to maintain their moral authority, it is important that rules are legitimate and that they work in the best interests of children. Punishment is effective if it is fair, consistent, and not overly strict. Expanded surveillance in poor communities has done much to injure the moral authority of public schools, which increasingly adopt the logic of crime control. Zero-tolerance policies, which originated in the Gun-Free Schools Act of 1994, demand harsh and swift punishments for school infractions.[61] They have had an especially harmful impact on young men of color and have helped funnel Black boys from failed school experiences into jails, prisons, and other forms of state control.[62]

As discussed in chapter 1, Mr. Pierce clearly wished to distance Northside from stigmatized all-male institutions, such as juvenile prisons and the city's disciplinary high schools. The severity of discipline does not necessarily change, however, in respectable institutions. It is rather packaged as what Martin Summers has identified as a "missionary paternalism" foundational to early elite Black colleges and high schools at the turn of the twentieth century: precisely those "role model" institutions described earlier in the book. Drawing on Victorian ideals, missionary paternalism relied on "mechanisms of control" to produce disciplined, racialized, gendered, and sexualized subjects. These mechanisms were needed to cultivate respectable character and ease the assimilation of Black students into a white-dominated society. As Summers has described, at institutions such as Fisk University in Tennessee (Du Bois's alma mater), the administration hovered over their students and standardized nearly every facet of life. Black male students were required to attend daily church services; were forbidden from consuming alcohol and tobacco; and were not allowed to listen to jazz or the blues, Black musical genres that captured the "tempestuous spirit of rebellion" among many young African Americans.[63] Many observers critique today's "no excuses" charter schools for their boot-camp culture.[64] This, in fact, has a long history. Indeed, early elite Black institutions were modeled after the military.[65] In a similar fashion, the student handbook at Washington, D.C.'s illustrious Dunbar High School left no doubt about how their high-achieving Black children were expected to behave. Among other things, the handbook instructed the pupils to have impeccable manners, to avoid gossiping, to get at least eight hours of sleep a night, and to avoid "as companions" those "who are unsatisfactory in deportment or careless in their habits."[66]

Northside Academy was not a military institution, of course, but the "regimented lifestyles" and "martial logic" that were the pride of Fisk University operated also at Northside. There were many reasons why the Northside students felt they were under the careful watch of school officials. One was the rigorous schedule, which included an extended school day (including required extracurricular activities, or for some students, detention and study hall) and occasional school on the weekends. Even for the eleventh graders, who were accustomed to the long schedule, the hours could be grueling. In fact, a few students even took it upon themselves to do research into the optimal number of school hours for high school students. They brought it up with the principal, Mr. Green. He thanked them for their research, and asked that the students trust the administration's methods. The young men at least understood that the extended hours were not simply extra time to work.[67] They were meant "to keep us from the danger and all the other guys that's out there," Trevon, a tenth grader, told me.

The school's many rules were spelled out in the "Code of Conduct." A three-tiered system assigned a certain number of demerits to violations of increasing severity. A Tier 1 offense, for example, included violations such as chewing gum and showing up to school without the student ID. School officials had several "corrective actions" at their disposal to punish students for accumulated demerits, including detentions and a phone call home. These comprised the vast majority of the offenses I observed. Tier 2 offenses included fighting, sexual harassment, and theft. The highest tier included offenses such as possession of a weapon, indecent exposure, and assault on school personnel. Tier 2 and 3 offenses often resulted in suspensions and possible expulsions.

A few weeks into the school year, I was having lunch with a few ninth graders. Mr. Holmes, the assistant principal in charge of school discipline, was across the lunchroom, moving quickly from table to table. He was in charge of discipline and was known to rule with an iron fist. He appeared to stop only to point out possible violations and hand out demerits. Impersonating Mr. Holmes, Terrell pointed to a friend and said, "Fix that tie, boy!" The boys laughed. "This man *does not smile*. He is *too serious,*" Terrell continued. "Everywhere I go, he's always there!" Among the first things new students learned was to be on their absolute best behavior around Mr. Holmes. While Mr. Green was still trying to carve out his role as the school's new principal, the school seemed to view Mr. Holmes as playing the "bad cop" to Mr. Pierce's "good cop," as the charming school founder and CEO was more likely to crack a smile and joke with the students. I interviewed two tenth graders, Trevon and Kevin, together. "I think it's too easy to get a demerit," Trevon said. "You can get a demerit for any little thing you do." Kevin added, "It's like, you have to be real careful, because if one of the teachers don't get you for something, then Mr. Holmes definitely will." Ms. Spring knew she could trust Mr. Holmes and his staff but conceded that they "operated on fear."

Ultimately, there was little the students could do. If the students were vocal in their frustration over school discipline, the administrators would remind them that attending Northside was a privilege or, drawing on the language of "choice," would tell the students that they (and their families) were the ones who chose the school and were therefore the ones choosing its culture of discipline. The choice was always theirs. For students who did not consent to rules, coercion in the form of punishment—sometimes severe—was always there in reserve.

Diverse Masculinities

The school's disciplinary regime ultimately posed several paradoxes: the boys felt that the culture was both restrictive and liberating, based on fear while also promoting the kind of hard work and success that would raise hope of getting to college. Mr. Pierce wagered that if the students felt protected and safe, then that would free them to be themselves. Indeed, this was precisely the message Du Bois shared with his alma mater, Fisk University, when he condemned its strict in loco parentis mission: too much discipline could choke freedom, but providing just the right amount of order could give children the space to reach their potential.[68] They could pursue their interests and take risks without fear of judgment. Jack, whom we heard from earlier, captured this sentiment best:

When I was young, I was like, "all-boys?" But now I see the good in coming here. I see the whole point. I get it. I can tell you, this school saved my life. If I had gone to East [Morgan High], I'd either be locked up or probably dead by now. Because the people I was hangin' out with, they locked up. I know there ain't too much learnin' in East. You can pretty much do what you want. It's like a mini placement camp. Here, you're on restriction, but you're free. You don't have to worry too much about nothin'. You don't have to worry about fightin' everyday, you don't have to worry about people jumpin' you or stuff like that. So this school saved a lot of people. It put people on the right path.

Edward Fergus has endorsed "the freeing powers of single-sex education," which helps to "chang[e] notions about a one dimensional image of masculinity."[69] Northside promoted this very idea. It was so strong, in fact, that middle schools used it as a selling point to their own students. Jim Chambers, the CEO of a local charter middle school whom we met in chapter 1, said:

When they get to high school, they could take it to the next level, and [Mr. Pierce] does that with the Latin. He does that with the rowing team. I mean, like I said, most urban settings, it's basketball or hang out on the corner. For girls, it's jump rope. But we need more boys to be nontraditional. So just an opportunity to have a jazz ensemble, to have a rowing team, and they're good at it. It just helps them see the world in a lot of different ways because there are other people that do those things as well, and they're into different things, and that's going to expose you to a lot of different things as well.

Northside officials desired conformity to school rules but otherwise encouraged their students to pursue many different interests. And school officials went out of their way to celebrate all student achievements, including those of the debate team, which placed well in citywide tournaments; a mock trial team that received rave reviews from the law school students who advised the team; and the basketball team, which was winning games despite not having its own gym. Teachers expressed enthusiasm for the boisterous anime club, as well as the school's new rowing team.[70] Northside, therefore, alongside its strict disciplinary system, nurtured the idea that its students were still children who should be able to play and experiment freely.[71] And although Northside did not publicly advocate for the group, there was a thriving GSA (sponsored by Ms. Spring), which had seen increased interest from students who wished to participate as allies.

School Moms and White Saviors

Perry High

What role did women play in the schools' caring regimes? This section examines the performance of female teachers as "surrogate" moms, or "school moms," for the young men. While the two schools nurtured different forms of belonging, they converged in one important respect. White women held a disproportionate amount of influence at the two schools. In fact, fifty-one of the sixty-four students I interviewed at the two schools (80 percent) identified a white or Asian woman as their favorite teacher.[72]

In the last chapter, I described how teachers with more experience working with disadvantaged populations (at these two schools and others) were more likely to practice a culturally relevant pedagogy. Yet given the reality of many Black and Brown schools with a predominantly white teaching force, it is important to consider how teachers will move from being "unaware of their culture," meaning how teachers fail to see how whiteness grants privilege and is therefore taken for granted, "to a critical understanding of the role of culture, power, and oppression."[73] Indeed, popular discourse has circulated a "white savior" narrative where the heroic efforts of a white individual helps lift up a Black and Brown school or community and helps students find their voice and beat the odds. Popular white savior teaching films include *Freedom Writers* (2007) and, most famously, *Dangerous Minds* (1995), starring Michelle Pfeiffer as the renegade teacher (who just so happens to be an ex-Marine).

The race men of Perry High recognized the influence of the non-Black female teachers in the building, and their feelings about these women ranged from frustration to resentment. For instance, Mr. Sharp spoke at length about the "School Moms," a group of three young white women and one Asian woman who were friends and were especially popular among the students. (This included one teacher, Ms. Channing, whom we met in chapter 1, who had recently left the school.) Mr. Sharp had taught for years in schools with faculty that were disproportionately white women. He recognized some of their efforts and achievements but thought it damaged young men to be surrounded by so many white women:

> The "optics" aren't good. See, you have these women coming from
> college or recently out of school: these do-good, "save-the-world" types.
> At every grade, you see these women. And our boys gravitate towards
> them. They latch onto these women; you see them following them
> around the hallways. Our young men only come to trust these white
> women, and they won't give other teachers a chance. I think in a

school like this, we need less of those women, you understand? They need to learn from people of their own race, or from other men.

Mr. Sharp seemed to resent the success of these School Moms and even saw them as a threat. He felt they sucked up all the attention of the young men, which presumably drew attention away from other teachers (Black women, and Black and non-Black men). They were *doubly* inappropriate for boys in Black male academies because they were white and they were women. And he saw these women as white saviors: through their hard work and sacrifices, the students were supposed to be "transformed, saved, and redeemed."[74]

Mr. Richards, whom we met earlier in the chapter, had not been at the school long, and he was something of a curiosity for the students. The boys were known to "test," or provoke, new staff members, but Mr. Richards was ready for them, showing an unflappable demeanor that earned him the nickname "Mr. Serious." "Our biggest issue are the teachers," he said. He was especially concerned with the influence of the School Moms.

> MR. RICHARDS: Many of these female teachers are too young and don't have children of their own. And so their point of view and their lack of knowledge is sometimes damaging. So you're going to have an all-boys school, but they don't have male teachers. How can [these female teachers] relate? Especially if they don't have sons and they don't have children of their own. They can't relate in a maternal way.
> FREEDEN: "A maternal way"?
> MR. RICHARD: A mother knows exactly what her child needs. These are needs that aren't all about academics. Are you healthy? Are you safe? In the same way a good teacher knows what her students need. And a mother doesn't leave her child.

Mr. Richards had strong words for the School Moms. He concluded that they did not practice a culturally relevant pedagogy, and he even drew on an essentialist argument to claim that mothers were naturally better and more caring than women without children. And as his last statement conveyed, he even blamed teachers for abandoning their students (by teaching for a short while and then leaving the school).

I did not observe any confrontations between the School Moms and the administration, but this tension was widely rumored to exist. Ms. Channing said:

> Black male teachers got away with not doing stuff that white females would be called out for. So there was a lot of tension around that. And we sort of brought that up at the end of last year, like, "There is some serious racial tensions happening in this building that need to be addressed."

Ms. Channing felt that Black male teachers were receiving preferential treatment from the administration, and she shared other stories about Black men who were being promoted and supported in a manner that other teachers were not. The larger issue was that officials and teachers never had an opportunity to openly address how they were implicated in, and helped to reproduce, these racial and gendered dynamics in the building. It appeared it would have been especially important for the race men to articulate why they felt it was crucial that Black men play a leading role in the building, to discuss the historical underrepresentation of Black men in the teaching force, and to ask the white women to reflect more carefully on how the white savior narrative had shaped their subjectivity.

Northside Academy

While men outnumbered women on the staff at Northside, as they did at Perry High, two white women carried enormous influence and were widely adored by the students: Ms. Spring and Ms. Holden.[75] Thirty-five of the thirty-nine students I interviewed called at least one of these two "Mom." They shared many qualities that were interpreted as maternal. They were tender and firm and rarely raised their voices. They did frequent check-ins with their students and often connected nonverbally through soft, physical touch. The boys seemed especially taken when Ms. Holden referred to them as "darlin' " (she had lived for a while in the South). The two teachers referred to the students as their kids.

School community members also acknowledged the white savior narrative. A few days before the holiday break, the staff surprised the boys with a trip to a movie theater to watch the movie *The Blind Side*. Based on the best-selling book by Michael Lewis, the movie chronicles the real-life story of a homeless African American teenager, Michael Oher, who is adopted by the Touhys, an affluent white family. Michael is shy and suffers from past trauma. His new family, and particularly the mother, encourages Michael to pursue football, where he quickly proves to be an elite player. He goes on to be a star in the college ranks and then in the National Football League.

The administration seemed to think the movie was harmless, that it would engage the young men's interest in sports, or that it would be uplifting to see a movie about a disadvantaged Black man who went from "nothing to something." The movie, however, threw into sharp relief two consequential issues for Black male identity. Tamar, a tenth grader, had struggled academically and had nearly left the school after his first year. But he had grown to think fondly of the school. He used the film to make sense of his time at Northside:

It got to me and I thought maybe seeing *Blind Side* movie taught us about how you leave from one place . . . you left . . . but you always got a place *in your heart* sort of. Because the guy, Michael Oher, he left out of the urban community, the city or whatever, the bad part, where all his friends and his family was, and moved into a suburban home, or a suburban family home, and he never forgot about his friends. He never forgot about his mom, his family, his brother. But, on the other hand, there was some bad things there that he tried to let go of, so I sort of took it as that's me leaving this community.

Like Jack before him, Tamar was trying to reconcile the two opposing forces of his community and Northside. He was torn (his comment "in your heart" stuck with me), but Michael Oher offered hope. Maybe hard work and future success were a worthy trade-off for leaving behind a community that had raised him. Yet I heard few school discussions about how the young men could work to improve their communities. As Kenneth Saltman has written, grit and resilience promote " 'getting out' of the context of poverty rather than learning to comprehend and confront the forces that produce it."[76]

Shortly after the screening, Lila Larkin, a tenth-grade English teacher, gave her class space to chat about the film. Some boys enjoyed the film. Their comments included these: "They take in a kid less fortunate than themselves, and raised them as their own. I really like the movie." "[Ms. Touhy] really believed in him. Not everyone will do that for you if you're Black." "If you work hard at your dreams, you can become great." Ms. Larkin then asked the students to read a scathing review of the film. The reviewer argued that it depicted Michael as largely passive and mute, and Ms. Touhy as the white female savior who goes on her own personal odyssey to quite literally give Michael a voice.[77] It generated a productive, if difficult, conversation among the students. Ja'quan applauded the reviewer and mockingly said, "I guess Black boys are fine if we're saved by a rich, white lady." Trevon agreed and made a connection that had an impact on his classmates. "It's not just that white lady. I think [the reviewer] is saying, why do Black kids have to follow white people to get somewhere in life? That's like Latin, right?" This conclusion was disorienting, but Trevon's classmates clearly respected him for articulating it.

In our interview later, Ms. Larkin told me that she was "totally appalled" by the symbolic act of taking the entire school to see a white savior film (and one that glorified sports):

> There was the message that he got there because this rich white couple felt bad for him and picked him up on the side of the road like a stray.

There was just something about carting a whole school of African-American boys to this story of someone who didn't succeed through mental, work or academic perseverance. And it just threw up a lot of red flags for me.

Unlike the race men of Perry High, the Northside administrators appeared unbothered by the racial and gender dynamics of their staff and the quite evident racial politics behind their selection of the dead language of gods and gladiators. Yet the discussion of the film in Ms. Larkin's class laid bare the contradictions behind a respectability politics that was entrenched in the school but that the young men rarely had a language or an opportunity to discuss. Once a popular explanation for Black academic underperformance, researchers have undermined the "acting white" hypothesis that Black children oppose schooling because they associate it with a white identity.[78] The culture of the school, however, passed along the implicit and distressing message that being adopted by white women, and that adopting a "white" language, was their ticket to success.

Conclusion

This chapter opened by highlighting the central role that the church has played in African American history. The significance of the church's primary unit—the family—becomes clear when we consider that the Black church has long promoted a respectability politics that symbolically divides the church and the street.[79] Both Perry High and Northside promised to build new kinds of families for their young men, ones that would steer them from the dangers the community posed.

Identifying themselves with the legacy of Black male leadership, the race men of Perry High saw themselves as surrogate fathers who could offer care, tough love, and empathy. Acknowledging the dearth of men in the classrooms, they were committed to surrounding their students with male role models. These efforts sometimes did more harm than good, but a new mentoring program brought men and boys together to give and receive care, and to give the students a chance to be vulnerable and to be children. However, in this school's gender regime, celebrating the mentoring program highlighted the relative lack of administrative support for the school's new gay–straight alliance.

Northside asked the boys to turn to one another. As members of a college-bred community, they came to see themselves as a Talented Tenth of sorts, a select group of young men with bright futures. The young men were tasked with protecting themselves and the school's status and resources from outside threats, in a process akin to what Charles Tilly calls "opportunity hoarding." In this process, "members of a clique of a categorical boundary seize control of a value-producing resource of limited availability and allocate a large share of the value produced to themselves, devoting some of the value to reproducing the boundary."[80] The administration felt they cared for their students by offering them protection: by keeping them safe so they could pursue their interests and be their best selves within the symbolic and physical borders constructed by the school. The young men of Northside may have had some freedom to assert their wishes (as when they proposed cardigans as an alternate uniform), but they largely had no choice but to follow the strict rules and accept the school's disciplinary culture. These shared bonds of struggle may have strengthened the brotherhood, but they came at a cost. Some students struggled to reconcile a brighter future with a connection to a community that was characterized as desolate, traumatizing, and in need of abandoning and of "getting out." The next chapter examines the future trajectories of these two groups of young men.

CHAPTER FIVE

Heroic Family Men and Ambitious Entrepreneurs

The Making of Black Men

How do we understand the future lives of young Black men? As Elijah Anderson has written, Black boys growing up in violent neighborhoods perceive their own lives in existential terms, taking life one day at a time and acknowledging that tomorrow is not guaranteed.[1] Schools, however, can have a profound effect on how young people project their futures, their hopes, and their visions for the identities they will grow into. As I have described in these pages, the young men of Perry High and Northside Academy felt their lives had volition, or a sense of movement with respect to the future.[2] While the scholars of Northside had forward momentum in the race to college, many of their peers outside the school's Safe Zone were not as lucky or hopeful. In linking young Black men to futures, research shows again and again that young Black men are tracked away from higher education and into the criminal justice system. School officials "adultify" young Black boys, or treat and punish them like men, which denies this population the privileges of childhood.[3] Indeed, we so often look ahead to the (presumed ill-fated) futures of Black boys that Black boyhood itself is rendered unimaginable.[4]

How, then, might we imagine Black male futures in a contemporary neoliberal era? Jennifer Randles and Kerry Woodward explain how the neoliberal state participates in the practice of governmentality. The state not only manages and disciplines but also trains people to become particular kinds of subjects, or "good neoliberal citizens" who will acquire and hone the requisite skills when self-sufficiency is demanded of them.[5] Having examined why Perry High and Northside Academy separate their boys from girls, and how the schools teach and promote belonging, this chapter looks ahead and considers the young men's futures. While Perry High asked their young men to be good (surrogate) fathers and family men, Northside groomed its young men to be good workers in a global economy.

Perry High

The Good Life

While newer to Perry High, Mr. Gardner, the social worker, had quickly ingratiated himself to a wide swath of young men at the school. Unlike other men in the building, he never yelled; instead, he spoke in a deep and calming voice that made him, as various students and adults at the school told me, seem "wise." During our interview, I asked Mr. Gardner if he could share some wisdom on the emotional and psychological lives of the young men in his care. Given that graduation was around the corner, he asked me to consider the boys' futures. Graduation, he said, brought with it a strange mix of feelings. The students were excited to be done with school, but he suspected many were also afraid to have so much unstructured time. Especially for the graduating seniors, "it almost feels like they're suffering from a Peter Pan Syndrome," Mr. Gardner said. "And what I mean by that is a lot of our kids are about to embark on the work world, but I think that there is this overall sense of fear that underlies a lot of their actions." A feeling of trepidation sunk in as the young men entered a world after high school that offered few concrete opportunities for men of color.[6]

Only a handful of the seniors would move on to college that fall. Frank was the student body president and the class valedictorian. His two nicknames, "Obama Junior" and "The Reverend," perfectly captured someone who yearned for a career as a politician and who was active as a tutor in his church. (In conversation, he frequently cited Bible passages.) While his classmates struggled, Frank thrived in part because everyone saw him as exceptional inside the school: an identity that he embraced even as it implied that, as a group, his classmates were underachieving. Frank was the ideal student that *Northside* had in mind, and so it was no surprise that Frank was the only student I interviewed who had a clear plan for getting to college. Frank recognized his own status. He had thrived despite the culture of Perry High School and despite the challenges his community presented. He looked forward to joining the college-bred community. He shared an excerpt from a poem he had written:

> Our time has risen.
> In '03, 193,000 young Black men were in prison.
> That was definitely not cool but we're also getting knowledge.
> Because what they forgot to mention is 532,000 young Black men
>   were in college.

Uncertainty, however, marked the lives of most of the young men I interviewed. "Everybody got an expiration date," Jared, a twelfth grader, told me. "That's why you live every day like it's your last." Death and violence were never far from the minds of many of the young men I met. Throughout the school—carved on bathroom stalls, desks, and elsewhere—were living memorials for lost friends and loved ones. Jared and Leon wrote "R.I.P. Sneaky" on all of their paper assignments, to honor a mutual neighborhood friend who had been murdered the previous year. Through tattoos, the boys' own bodies revealed small memorials and permanent reminders of both the reality of violence and the kinds of men they wished to become.

Keith, a twelfth grader, had been placed in the Second Chance program for missing too many school days the previous year. He was soft-spoken and unusually introspective. He called his time in high school a "roller coaster ride." There were "ups and downs, lots of thrills," he said. "But eventually you gotta get off." He pointed out the window and told me that, when he was young, he used to live just a short walk from the school, before the school had become all-boys. School had let out a half hour earlier and some young women had walked down from Thompson High and were milling about with Perry students. Keith watched this scene and said he was grateful he had grown up with "lots of females"—in a family with his mom and four sisters, two older and two younger—because he had learned to be respectful of women. His two older sisters had started off at the local community college before moving on to the same state university. Keith was grateful he had a road map to follow, and for the first time he saw college as a real possibility. He above all wanted to make it there for his father. "My dad never went to college," he said. "So I feel like if he was still here he'd be real proud, like he saw that I had become a real man." Keith's father was murdered when Keith was ten. He rolled up his sleeve to reveal a tattoo and traced a finger across the ink: "Lost a dad, gained an angel."

Tattoos were a masculine currency both tragic and uplifting: a reminder of violence and death, yet a motivating force to be better men. Some tattoos were completed hastily and others elaborately conceived. Nearly all featured the phrase "R.I.P.," the nickname of the person whose life was being commemorated, and the date of death. They contained phrases such as "Got killed on these streets" and "In Loving Memory." Some featured Bible verses.

Even more common were T-shirts made to honor fallen brothers. At lunch one day, a group of students were talking about their plans for the weekend. They told me that a classmate was attending a funeral on Saturday for a friend who had just died. When Asad heard the date of the young man's death, he pulled up his blue polo uniform shirt to reveal a white t-shirt with a screen-printed image of a friend, Raheem, who had died almost exactly a year earlier. There were wings to show that his friend had ascended to heaven. Below the image was the word "sunrise" and his friend's birthdate, and the word "sunset" and the day Raheem died. Like Keith, Asad was a member of Second Chance. "I'm tryin' to make it outta here," meaning graduating from high school. "I'm doing it for the chance that Raheem never got." Tattoos formed intimate bonds with loved ones and they nearly always commemorated other men. While a few tattoos honored mothers and grandmothers, none featured girls or girlfriends. "You might not be with girls forever," Jared told me. "Honoring family and dead friends is forever."

Unlike their peers at Northside Academy, fewer young men at Perry High saw college as a possibility for after graduation. As I explain later in the chapter, Northside students projected futures as college students and as workers. My conversations with Perry High students, however, revealed stronger desires for what Alford Young Jr. calls the "good life": a peaceful, married life with children and modest material comfort.[7] These aspirations were basic goals and not grandiose ideals. Being a man meant being able to financially support yourself and your family. It was about "making good" in one's life.[8] "I want to have a family," Brandon told me. "I want to have like two kids and a nice house. I don't want to look like I'm rich, but I want to live how I want to live." Even younger boys had similar aspirations. When I asked eighth grader Gerald what it means to be a man, he responded, "To have a job and to be able to do important stuff like taking care of a family. Maybe one or two cars." The boys located "self-worth in their ability to discipline themselves and conduct responsible yet caring lives to ensure order for themselves and others."[9]

Tre had been dating a young woman for a little while, and the two of them had recently spoken about the possibility of having children together. But he had concluded that "I can't take in nobody's child." I asked, "Do you eventually want children?"

> Yeah, I do want my own children eventually, but no time soon. I probably have my first child when I hit like 25, 26 if my plans go right. I can't predict the future though, but hopefully it happen around that time. I'd be settled in, I got my money right, a crib [home], everything be settled because I can't bring my child in here and I can't clothe him. I ain't going to do that.

As Tre saw it, it was irresponsible to bring a child into the world without the means to support that child. Here, Tre wanted to be the man he felt his father had failed to be. He drew on the hegemonic ideal of men as providers, an ideal that has fallen further outside the grasp of men in periods of economic decline and one that has historically been denied to Black men.[10] Tre's dad had left him and his mom when he was in elementary school. The pain was still there in Tre's voice. "I can't never forgive him for walking out like that," he said. "But he taught me a lesson. I know I can't ever walk out on my own family."

Being Unknown

"There's a slogan around my neighborhood," Brandon, a twelfth grader, said. "You get it how you live." For Brandon, whose family struggled to support him financially, this meant hustling drugs in order to take care of himself. After several years as a "dope boy," he was caught with drugs in school and was assigned to a youth detention center. Back in Morgan, there were promising signs. He had developed good relationships with his reintegration officer and a teacher who was helping him develop his interest in audio engineering. For Brandon, who had never been away from Morgan, returning to his community began "a struggle for social belonging that is deeply patterned by human frailty."[11] The lure to return to hustling was strong, he said, in part because he knew he could earn back the respect he once had. But when I asked him about his future, he envisioned "aging out" of crime.[12] "Maybe with each passing day," he said, "the streets will be behind me."

"I thought," Brandon continued, "I was another nobody who leaves Morgan for prison." He had tried, in his own words, to "lay low" and "just follow orders" in the hopes that would expedite his release from the detention center. What he did not expect was to feel as much as he did his visibility as a young Black man. He was told that the majority of the young men there were Black and from Morgan. He quickly came to view the facility's population in those terms: the Black kids from Morgan, the white kids from other counties. "A lot of the staff there were cool," Brandon noted, but the treatment was still racially discriminatory:

> If a kid from Morgan do something, the kid from Morgan will get punished more than a different kid [from a different county]. And because there'll be so much Morgan kids up there, the staff don't really have a sense of guilt. It's like, "It's a Black kid. That's just how they are." I went up there thinking I was a nobody, but all they do is call us out for being Black!

As Brandon implied, the staff did not feel a "sense of guilt" for punishing Black boys more than their peers because they perceived that Morgan boys deserved it ("That's just how they are"). For Brandon, his time at the detention center threw into sharp relief a paradox: the simultaneous visibility and invisibility of Black masculinity. On the one hand, Black men and boys are closely watched and seen in their neighborhoods, and on the other, they are depicted as "missing" or "invisible" in the public eye. Brandon was caught in a seemingly irreconcilable position. He felt that going into prison he would be anonymous, but he found that more than ever his Blackness made him more visible.

A burglary conviction kept Tre away from Perry High for some time. Tre described being deeply invested in street life when he was younger, and he knew it would always be an important part of him. But he saw his future goals in a straightforward way: "Got to get my own job. Got to be able to provide for myself and my people. Got to get my own crib, pay my own bills." Tre's yearnings became clearer following Mr. Bradley's visit to the Second Chance program one day. The young men had just hung up a banner with the program's new motto: "Success Is the New Revenge." Mr. Bradley singled out Tre as one of "our leaders" and asked him what the motto meant to him. "People doubted us," Tre started. "Our success will prove them wrong." Mr. Bradley was ecstatic with the response and he asked Tre to share that message at an assembly. Just as the race men in his administration sought to be mentors for their students, Mr. Bradley hoped that older boys would help to look out for their younger peers. The principal felt this would raise the self-esteem of the Second Chance students and also support the administration's mission of cultivating stronger solidarity and male relationships in the school. In our interview later, I asked Tre what he thought of Mr. Bradley's proposal:

> TRE: They ask me to be a mentor, a leader, for [the younger students] . . . and that's fine, I get it. But for real, for real: I also don't want to be a leader for nobody. It just gives people more of a chance to slice me up, see me as bad. I don't trust that most people won't judge me as being bad.
>
> FREEDEN: If you don't want to be a leader, then what do you want to be?
>
> TRE: I don't think it's even possible. I want to disappear . . . but not be ignored. You feel me? Do right by my people, but not make it like some big celebration. Just be like everyone else, go about my business.

Tre expressed frustration: in one way, he understood why he was being held up as a role model and even embraced to some degree the chance to be "a mentor, a leader." Yet he also wished not to be highly visible in any respect. Crucially, Tre did not want to "be ignored," or invisible in a negative sense before others. Like Brandon, Tre invoked a paradox of being visible and invisible, and he struggled to find a measure of self-worth within it.

What Tre desired is what I call *to be unknown:* the privilege of anonymity in a wider community. Young men like Tre attempt to reconcile their paradox of visibility—they are constantly monitored and labeled as the subject of a crisis—and invisibility by carving out a space in the middle, a privilege they believed others possessed. Tre still wished to be someone (to take care of his family and to do right by others) and to be able to come and go outside the gaze of others. His was a yearning for a modest form of recognition. This contrasts with the dominant way researchers have described young Black men's pursuit of status: *to be known,* an aggressive form of masculine respect.[13]

My observations suggest that the assertions to be unknown were strongest among boys who had formal contact with the criminal justice system—a population similar to the "delinquent" boys in Victor Rios's study[14]—and who were older and were therefore thinking more carefully about their futures. The young men who as a group fit these criteria best were those in the Second Chance program. Asad had a stronger academic record than Brandon and Tre, but a drug conviction kept him back in school. When he returned to Perry, he was placed in Second Chance. He was progressing well in the program, and his teachers encouraged him to attend a college fair. There, he spoke excitedly about getting back on his feet. He envisioned starting out at community college and taking up a part-time job painting homes.

As a member of two communities—Second Chance and Perry High—that aimed to help Black boys, Asad had much to say about how he and others viewed his racial identity. Like his peers, Asad shared aspirations for the good life: "a nice home somewhere, a job to go to each morning, one that pays for all the things I got back at home." Yet he desired more. By way of introducing this, he described ongoing conversations he had with a teacher, Carrie Swanson. Asad and Ms. Swanson used the plot behind the movie *The Sixth Sense* to discuss racial privilege. (In the film, the protagonist, Malcolm Crowe, played by Bruce Willis, is unaware that he has died and is a ghost.) Asad observed:

> [Crowe] don't know nobody can see him. But he thinks he's being seen, right? At the end, it's like, "Shit, I been wrong this whole time!" Trick ending, right? What a shock, right? But what he don't realize is that, not having people look your way, that's an advantage. Shit, that's some power right there! Being Black mean I don't have that. If you're a Black man: the police . . . people see you and think you've done something

wrong. If they don't see you, they still think you've done something wrong. You lose both ways. What I want is for nobody to single me out and trust I'm not doing nothing wrong.

Asad understood his own identity as both visible and invisible before others. On the one hand, he was seen as a criminal. On the other, he was forgotten and lumped with "missing" and "invisible" Black men. Asad expressed a desire to be free of a paradox that deprived him of the presumption of innocence in two respects ("you lose both ways"). "Being unknown" is not a matter of status or standing apart from the crowd. While social invisibility normally implies disadvantage, it can also be a racial privilege. The heightened visibility and pervasive invisibility of criminalized young Black men, in fact, implied how young white men benefit from a "hyper level of invisibility."[15]

Becoming Fathers

As Marlon Ross observes, Black male subjectivity is defined by paradoxes.[16] Black men have historically been characterized as failed fathers but supermen in sports; they are disproportionately represented in the media but conspicuously absent on college campuses; mainstream institutions pit the respectable among them against their deviant peers. While some young Black men express a desire to be unknown, they are also always seeking positive forms of recognition: to be viewed as whole, honorable, and worthy. For some young men, fatherhood provided a path to dignity. But having kids was the last thing teachers wanted their young men to be thinking about. As Mr. Riles, an English teacher, said,

> Last year when I taught seniors, some of my seniors broke my heart because they were having children. Why are you having a baby? And then you go to more of a conversation about what it is to be a man and what it is to be a father. To know that this person that you're bringing into the world is really going to depend on you. What's your plan? "Well, Mr. Riles, we're . . ." If they don't have any answers, I'm like, "So you're not prepared to take care of a child or a small baby. *You're* still a baby."

Other male teachers strongly condemned teenage fatherhood. One time Mr. Youseff chided the boys for not being responsible students, then followed up with, "You talk shit, have babies, and you can't support them. For real, man to man. If you bust a nut, have a baby come out, and can pay child support without having the court tell you to, *then* you a man."[17]

Ms. Okoye, the director of Second Chance, recalled a conversation she had with Robert, a twelfth grader and the father of a two-year-old girl:

He said he had a child and he was being challenged about this because you have to be responsible for this child, and he was having some hardships and sleepless nights and all that, and I said, "Why in God's name did you get this baby?" and he said, "Ms. Okoye, by now don't you know?" And I said, "No, what?" He said, "Many of my friends have died. Many of us do not live until age twenty-five. By twenty-five many of us are dead, so I'm trying to leave a legacy here. I need to leave my children [behind]."

Elijah Anderson argues that inner-city teenagers may wantonly engage in sexual relations because they "see no future that can be derailed" and therefore "see little to lose by having a child out of wedlock."[18] Robert's thinking was similarly based on the notion that he could not see much of a future for himself. Yet he chose to have a child not so much because he has "little to lose," as Anderson writes, but because he has something to gain: "a legacy." Robert was desperate to maintain a presence in the world, through his child. In *Doing the Best I Can,* Kathryn Edin and Timothy Nelson vividly describe the complex and frequently tragic circumstances surrounding poor men who sought to be fathers. These men saw in children a hopeful beam of light that could cut through the negativity in their lives. A child represented a chance for these men to connect deeply with an "unsullied" version of themselves.[19]

Jared was another twelfth grader and a member of the Second Chance program. He had a young daughter, Kamila, who was ten months old at the time of our interview. He was on rocky terms with LaTonya, the child's mother, who was now out of school, living with her grandparents, and raising the child. Jared struggled to articulate his feelings about being a dad. He had no money to give but did not want to be seen anyway as an absent father who gives money and nothing else.[20] But he was afraid to ask for more time to see Kamila given that he had no money for LaTonya. "I can't win," he said. But he held out hope, even when the rest of his life offered few bright possibilities:

Kamila, that's my angel right there. That little girl is my sunshine. I want to take her to the park around my way when she gets older. I told Ms. Okoye about Kamila, and she said she'd help me find some kids' books I can read to her.

"The new package deal" is a hazardous situation where men "assign a high value to their relationships with their children but are hesitant to invest too much in the relationship with their children's mother."[21] While Jared and other young dads are unable to provide the "hard" instrumental side of fathering (providing money), "they have radically redefined fatherhood to sharply elevate the softer side of fathering: offering love, preserving an open line of communication, and spending quality time."[22]

Despite the strong feelings of pain evoked in having to talk about their fathers in interviews, or dismissing their fathers outright, the boys themselves did not reject the possibility of fatherhood. As the "man of the family"—growing up in a household with five women—Keith already felt like a father of sorts, as he often had to look out for his baby sisters. He expressed great joy for the chance to one day have his own child. Like the men in *Doing the Best I Can,* Keith saw in a child a way to have a profound connection with another human being; someone who was "pure," he said. But he made it clear that he only wanted a daughter. Despite missing out on a chance to have a relationship with his own dad, who had died when he was young, Keith saw too many strained relationships between young men and their fathers. In a heart-wrenching way, Keith saw in a daughter not only someone who was completely unlike the violence and negativity he observed in Morgan but also someone whom he was tasked with protecting from that violence and negativity at all costs. "If you have a boy and you push too hard," Keith told me, "they could go the other way. But a girl you can take care of. *Girls need that protection.* I'm gonna have 'daddy's little girl.'" Offering protection to daughters gave Keith's life meaning and affirmed his own sense of manhood. Compared to other young men I spoke with, Keith was less trustful of women as romantic partners, and he spoke little about settling down and getting married. Keith's desires reflect "the new package deal."

Perhaps because he was more focused on college and work, Asad spent less time in our interview talking about being a father. Yet he, too, described how having girls was preferable to having boys. This came as a bit of a surprise to me, given that Asad had such good rapport with the younger boys. I noticed that many of these students went out of their way to greet Asad and appeared to be seeking his approval. But like Keith, Asad believed that girls needed more protection from their fathers. "A boy has to learn to take care of himself," Asad told me. "But a girl you can be that shield for." "Why does a girl need a shield?" I asked. "Girls have that innocence and that purity. Men can shield them from that danger. Boys get eaten up by the streets."

Keith and Asad embraced a hegemonic ideal of the protector. Distinct from an expression of masculinity as aggressively dominative, here a "good man" keeps "vigilant watch over the safety of his family."[23] In addition to its paternalism, Asad and Keith revealed another gendered layer to this discourse: fathers were especially needed for—were even responsible for—protecting their daughters, who could not look out for themselves the way boys could. While Asad and Keith asserted a measure of dignity by describing themselves as responsible fathers, a "promise of protection" in Black communities has historically been linked to a politics of respectability.[24] In a racist and patriarchal society, Black activists and intellectuals developed this discourse as a way to offer emotional and physical safety to Black women and girls. But this discourse has often replicated patriarchal norms on the path to racial emancipation, as men are asked to assume their rightful place as the protector of subordinate and dependent others. Moreover, as Farah Jasmine Griffin writes, Black men have equated protection with possession, and in doing so have "place[d] limitations on women's freedoms."[25] In fact, researchers have found that the reality of inner-city violence means that girls as well as boys learn from a young age that they must learn to protect themselves. In her ethnographic study of Philadelphia, Nikki Jones found that the same "code of the street" that regulated interpersonal violence for poor Black boys applied to their female peers as well.[26] Even as a "cult of womanhood" demanded that girls adhere to a middle-class respectability, they were still prepared to use violence to defend themselves and their friends. This reality contradicted Keith and Asad's depictions of girls as passive individuals in need (and deserving) of male protection.

Heroic Family Men

A critical phase in the caregiving process is responsiveness.[27] Care recipients assess the quality of the care and respond in some way. In the last chapter, I described how Mr. Jeffries wanted the mentors to step inside the shoes of the mentees. For him, a role model is not simply someone to be imitated. Yet it is, in one respect. Care recipients respond by emulating the care they received. Put another way, they affirm that care by feeling an obligation to be a care provider themselves. The cycle of care then begins anew. Mr. Westbrook saw this as a long-term goal of the mentoring program:

> I imagine a year or two from now. What kinds of people will [the young men] be? Meeting once a week isn't always sustainable. What kinds of people will our young men be after their mentors are no longer there? If they are better men and have learned to improve their own lives, then we can hang our hat on that. But we have to aim for more. Our community is depending on it. How can we teach our young men to improve the lives of others? Other boys who don't have the luxury of a mentor? I believe that's our utmost task.

While there were examples of camaraderie (e.g., the mentoring program and the GSA), the Perry High students did not form a tight-knit brotherhood like their counterparts at Northside. There was, of course, the legacy of turf wars that harmed the building of school solidarity. And the race men of Perry made little effort to bring their students together. (The Northside community, of course, bonded over the shared struggle to protect the school's status and resources.) What the school did promote was a vision that their students could be valiant care providers themselves one day—for their wives, their children, and fictive kin—or what I term *heroic family men*. For young men at a school with a stigmatized reputation that it was never fully able to shake, being good role models would bring the young men a measure of respectability. Black feminist scholars, however, have been critical of how all-boys schools and similar interventions place a strong emphasis on grooming boys to be good husbands and fathers.[28] The supporters of the Detroit plan believed that all-male schools would specifically help boys grow up to be better "providers" and give young Black women "some positive African American males to choose from when they get married."[29]

Perry High officials reconciled this by suggesting that their own communities would need the boys one day. This differed widely from Northside Academy, which tracked their young men *out* of the community. Promoting heroic family men was on display at the Education over Incarceration event. Kevin Oakley, a local congressman, told the students:

> But the females are looking for a man, right? The females are looking
> for a man. They say now it's harder and harder to find a man. They say
> a lot of the guys, rather, are in jail, they're not about nothing, or they're
> dead. We're going to stop that. We're going to see if we can help them
> find some men. Because I see a lot of men *(points to the boys in the
> audience)* inside of here.

Staff members applauded. Mr. Oakley's comments were deeply heteronormative and conservative: he implied that the boys could grow up to be respectable men who would care for their women and assume their rightful place at the head of the family. They could be providers and protectors. Mr. Oakley had rehashed a principle of uplift ideology: that Blacks can prove their worth by building patriarchal families. Mr. Bradley then added:

> Our women are counting on you all! We need you to one day be
> mature family men, to help raise our boys and support our mothers. I
> can picture these men *(points to the boys in the audience)* leading our
> community. It's *the men you will become.* But we need you to get your
> education and to get a job.

According to Mr. Oakley and Mr. Bradley, it was the responsibility of the Black boys to grow up to be heroic family men, providers for women and providers for the local community. And getting "your education" and "a job" seemed to fit awkwardly in Mr. Bradley's comments. It seemed overwhelming for the students (who included the school's youngest seventh graders) to be told to get their education (or to go to college), work, and then commit their lives to caring for dependents. There was also the strong message that the boys should become responsible fathers who were an active presence in their own sons' lives, or at least care for other young Black men in crisis. (No women attended the event outside of the radio station representative who was the emcee for the event.) In doing so, as fathers, those men could save their own sons from the streets and incarceration. Or to borrow a phrase that Mr. Bradley's brother used at the father-son breakfast (which we heard at the start of chapter 4), the school tasked its young men with being the community's future "homeland defenders."

Northside Academy

Ambitious Entrepreneurs

Ms. Holden had long admired Howard Zinn's book *A People's History of the United States,* which famously reinterprets the country's past through the eyes of the historically disenfranchised. She was therefore delighted to assign the teenager's version of the book for class. The book was a huge hit among the students. During a lesson on the civil rights movement, Ms. Holden and her tenth graders discussed voting rights and the importance of political participation. Ms. Holden asked her students not to forget that one of the earliest and most passionate defenses of a flourishing democracy was Alexis de Tocqueville's celebrated 1835 tome, *Democracy in America.* She hoped her students would one day read and be inspired by the book. In it, Tocqueville traced the country's democratic roots back to its (white) Puritan origins. I found this particularly interesting since, as I explained in chapter 2, Mr. Pierce, the school CEO, had also drawn inspiration from Puritanism. He had traced his school's Latin origins to a TV segment he had watched on Cotton Mather, the Puritan leader and early graduate of a school founded by Puritans, the Boston Latin School. While Ms. Holden had wanted her class to discuss Black mobilization in the civil rights era, whiteness remained an unmarked category in the lesson. In any event, few students seemed to be familiar with *Democracy in America.* In the text, Tocqueville also observed how an entrepreneurial spirit suffuses the American national character. Americans, he wrote, were a restless and industrious lot who had their eye on material gain.[30]

As Michael Kimmel notes, the entrepreneurial spirit that captivated Tocqueville has a uniquely gendered history in the United States. This spirit captured the heart—or, better yet, the character—of the Self-Made Man, the defining archetype of American masculinity. By the turn of the nineteenth century, the Self-Made Man was beginning to replace two holdovers from European rule: the Genteel Patriarch, the aristocrat and landowner with his refined manners; and the Heroic Artisan, the hard-working, modest, independent craftsman. According to Kimmel, while the Self-Made Man was not unique to the United States, this version of manhood was well suited to the country's cultural and political history.[31] The Self-Made Man is "on the go . . . competitive, aggressive in business," and "temperamentally restless, chronically insecure, and desperate to achieve a solid grounding for a masculine identity."[32] Interestingly, as Du Bois promoted his aristocratic vision of the Talented Tenth in the early part of the twentieth century, it was a militant strand of Black Nationalism that most nurtured the entrepreneurial spirit. The ideology of the Self-Made Man permeated Marcus Garvey's Universal Negro Improvement Association (UNIA), founded in 1914. A Garveyite vision of racial uplift rested on "strong character, an enterprising mentality, and an independent will," and an eagerness to exploit economic modernization.[33]

The entrenchment of neoliberalism today has had a structural effect on the formation of masculinities around the globe, and in particular has breathed new life into the ideology of the Self-Made Man. The "concentrated profits of development," Raewyn Connell writes, have "created conditions for the growth of entrepreneurial masculinities."[34] Today's entrepreneurs are business elites. And what separates them from earlier entrepreneurial masculinities is their keen interest in exploiting new technologies and "being closely integrated with corporate intranets and high-technology communications."[35] In a globalized world, expertise in advanced technologies is seen as vital for profit-making and power. This is a masculine enterprise because technology becomes the new, constantly evolving "frontier" waiting to be exploited, one that requires actors who are bold and willing to take risks.[36]

While Perry High School nurtured a vision of heroic family men, Northside Academy had a starkly different aim. The school was grooming their scholars and future college-goers to be what I call *ambitious entrepreneurs*: fiercely independent working men and leaders in a globalized economy. It is important to distinguish between two meanings of "entrepreneur." The first reflects my use of neoliberal governmentality throughout this book. Neoliberalism demands that modern subjects always be works in progress: never satisfied, continually experimenting, and therefore always reforming themselves. In the words of Paul Du Gay, this neoliberal governmentality produces subjects that are "entrepreneurs of the self."[37] These Northside

Academy scholars learned to be resilient precisely because they were entering a competitive economy. The second meaning of "entrepreneur" is consistent with Connell's formulation: corporate elites with fluency in advanced and profitable technologies. While Ms. Holden extolled that day in class the virtues of democratic participation, her lesson mostly took a back seat to the school's larger message that financial success was there for the taking.

Becoming Leaders in a Globalized Economy

The entrepreneurial spirit was right there in the school's motto: "A man builds his own worth." The phrase stuck with the young men. When I asked students what it meant to be a "Top Gladiator" (the name of the weekly award the school gave out), over 80 percent of the students mentioned the motto. This simple phrase communicated powerful messages. "Worth" can mean self-worth and a sense of honor. It can also mean riches. And in both cases, each student would not inherit or be given that worth but would have to build it himself.

While many of the young men at Perry aspired to the good life, their Northside counterparts were able to articulate more ambitious, yet concrete plans (especially, though not surprisingly, the eleventh graders). In chapter 3 I described how the race to college provided the young men with a certain volition, a pace and sense of movement with respect to the future. It was a test of endurance. There was a second dimension to their "imagined futures," as Ann Mische has called it: clarity.[38] The highly structured nature of the school day and curriculum helped the boys see the concrete steps they would have to take to reach college. Northside students answered my prompt, "Tell me about the future you see for yourself," with checkpoints and milestones. Take the SAT. Apply to college. Enroll in college. Graduate from college, ideally in four years.[39] Get a good job.

There was stiff competition for getting to college. And teachers told the young men that the competition would only become stiffer once the young men entered the workforce. The competition came from all corners of the globe. As the community began to emerge that year from the Great Recession, which had crippled Black wealth, staff members shared that U.S. schoolchildren were losing ground to their peers around the world.[40] The students viewed themselves as being in a race to college in an era of globalization. In his science class one day, Mr. Tomlinson asked the boys to focus because "science is the great equalizer." By this he meant the way his own Black male students could compete with their peers around the world. They were watching a film about the scientific revolution, which conspicuously featured only white men: Copernicus, Galileo, Newton, Planck,

Bohrs, and Einstein. He asked his students to "get your mind right" (a favorite line of his):

> These men changed the world using science. Follow their lead. They took risks and made lots of mistakes but made big discoveries and solved big problems. And today there are high school students all around the world who are solving problems and becoming the next great scientists. Don't get left behind.[41]

Mr. Tomlinson characterized these scientists as entrepreneurs at their core: they took risks and were at the cutting edge of their fields. More than that, these entrepreneurial leaders embodied a respectable form of Black manhood set apart from hip-hop culture, which many adults in the school derided. Ambitious entrepreneurs embraced what Martin Summers identified as the "producer values" that were important to upwardly mobile Black masons and small business owners in the early part of the twentieth century.[42] These producer values—including sobriety, thrift, and strict discipline—rejected the lavish and increasingly pervasive consumer values associated with deviant jazz culture and rebellious youth cultures. Alongside the message that his young men should be industrious risk-takers and leaders was Mr. Tomlinson's observation that hip-hop "seduced" young Black men into desiring all the wrong things: "bling, all this awful commercialism." Implicit in Mr. Tomlinson's statement was a rejection of "the racialized stereotype of African Americans' overconsumption and inability to delay gratification" in favor of a rational, hardworking manhood.[43]

Mr. Davidson, the math teacher we met earlier in the book, was fond of telling his students that real money could be earned in technical and science fields. Like Mr. Tomlinson, he supported a vision of ideal manhood distinct from "bling culture" and "the easy money from selling drugs on the streets. Or how rap culture sells these kids a life of cars and women." Mr. Davidson also asked his students to envision a future far beyond the city of Morgan:

> We live in a globalized world. What this means for our students is that they need skills that will assist them for jobs here and around the world. I think it's good we're sending kids to different parts of the world, to places like Rome. They have to see that the world's at their doorstep. They also have to understand they can expect competition when they pass through that door. We have teachers here who went to good colleges. Ask them and I bet they'll tell you that some of the best students are foreign students, international students. They're smart, they work hard.

Mr. Davidson drew on an old narrative—that American students were being outpaced by their peers abroad, spelled out in *A Nation at Risk* (1983)—that helped to lay the groundwork for the neoliberalization of public schooling.[44] Moreover, he hinted that his own students could get "left behind," to borrow Mr. Tomlinson's phrase, in a globalized world. Indeed, other seemingly progressive initiatives aimed at helping young men of color have drawn on this narrative. They include the Obama administration's My Brother's Keeper initiative, which has introduced job-readiness, mentoring, and other programs targeted to young men of color. As Michael Dumas writes, this program views a Black male crisis as a "state of affairs requiring paternalistic intervention to eradicate deficiencies of character and provide psychological uplift for those willing to overcome the damage inflicted on them largely as a result of their failure to adapt to shifts in the global economy, and who have, it is asserted, chosen an anachronistic cultural identification with blackness over racial and national identities more consistent with social cohesion and economic mobility."[45]

While Afrocentric curricula were the defining feature of the first-wave academies, they also aimed to be "futuristic": to prepare young Black men for "21st century careers" in "high demand" sectors of technology.[46] Northside wanted to do the same. They therefore combined the old (Latin) with the new (advanced technologies). The emphasis on technology conveyed that the school was forward-thinking. Tenth graders were given used laptops, and teachers and students were encouraged to use them in lessons. (The laptops were much sought after by the students, and their widespread use gave the school an added college feel.) Northside students took a computer technology class and learned how to use various software programs. Students gave PowerPoint presentations in their classes. These scenes were rare at Perry High. Northside Academy aimed to integrate technology as seamlessly as possible throughout the building and to eventually make technology a second native language for the school. Peter James was an English teacher who was tapped to lead the effort to fully integrate technology into the school:

> I'll be helping to incorporate more technology into the classroom; not only just technology, but more twenty-first-century skills, as far as collaboration goes in different kinds of online media, being able to filter through the internet and understand how it actually works, and be able to search and discern between good information and bad information.

The science department partnered with a not-for-profit STEM program to start a robotics club that later participated in competitions. The administration seemed particularly excited about this group's future. It not only got young men excited about engineering and the STEM fields, but emerged as an "applied science," which the school seemed to idolize. Ultimately, Latin held a contradictory place in the school. It had an instrumental function (to help improve test scores) and a symbolic purpose (to give the school prestige). Latin defined the school from its inception, but my sense was that in the face of an increasingly globalized world, the engineering sciences were the language of the future. The school would adapt with the times, just as any good entrepreneur does.

Entrepreneurs seek to break new ground, make new discoveries, and be on the cutting edge of their industries. They could be scientists, or they could be corporate leaders. But they were, above all, leaders. Michelle Rollins had two sons, Rakeem and Jayce, at the school, and so she was quite involved and invested in Northside. She left little doubt that the school was training the country's next generation of great leaders:

> I think [the school is] really, really preparing the future leaders. Because with Rakeem's friends, and Jayce's friends, I always get to know their names and stuff, and they're like, "Why attend Northside?" I was like because whenever they're in *Time* magazine, I want to go, "Oh, I knew that kid," because I really do think that they're going to be the future leaders.

Just as important, the young men of Northside had to lean on their brothers *now* and train to become diligent workers because once they graduated and left Morgan (and presumably entered the global workplace), they could only rely on themselves for help. Ms. Rollins continued:

> The world out there is cruel. It really is. Rakeem and Jayce have a good thing here at Northside, but college and the real world might not be so kind. So they're learning to assert themselves now and to do the right thing, to learn that hard work that will carry them wherever they end up.

Indeed, in response to the question "What does it mean to you to be a Top Gladiator?" over half of the young men mentioned leadership. It was crucial for a Gladiator to stand apart from the crowd, to assume extra responsibility, to make important decisions, to help others to help themselves. Just like Ms. Rollins, they connected leadership and hard work. Thomas, an eleventh grader, told me that being a Top Gladiator "is like being the ultimate man." The ideal man rejected what Thomas called a "hardcore" style (which resembled a street masculinity) in favor of a leader who went against the grain:

What does it mean to be a Top Gladiator? Don't follow others. Be a leader. And if someone's doing something in school and it's like really messing with their grades, help them out. Tell them what they need to change themselves.

His classmate Justin added, "A leader gives 110 percent. He shows others the right away. A leader shows others how to work hard." He reflected later on where he might end up after college. "I feel like Northside is helping me get wherever I wanna go." He mentioned being an owner of an NBA team but seemed most enthusiastic about being an engineer. Justin returned to what it meant to be a Top Gladiator. "I feel like, me and my brothers," meaning his Northside classmates, "we'll be Top Gladiators *for life*. After graduation I'll go my own way. But I know me and my brothers, we'll be successful wherever we go." Some of the young men of Perry High also had big aspirations, but they mostly steered toward a modest good life. And while they were being asked to take care of their own families and communities, the Northside Academy scholars turned their futures and their gaze to a larger stage beyond Morgan. They would be Top Gladiators for life, wherever they ended up.

Conclusion

This chapter has examined young Black men as *beings*, as agents in their own right, making sense of their social worlds and present lives as they forecast themselves as *becomings*, or people on future trajectories.[47] Both Perry High School and Northside Academy communicated visions for the kinds of men they wished their students to become. Having struggled throughout its tenure as a single-sex school, Perry High officials passed along a vision of Black men caring for vulnerable others as providers and protectors. Some of the young men embraced these ideals themselves and saw providing for their families and protecting vulnerable daughters as paths to securing masculine dignity. Linked to a promising male mentoring program, the discourse of heroic family men had an emotional appeal, however far-fetched. Lifting up others demanded much from the school's already vulnerable young men. Yet it was still consistent with a neoliberal ideology. Framed differently, the students were being asked to be their community's strongest and most resilient young men, as the community could only rely on its most exceptional men to save it.

While as an institution Northside Academy largely emulated elite schools, in the school's third year of existence school leaders envisioned their young people graduating and becoming entrepreneurs and leaders of industry. Northside officials sought to cultivate "good neoliberal citizens" who were industrious and hardworking young people and who possessed the skills to survive and thrive in a post–high school world that would not offer the protection of the Northside brotherhood. School officials wanted their young men to dream big, and they laid out a clear path to college. Yet situating the boys in a competitive and globalized world further displaced young men from their own local community. This heightened the challenges the boys experienced in navigating the street and their school, their home community and their male academy, their past and their future. But they could not lose sight of a rare promise for young Black men in the city of Morgan: to be a Top Gladiator for life.

Hoping and Hustling Together

The fate of these two schools will not come as a surprise.

Despite committed school officials and some promising initiatives, turmoil was never far from Perry High. Rates of student punishment had declined, but the school's academic performance never rose appreciably. The school had also become less of a priority for the school district, which was mired in other conflicts. The district had doubled down on its commitment to privatize education. Confronted with a ballooning deficit, it shuttered several of the city's largest schools. Smaller (and more cost-effective) charter schools replaced them. The city's teachers' union and the City School Board sparred frequently. After the school district restructuring, the union's leadership had won a number of important protections for its rank and file (including a majority of the teaching staff at Perry High), but these protections were threatened by the school district's larger cost-cutting efforts. A decade after first experimenting with a split academy model, the school district closed Perry High's doors for good.

Over in North Morgan, by the time the school had graduated its first class in 2011, the "buzz" around Northside had reached a near fever pitch. College acceptance letters poured in for its seniors, a local paper lauded the school as having some of the best extracurricular programs in the city, and the school secured a second contract with the city as other charters came and went. Even as the country was beginning to confront the disastrous effects of the financial crisis of the late 2000s, Northside continued to press forward with its fund-raising efforts. A large endowment added to the allure of a school that had become a truly singular option in the city. The school moved ahead with plans to open a lower school for younger students. Some staff members likened the expansion to a company growing to meet client demand without sacrificing performance. The idea of "scaling up" the school, as it was described, was met with excitement. Tristan Davis, the school's computer and technology instructor, felt the expansion only reinforced Mr. Pierce's "aggressive growth plans."

This final chapter sheds light on hope, peril, and possibilities for caring in all-male public education. I consider the implications of my findings for teaching Black boys apart from their peers, examine the consequences for the synergy between neoliberalism and respectability politics, consider what is likely to come for Black male academies in the post-Obama era, and finally turn to Du Bois's vision of abolition democracy to carve a path forward.

Rethinking Black Masculinity, Racial Uplift, and Respectability

Jeremiah had promised to be my "assistant" during my year of research. He was a wonderful guide.[1] We caught up one final time at the end of my research, during the first week of Northside Academy's summer session for the incoming ninth graders. It had been an up-and-down year for Jeremiah. He and Terrell were not talking much anymore, for reasons he was not interested in sharing. "Mostly dumb stuff," he offered, though it clearly weighed on him. Changing topics, I asked him what the highlight of his year was. He answered, without a second's thought, being recognized as a "Top Gladiator."

Jeremiah asked me if I had seen the shirts the new students were wearing. I had. The polos featured the Northside logo with the words "Class of 2014" beneath it. "I'm no longer one of the youngest boys here," Jeremiah beamed. "I'm Class of 2013. I'm a seasoned vet!"[2]

I asked the seasoned vet how he was feeling now with his first year behind him. Latin still gave him fits, but he trusted Ms. Spring. He was tired and was glad to catch up on sleep. He had trips lined up to a local water park. But he was already looking forward to tenth grade and to being back in school. Despite sharing all the fun things he wanted to do, he still said, "I feel like I got too much time now. There's nothing to do."

His statement did not surprise me. What he meant was that Northside had given him a sense of purpose. Mr. Holmes may have ruled with an iron fist, and the hours may have been long, but the school's rigid schedule made him feel productive and that he was moving forward.[3] College was a reality. He was excited to get a laptop next year. He was a member of a Black brotherhood that was truly set apart. The school made him feel special. It made him feel protected. It had become family.

Jeremiah was not aware of this, but that year Perry High had started a new mentoring program for ninth graders like himself. As I explained in chapter 4, the program targeted this grade because of a troubling dropout rate between ninth and tenth grade. Perry's student population was highly transient, with many students coming and going throughout the year, but administrators there estimated that a full 20 percent of ninth graders who began the year at the school would not return to school, either to Perry or to another high school. The students at Northside traveled a different path. When Jeremiah's class graduated three years later, over 80 percent of his peers would enroll in college.

What explains this difference? Certainly institutional-level differences matter. Northside had a bevy of resources that Perry High lacked. Selection biases were also important. Northside attracted and recruited academically oriented young men. But my goal here has not been to compare these two schools by assessing their successes and failures and to offer one up as a model for school reform. Rather, this book's task has been to examine what teaching Black boys apart from their peers ("successful" or not) can tell us about ongoing, historical efforts to reform Black masculinity. Seen in relation to one another, we can best understand Northside's attempt to groom an exceptional class of young men and to protect them from their criminalized peers: precisely the stigma that befell the young men of Perry High School.

As of this writing, the California State Assembly is considering a bill that would approve single-gender instruction across the state's public schools. Sponsored by a Democrat, Sebastian Ridley-Thomas, the bill has strong bipartisan support.[4] In a strongly worded rebuttal, the leading feminist scholars Kimberlé Crenshaw, Diane Halpern, and Juliet Williams called the bill a "civil rights assault."[5] For these scholars, addressing deep-seated structural racism with a gender-based intervention would invite more inequalities: on the one hand, they argued, these schools would lean on flawed beliefs in biological sex differences to teach; on the other, the focus on boys of color would take away much-needed help for girls of color. The findings in *Black Boys Apart*, however, underscore how the pursuit of Black male advancement has promoted inequalities *within* the Black community and among Black boys themselves, as well as between Black boys and girls. The Northside community's performance of class exceptionality underscored that the upward mobility of its students rested on the physical, symbolic, and material exclusion of unsalvageable Black boys outside the school doors. The school embraced the hypercompetitive environment wrought by the Morgan school district's turn to the market, viewing the race to college as a test of endurance with threats at every turn.

These findings challenge the resilience perspective on Black male academies, which has become commonplace more generally in studies of

Black youth. This perspective holds that Black male academies are virtuous because they aim to build resilience—self-esteem, optimism, and
persistence—in their students. This perspective fails to identify what is distinctive about these academies. And as I have argued, while this research
has tried to clarify the assumptions behind these academies, it fails to in-
terrogate their very commonsense ideas: the need to protect students—from
the outside community, defined strictly in deficit terms—by helping them to
build resilience from within, to be individuals who can take on any challenge. Cultivating inner strength to help inoculate vulnerable schoolchildren from "the streets" makes for good policy across the political divide.
Yet the task, as Antonio Gramsci wrote, is to find the kernel of "good
sense" within the everyday consciousness of common sense.[6]

   Black Boys Apart has therefore attempted to bring history fully into
view, to demonstrate the circumstances under which today's male academies have emerged. Black male academies are less a "school reform"
effort and more a poignant example of the continual institutional efforts
to reform young Black men during periods of stark inequality. This book
situated today's Black male academies in a long history. All-male education
has been embraced as a strategy to defend and restore gender and racial
hierarchies. Academies such as Northside have found inspiration in the
old Dunbar High School, once the nation's finest Black high school. Yet
Dunbar thrived in the Jim Crow era by enrolling only the most academically gifted students and by promoting a respectability politics where upwardly mobile Blacks used cultural and moral distinctions to exclude their
more marginalized Black peers. This history also includes a community
control tradition in which Black communities in the post–civil rights era
have fought for control over their schools.

   My analysis has situated today's Black male academies in the "neoliberal turn in Black politics."[7] I began research in the city of Morgan at a
pivotal time for Northside Academy and Perry High School, when the trajectory of each was clear: in 2009, in the fallout of the Great Recession
and amid a global economic crisis that represents the peak of the neoliberal era. While Perry High and Northside took radically different courses,
they each aimed to groom more respectable Black boys. What explains this,
I have argued, is the entrenchment of a market fundamentalism that has
revitalized a politics of respectability that has long proved divisive for
Black communities. As Fredrick Harris has written, racial uplift theory first
promoted the need for Blacks to "lift as we climb."[8] However, today's respectability politics "commands Blacks left behind in post–civil rights
America to 'lift up thyself.' " Today, the transition of power to technocratic

elites and the Black professional class in public schools "only promises to exacerbate differences between the worldviews and interests of Black elites and the Black poor people they serve or, in neoliberal terms, *manage*" amid "the growing intraracial economic divide."[9]

Therefore, at this neoliberal turn in Black politics, neoliberalism and a politics of respectability have conjoined in what Max Weber famously described as an "elective affinity," or a strong magnetic attraction between ideas and interests.[10] Behind the veneer of freedom of choice and an unbiased market, neoliberalism encourages a zero-sum game of schooling where a privileged minority are empowered through the symbolic exclusion of others. Growing up in an era of a neoliberal respectability politics, each of the young men at Northside knew he had to work hard. Yet he had his brothers, his fellow Gladiators, to lean on. This was a very particular form of individualism: the school was cast as a singularly safe harbor in a community viewed in overwhelmingly bleak terms, to protect a special class of young Black men who would go on to college and become ambitious entrepreneurs. Thus, Northside Academy was its own "entrepreneur of the self," tasked with caring for, managing, and reforming its own young people, while doing little to contest or question the political and economic conditions that gave rise to this unique institutional entrepreneur in the first place. These findings allow us to revisit the topic of segregation. In research on the spread of competition under neoliberalism, researchers have focused mostly on interracial inequality and on the segregation of Blacks from whites.[11] However, the boundary work performed by respectable Black male academies shifts attention to a relatively overlooked outcome of educational stratification: how "intra-racial inequality has been perpetuated and created anew" under competitive neoliberal regimes.[12] Given hyper-segregation in the city of Morgan, pro-charter policies would have done very little to create more racially integrated schools, given that families frequently choose among racially homogeneous schools.

As neoliberalism's politics of dispossession has starved the public of wealth, it has had an especially harmful impact on communities of color.[13] For this reason, some of the most vehement critics of neoliberal policies maintain that neoliberalism destroys the very notion of democracy and a public.[14] Yet history tells us that Black democratic empowerment and the market have often been odd bedfellows, which is in line more generally with neoliberalism's contradictory cultural politics.[15] Indeed, I am sympathetic to a longer history of Black families using the market to their advantage.[16] However, my findings support the view of an increasing hegemony of market principles in Black politics. As the historian Cedric Johnson notes, the commitment to liberal social provision has waned since the achievements of the civil rights movement. "Since that moment," Johnson writes, "Black politicos, especially at the level of city governance, have veered toward an embrace of neoliberalism—the ideological rejection of left egalitarian, public interventionism in favor of those modes of state regulation that enhance capital flows and profit making."[17] This middle, or "third way," treads between older forms of liberalism and conservative policies, and this third way crystalized in the United States in the formation of former president Bill Clinton's "New Democrats." In this book, I have situated today's Black male academies in this precarious middle path, in a community control tradition that has, dating back to the post-*Brown* era, evinced a strange and at times perilous relationship between progressive racial politics and the market. Neoliberal ideologies and austerity measures are only aggravating this already precarious relationship.

I do not want to dismiss the good intentions behind seeking to lift up Black boys. Rather, this analysis has sought to properly contextualize the "ideological foundations of racial uplift social policies" and raise "critical questions about how the framing of the 'problem' legitimizes interventions that neither disrupt the White supremacist racial hegemony, nor threaten the capitalist economic order."[18] Indeed, the racial uplift at work in *Black Boys Apart* can tell us something about Black masculinity in a neoliberal era. Past research has examined how a carceral apparatus exacts violence on the bodies of poor young men of color. Since I completed my research, the brutal deaths of Black men at the hands of police officers have drawn national attention.[19] Yet hegemony operates insidiously through a combination of consent and force. Through a process of neoliberal governmentality today, we find the shaping of young Black men's character, sensibilities, and habits within institutions driven by the commonsense market imperatives of standardization, accountability, innovation, entrepreneurialism, and competition. The "forward-looking" language of markets joins forces with other regressive narratives claiming that structural oppression is behind us (such as post-racialism). In doing so, they ignore how hegemonic power morphs and endures, and further naturalize inequalities not only between men and women, but among groups of men and boys.[20] By emulating a time-honored, respectable identity, Black male academies "represent both the structural conditions of hegemonic projects now and the sedimented consequences of gender projects in the past."[21] Still, as hegemony is a field of struggle, members of both school communities also actively contested the assumptions that guided their schools: concerning whiteness, testing, and the need to be saved.

Democracy and the Market

What lies ahead for all-boys education?

In December 2014, the Department of Education's Office of Civil Rights (OCR) released a Q&A document that clarified legal ambiguities around single-sex education. While the document focused explicitly on single-sex classes, these guidelines should have important repercussions for single-sex schools. Several are worth mentioning. First, the OCR emphasized that schools "may not . . . assign a male teacher, on the basis of his sex, to teach an all-boys class because the school thinks male students will prefer, respond better to, or learn more effectively from, a man."[22] In fact, rather than focusing exclusively on hiring Black men in public schools, school districts should do more to recruit Black men *and* women. Scholars have found that for low-income Black boys, having at least one Black teacher in elementary school correlates with lower high school dropout rates and higher interest in attending college.[23] Moreover, an effective teaching formula links cultural relevance with high-impact methods that challenge students, but this formula is certainly not specific to single-sex education.[24]

A shifting political climate, however, appears amenable to the all-boys schooling movement. In December 2015, President Obama signed the Every Student Succeeds Act (ESSA) into law as the successor to No Child Left Behind. The new law received bipartisan support and is intended to be a clear departure from NCLB. In a report introducing ESSA, the White House did not hide its disdain for the old law: "Under NCLB, schools were given many ways to fail, but very few opportunities to succeed, by forcing schools and districts into one-size-fits-all solutions, regardless of the individual needs and circumstances in those communities."[25] We are, however, likely to see more of the same. The start of Betsy DeVos's tenure as secretary of education in 2017 is a victory for the privatization movement. In her first major policy address as education secretary, DeVos, the former head of the American Federation of Children, stressed her commitment to expanding school choice. "I'm not in favor of any one form of choice over another," she said. "I'm simply in favor of giving parents more and better options to find an environment that will set their child up for success."[26] Likely anticipating criticism of her nakedly corporate agenda, DeVos stressed that "throwing money at the problem isn't the solution" and that "we must invest in children, not in buildings."

But DeVos ran into trouble when she lapsed into the language of markets. She drew criticism for drawing a parallel between school choice and popular ridesharing options such as Uber and Lyft. Her rationale was that the success of ridesharing demonstrates that "people like having more options." More educational choices for consumers would, by this logic, lead to similar success. "Just as the traditional taxi system revolted against ridesharing," she continued, "so too does the education establishment feel threatened by the rise of school choice. In both cases, the entrenched status quo has resisted models that empower individuals."

But DeVos's own logic—and the comparison between ridesharing and public schooling—is flawed. While she argued that more choice would serve "the greater, common good," it is only likely to empower individuals "who have the economic, social, and political power to make the market work for them."[27] The healthy and seemingly natural form of competition that DeVos seeks—or what Foucault called "pure competition"—assumes that everyone enters the competition on equal footing, or in this case, that everyone has equal access to ridesharing.[28] In reality, many have never heard of ridesharing, only a small percentage of Americans use it, and those who do use it tend overwhelmingly to be financially privileged.[29] In an ironic twist, the poor students DeVos has in mind come from families that disproportionately rely on public transportation.[30] With this in mind, DeVos's critique of the "traditional taxi system" also falls flat. The education secretary imagines this constituency as comprised of those who oppose privatization and expanded choice (such as liberals and union leaders) and who are hurting the very people they claim to help: disadvantaged kids. But DeVos fails to see that those who hail cabs are a privileged group to begin with. But under the terms of school privatization, it is out of the question to invest more in buses, light rails, and other affordable forms of public transportation that serve a greater percentage of a city's poor residents.

Charter schools remain a divisive issue, but their numbers will likely see a steady climb in the coming years. I agree with Eric Rofes, Lisa Stulberg, and other progressive educators that there is a need to "step beyond the 'all charters or no charters' polarization" in contemporary debates.[31] Here, more robust discussions are needed on the impact of segregation on charter school education. Critics take issue with the increasing segregation of charter schools. But taking inspiration from Du Bois, progressive educators have supported efforts to found schools by and for Blacks. This perspective is now increasingly shared by communities serving children of diverse backgrounds. As Christopher Stewart, of the nonprofit organization Education Post, observed of recent efforts in Minnesota, "We have Somali schools, we have Hmong schools, we have schools for Native American kids . . . [a]nd those communities don't really see their schools as segregated or as isolated, they see them as kind of culturally affirming environments for kids that they can't get in a very white state like Minnesota."[32] Here, these schools seek neither full separation from white society nor full assimilation into it. Indeed, as Du Bois's biographer David Levering Lewis writes, Du Bois affirmed this "permanent tension," pointing the way to a freedom with a "proud, enduring hyphenation."[33] At the same time, the findings in *Black Boys Apart* encourage caution for supporters of Black-controlled institutions. They point to the need to take seriously the increasing impact of market principles on community schools and to consider how those principles increasingly aggravate divisions between upwardly mobile Blacks and those who are more severely disadvantaged. By defending the right of Black empowerment in schools, the community control tradition has mostly avoided an association with controversial, "ultra-competitive charter schools."[34] I found, however, that Northside Academy saw little choice but to join a high-stakes, competitive race. It is the task of Black male academies to recognize and honor the tensions on which these schools rest—between integration and separation, democractic empowerment and market principles, Black Nationalism and Black feminism—and work to find the proud, enduring hyphenations.

Abolition Democracy

In these pages, I have shown how the "discourse of Du Bois" has played out in all-male public education.[35] *Black Boys Apart* has revealed W. E. B. Du Bois "as a champion who can be appropriated on an equal basis by any and all political tendencies."[36] Yet if Du Bois can offer a lesson to proponents of single-sex education, it is the need to thaw the "frozen" ways that his ideas have been invoked, detached from history and without an understanding of how Du Bois himself revised his own ideas.[37] Today's Black male academies seek what Du Bois pursued when he outlined the vision of the NAACP's magazine, *The Crisis,* in its inaugural issue: "the advancement of men." Adjudicating a Black Nationalist perspective (which supports all-boys schools) and a Black feminist approach (which argues that gender inequality is often reproduced under the banner of racial uplift) first requires acknowledging a contemporary moment that threatens to splinter Black communities further. A Black feminist reading of Du Boisian ideas seems especially helpful in this regard. As Hazel Carby has argued, if "as intellectuals and as activists, we are committed, like Du Bois, to struggles for liberation and democratic egalitarianism, then surely it is not contradictory also to struggle to be critically aware of the ways in which ideologies of gender have undermined our egalitarian visions in the past and continue to do so in the present."[38]

For educators (and entrepreneurs) choosing to press forward with Black male academies, my findings come with several recommendations. First, educators should ask what is gained and what is lost with efforts to institutionalize respectability. Neither school in this book could escape the elitist ideology of the Talented Tenth. It provided the men of Perry High and the students of Northside with a much-desired status. Uplift ideology, as Kevin Gaines has written, has always recognized "African Americans' quite understandable desire for dignity, security, and social mobility."[39] The problem, rather, has "stemmed from the construction of class differences through racial and cultural hierarchies that had little to do with the material conditions of African Americans," as well as "the active complicity of the state and opinion-making apparatuses of civil society."[40] To put it another way, by acquiring success through imitation, Northside Academy learned to deride those boys and schools that failed to imitate Northside. Yet school officials can still cultivate school pride without promoting a "winner-take-all" mentality. Male academy officials can dampen competition by creating stronger community partnerships and opportunities for their own students to collaborate with students at other schools. It will take the collective efforts of school officials to set an example for their students.

If single-sex schools are to be empowering spaces for young men, then they must be inclusive of multiple masculinities. A truly empowering culturally relevant pedagogy would honor the range of gender and sexual identities of young Black men. They should aim to nurture progressive Black masculinities, a feminist vision that nurtures strength that does not rely on the domination of others.[41] Despite a disciplined culture that stressed conformity to rules, Northside leaders encouraged their students to pursue a range of activities and extracurriculars that were celebrated nearly equally, including debate, drama, and sports. A progressive framework supports the work of schools that prepare young people for adult futures but also encourage children to play and experiment and to try different things.[42] This should be a core goal of all male academies. Committed students and adults also formed a gay–straight alliance at Perry High and Northside Academy. Compared to schools without these student groups, schools with GSAs have been shown to promote stronger student-administrator relationships and more friendships across sexual identities.[43] Yet more can be done. In particular, young men wanted to see more teachers and other adults participate as allies. This sort of participation would dignify the students, and the message of nurturing inclusivity would reverberate across schools that remain strongly heteronormative. Intensive, long-term mentoring may also help create more successful and confident young men, and this reveals the power that adult men have to inculcate messages about sexuality and manhood.

Schools everywhere will continue to tell their students to work harder, in all its guises: to be resilient, to be grittier, and to hustle more. They all shore up "the cultural logic of neoliberalism" that "resonates at the deepest level of the self."[44] But it is crucial to ask young Black men to see themselves as more than just "winners."[45] Following Angela Davis, Jordan Camp, Joel Olson, and other critical scholars and activists, I see a productive path forward that draws inspiration from what Du Bois called "abolition democracy." For Du Bois, an "abolitionist democratic strategy seeks to abolish explicit and normalized white advantages in housing, education, employment, asset accumulation, health, criminal justice, and politics."[46] Rather than promote competition among schools, city officials should use schools to promote alliances among social movements fighting urban problems that disproportionately afflict Black communities.[47] A better path is to support the cause of social movements, and particularly radical youth movements, that hope and hustle together. This politics should bear in mind what Du Bois himself preached near the end of his life when he reflected on his Talented Tenth ideology:

> Some years ago I used the phrase "The Talented Tenth," meaning leadership of the Negro race in America by a trained few. Since then this idea has been criticized. It has been said that I had in mind the building of an aristocracy with neglect of the masses.[48]

Du Bois conceded that his early vision of race leadership had invited "self-indulgent, well-to-do men" into its ranks, which only fractured rather than mobilize the Black masses.[49] Du Bois called instead for race leadership based on sacrifice and not selfishness. He closed by saying:

> This, then is my re-examined and restated theory of the "Talented Tenth," which has thus become the doctrine of the "Guiding Hundredth." Naturally, I do not dream, that a word of mine will transform, to any essential degree, the form and trends of this fraternity; but I am certain the idea called for expression and that the seed must be dropped whether in this or other soil, today or tomorrow.[50]

Du Bois acknowledged the elitism of the Talented Tenth and pushed instead to democratize the path to Black liberation.[51] And as Du Bois himself frequently revised his work and imagined different paths to racial liberation, so too must we imagine an alternative to neoliberal education. A path forward requires coming to grips with history: precisely what neoliberalism itself denies as it pursues quick fixes, transfers risk from states to schools, and places the burden for change on the choices and willpower of individuals. As the Du Boisian scholar Brian Lozenski has written, while crises are real in their consequences, a focus on the contemporary miseducation of Black youth overlooks the historical and structural causes of Black disadvantage, dating back to slavery, which have collectively produced today's racial disparities in education. "How do we keep the urgent aspects of crisis," Lozenski asks, "while not reducing ourselves to historical illiteracy?"[52]

Widening the historical aperture reveals that today's "crisis" of young Black men is the most recent fight in a continuous struggle against white hegemony. An abolition democracy demands being skeptical of a politics that preaches a repackaged version of rugged individualism, and instead is open to a politics that embraces a rugged collectivism. Even as groups turn away from a politics of "lifting thyself" to one of "lifting as we climb," they should be especially aware of how a "we" can adopt an us-versus-them logic, or how a "talented" few is lifted in part by rejecting the perceived "submerged" among them.

In a present when Black youth are victims of an alliance between state violence and racial capitalism, the Black Lives Matter movement is sowing the seeds of the counter-hegemonic struggle that Du Bois envisioned. In the words of Alicia Garza, one of the cofounders of this movement:

> Black Lives Matter is an ideological and political intervention in a world where Black lives are systematically and intentionally targeted for demise. It is an affirmation of Black folks' contributions to this society, our humanity, and our resilience in the face of deadly oppression.[53]

Indeed. Counter-hegemonic struggle requires resilience, but it is a collective resilience that works to undo systematic oppression. While a much-needed radicalism has escaped the NAACP, its spirit of counter-hegemonic struggle can be found in a constellation of youth organizations including Black Lives Matter and the Black Youth Project 100.[54] Especially relevant is how the Black Lives Matter movement has made "anti-respectability the center of its politics" by holding the criminal justice system equally accountable for the deaths of all young men of color at its hands, whether they are "respectable" or not.[55] Black Lives Matter reimagines a Black liberatory politics that is not led by "the charismatic Black men many are rallying these days," and instead recognizes the Black queer women and the multiply marginalized people within Black communities who are working to dignify the rights and lives of all Black Americans.[56]

In that vein, Black male academies should resist absolute conformity to predetermined rules and instead foreground the voices of the students those schools purport to serve. Northside Academy preached a politics of "getting out," but it was clear that the young men also loved much about their communities. Instead of being an "island" in the community that fought off perceived intruders and other threats that made their way ashore,[57] perhaps school officials could have acknowledged their young men's struggles to navigate the school and the streets and instead created a community school and not a school set apart from the community. These academies would also be well served by listening to those organic intellectuals—who may not always have the respectable educational credentials these academies valorize—who come from the communities of these young men and who work valiantly to help the young men articulate their struggle. These are hallmarks of a participatory democracy. While the race men of Perry High School fell short in their caregiving efforts, their desire to fight an unfair school disciplinary system should be applauded. Their young men may not have been "respectable," but they recognized they should not be punished for this reason. Even after its doors closed for good, what Perry High can teach us is to focus on these counter-hegemonic struggles, to investigate and take action against "the coercive hegemony of the carceral state."[58] "Rather than a framework of individual accountability," Gilda Ochoa has written, "there would be *societal* accountability."[59]

School officials and their students should remove their blazers and roll up their sleeves: to have meaningful conversations and develop lessons around historical and structural causes of racial capitalism, and how hegemonic formations especially disadvantage young people who stand little chance of ever setting foot in a school like Northside Academy. Collective, feminist, and anti-racist mobilization seems especially necessary with a new presidential administration that is committed to the unjust rule of "law and order."[60] As I have shown in these pages, Black male academies do not so much innovate as imitate elite schools. Leaders of future all-male academies should find a feminist and anti-racist politics worthy of emulation in their schools. This reveals how an abolition democracy is at its core a caring democracy, to borrow from Joan Tronto.[61] The self-interested behaviors behind a market fundamentalism will always threaten to undermine the responsibility of institutions to care for their most vulnerable citizens. True justice is grounded in care, and the caring principle of plurality resonates most here. It is a care that is practiced collectively, as citizens are always givers and receivers of care. It is a care that spreads widely, as individuals affirm the care they have received by finding ways to care for others. It is a care that actively resists the temptation to assert dominance, and a care that sees all young men of color as having the potential to grow and to contribute to their communities.

The Seed Time

W. E. B. Du Bois died on August 27, 1963, in Ghana, at the age of ninety-five. The next day, and across the Atlantic, thousands gathered in Washington, D.C., for the historic Civil Rights March. Hours before the Reverend Martin Luther King Jr. gave his "I Have a Dream" speech, Roy Wilkins, a representative for the NAACP, shared the news of Du Bois's death with the audience. While Du Bois had "chose[n] another path," Wilkins remarked, it was "incontrovertible that at the dawn of the twentieth century this voice was the voice calling you to gather here today in this cause."[62]

Just over a half century later, in August 2016, the nation's capital welcomed a new all-male public high school to the city. By all accounts, the Ron Brown College Preparatory High School was a model second-wave academy. Washington, D.C., like the city of Morgan, had embraced school reform, though many changes drew scrutiny. But the school district chancellor, who had called Ron Brown Prep her "pet project," was a firm believer in expanded choice. "We're not," she attested, "a one-size-fits-all school district."[63] Blessed with a new, state-of-the-art building, Ron Brown Prep blended (to borrow words from first-wave academy pioneers Clifford Watson and Geneva Smitherman) a "futuristic" approach, with a special focus on science and technology, and a more classical curriculum that included Latin. Maybe the school had modeled itself after Northside, or perhaps it had been influenced by the character and pedigree of Washington, D.C.'s Dunbar High School, the country's first high-achieving Black school. In this respect, Ron Brown Prep may have pleased Du Bois, who a century earlier had been passed over as assistant superintendent of Negro Schools in Washington, D.C., and thus denied the opportunity to help look after Dunbar High.

Within weeks of opening, the school hosted students from Morehouse College. During one activity, the Young Kings (as the school referred to its young men) linked arms and formed a circle around their mentors from Morehouse. Charles Curtis, the school's psychologist, remarked that "the power of forty, college age Black men telling you that you are a God is what our Young Kings felt today. My head is bowed at the greatness I am charged with serving."[64] The task at hand was urgent. The motto for Ron Brown Prep declares:

Now is the accepted time—not tomorrow, not some more convenient season.

The adage is the first line of a prayer written by Du Bois. The race man had composed homilies and prayers for his students at Atlanta University between 1909 and 1910, when the institution was also home to an elementary school and a high school. Atlanta University was one of the proudest examples of a legacy of Black community control, which, Du Bois wrote, are not "simply separate schools, forced on us by grim necessity," but "centers of a new and beautiful effort at human education, which may easily lead and guide the world in many important and valuable respects."[65] Du Bois understood how the Bible's emancipatory spirit nourished the families of the young people in his care at Atlanta University, who were descendants of slaves. His prayer was inspired by passages from the Book of Isaiah, which offer hope in a coming salvation. But that salvation would not be easily won. The students and their caregivers would have to work for it. The prayer continues, in language reminiscent of Du Bois's reflections on the "Guiding Hundredth":

Today is the seed time.
Now are the hours of work and tomorrow comes the harvest and
the play-time.[66]

Exactly a century after Du Bois penned these words, prayers were shared on the occasion of Perry High School's inaugural father-son breakfast. Community leaders implored the adults to nurture the seeds in their care.

The children smiled all morning and felt loved. May they one day reap the harvest.

ACKNOWLEDGMENTS

This book would not exist without the many people who offered me their support, expertise, hard questions, laughter, and love.

I cannot thank enough Barrie Thorne, my dissertation chair at Berkeley. Barrie helped bring creativity, passion, and rigor to my work, and reminded me never to take myself too seriously. Above all, she encouraged me to "sing my song." Dawne Moon first taught me the joys, challenges, and responsibilities that come with being an ethnographer. Raka Ray welcomed me into the sociology department's community of gender researchers and helped me develop a confident voice. Sandra Smith had high expectations from the start, and she never let up. In the Graduate School of Education at Berkeley, Na'ilah Nasir and Zeus Leonardo offered support at early and critical stages in my work.

Many friends read and offered generous feedback on various parts of the book. I had the good fortune of being in a writing group with stellar qualitative researchers, including Jessica Cobb, John Kaiser, Louise Ly, Rafael Colonna, Emily Gleason, Ingunn Eriksen, and Stian Overå. Kate Mason was my comrade when we were teaching assistants for Raka's Sociology of Gender course. My office mates Juan Fernandez and Malgorzata Kurjanska were sources of much-needed humor and were gracious sounding boards during the throes of writing. At Berkeley, I got to know many talented graduate students who have become good friends, including Julia Chuang, Paul Albertus, Chris Chambers-Ju, Nick Wilson, Ryan Calder, Damon Mayrl, Kate Maich, and Kimberly Hoang. Werner Ju, Deborah Shoub Ju, Angela Campos, and my surrogate grandmothers Nancy and Jennie welcomed me into their homes and became my California family.

My colleagues at Tufts University have been the absolute best and have offered encouragement every step of the way. I express my deep appreciation for Paul Joseph, Helen Marrow, Sarah Sobieraj, Rosemary Taylor, Paula Aymer, Susan Ostrander, Orly Clergé, Jill Weinberg, Cedric de Leon, Sabina Vaught, Steve Cohen, David Hammer, Ryan Redmond, Laura Rogers, Cynthia Robinson, Bárbara Brizuela, Donna Qualters, Annie Soisson, John LiBassi, Victoria Dorward, Carla Walsh, Pearl Emmons, Phil Gay, Peggy Hutaff, Liz Canter, and Sol Gittleman. A special thanks to Pawan Dhingra, who has helped me in more ways than I can count. Outside Tufts, Edward Morris has been a model researcher and a wonderful collaborator. He carefully read the entire manuscript and offered feedback that improved the book substantially. Poulami Roychowdhury, Tina Fetner, Andrew Bond, and Letta Page also offered generous feedback on parts of this book.

Long before I embarked on the research for this book, various faculty in the anthropology and sociology department at Williams College took a nervous kid under their wing. My love for teaching and for the study of the social world were nurtured in classes with Antonio Foias, Peter Just, and Michael F. Brown. James Nolan Jr. inspired me to pursue a career in sociology.

A generous junior leave from Tufts University gave me the time to revise this book. The ever-supportive Jim Glaser was instrumental in making that happen. During my leave, the sociology department at Portland State University offered me space and resources, as well as opportunities to share my research. A special thanks there to Matthew Carlson, Hyeyoung Woo, Bob Liebman, and Michelle Holliday-Stocking.

I'm grateful for several Tufts Faculty Research Awards, which supported my research and writing. At Berkeley, financial support from several sources helped launch my dissertation research, including a Eugene Cota-Robles Fellowship, a Dean's Normative Time Fellowship, a Lynnea Stephens Memorial Research Fellowship, and a Leo Lowenthal Fellowship. Selections from this book appeared in the journals *Socius: Sociological Research for a Dynamic World* and *Sociological Perspectives,* and in an edited volume with Peter Lang publishers. I'm thankful for the permission to reproduce that material in these pages.

The staff at the University of Minnesota Press have been class acts as I pushed this book through to completion. My gracious editor, Jason Weidemann, took a chance on me, was patient, and always supported the book's perspective. I also wish to thank Gabe Levin and Rachel Moeller for their assistance during the production stage, and Diana Witt for creating the index.

As an instructor, I've been blessed with the chance to work with and learn from many excellent students. From my Berkeley days, huge hugs for

Kristin Schoonover, Eivind Grip Fjær, and Vivian Chang. At Tufts, the same for Cecilia Flores, Ikenna Acholonu, Pilar Plater, Jimmy Zuniga, and Nick Whitney. Pilar and Nick also offered valuable research assistance. My students' insightful questions and comments—and their perplexed reactions to my own uninformed questions and comments—have pushed my thinking in this book in big and small ways.

Many friends brought much joy to my life long before and throughout the research and writing process. A special shout-out to Jay Lamar Harris, who showed me how to dream big. Justin Crowe and Chris Curtis have been close friends for many years. I'm lucky to have in my life Steven Kollar, Dan Reagan, Emilie Reagan, Matt Troha, Matt Mugmon, Damoun Delaviz, Mike Gann, Mark Lederer, Nicole Pagano, Ryu Yokoi, Rob Vargas, Max Greenberg, and Margaret Okada. Buzz Marcovici, Amy Blume-Marcovici, and Odin and Mae Marcovici became my new family as I wrapped up this book. I miss our Sunday dinners. When I was a sixth-grade teacher in Philadelphia, Sharif El-Mekki and Terrance Furin served as wise teachers and mentors and helped deepen my understanding of urban public education.

The incomparable Father Al Moser and I bonded over a Sufjan Stevens album during my first year of graduate school. A few years later, I thought often of Father Al when I had Stevens's Oregon-themed album, *Carrie & Lowell,* on repeat during writing sessions in Portland. I regret I never had a chance to ask Father Al what he thought of the album or to show him a finished copy of this book before he passed away in 2016. I dedicate this book to him, a man who showed me how to live with dignity.

My parents, Saran and Navy, arrived in the United States just weeks before I was born and have committed everything to giving me and my sister, Friday, a chance to be successful and to be happy. I'm still learning the full extent of the sacrifices they made and of the pain they have endured. Friday has been my biggest supporter from the start. I'm not proud of the fact that I can't speak to you all in our native Khmer. But I hope you are proud of my words in these pages.

I met Julie Blume the year I sat down to revise the version of the manuscript that would earn me my book contract. Her boundless love and enthusiasm nourished me during difficult stretches, and she was the first to help me celebrate the accomplishments along the way. Julie pored over nearly every word of this book (with our cats, Sesame, Tookie, and Widby, as her reading companions), and she helped me clarify things at pivotal moments. Thank you, Jules, for helping me find the confidence to release this book into the world. To our future together.

Finally, I could never fully express the gratitude I have for the people of Perry High School and Northside Academy. I remain humbled by the various officials and administrators who provided me with contacts and access; the teachers who welcomed me into their classrooms; the parents and grandparents who invited me into their homes; and above all the young men who welcomed me into their lives. For all the time they offered me, I regret how long it has taken me to complete this book. I understand that members of both school communities may read and disagree with what I have written, or see things differently, or wish a different story had been told. I have never doubted the good intentions of anyone I met. I hope that I have been able to situate those intentions in the larger social forces at play and that the conclusions I reach can help carve a path forward for young Black men.

Interview and Student Data

TABLE 1. Counts for Interview Participants

	Students	Parents	Teachers	Staff Members	Administrators	Totals
Perry High School	25	9	20	6	8	68
Northside Academy	39	15	16	4	1	75
Other	—	—	—	—	7	7
Totals	64	24	36	10	16	150

Note: The "Parents" category includes mothers and fathers, grandparents, and legal guardians. The "Teachers" category includes past and current instructors. The "Staff Members" category includes social workers, guidance counselors, admissions directors, and school police officers. The "Administrators" category includes principals, assistant principals, and school founders/CEOs. The "Other" category includes principals and CEOs of middle schools (n=6) that sent students to Northside Academy, as well as one school district official. Several participants spoke in multiple capacities. For example, a few parents in the study had been hired as staff members at the schools, but I categorized them here as parents. One woman was the mother of two boys: one child who attended Perry, and the other who attended Northside Academy. I included her in the counts of parents at both schools.

TABLE 2. Disciplinary and Criminal Justice Profile for Student Interview Sample

	At Least 1 Suspension since 6th Grade	At Least 1 Arrest	Sentenced to a Juvenile Detention Center 1 or More Times
Perry High School (n=25)	11 (44%)	6 (24%)	4 (16%)
Northside Academy (n=39)	8 (21%)	0	0

Note: This data was determined through a mix of student self-reports and parent reports.

TABLE 3. Academic Profile for Student Interview Sample

	Aspires to Attend College	At Least 1 Parent with a High School Degree	At Least 1 Parent with a College Degree
Perry High School (n=25)	15 (60%)	20 (80%)	2 (6%)
Northside Academy (n=39)	39 (100%)	37 (95%)	12 (31%)

Note: This data was determined through a mix of student self-reports and parent reports.

Introduction

1. Watson and Smitherman, *Educating African American Males*, 40.
2. D. Johnson, "Milwaukee Creating 2 Schools for Black Boys."
3. Hopkins, *Educating Black Males*, 9.
4. "Hostility Greets Students at Black School in White Area of Detroit."
5. Leake and Leake, "Islands of Hope."
6. While the first schools in the early 1990s—in cities such as Detroit and Milwaukee—enrolled girls, the language of "male academies" stuck because of the spirit of the original proposals and because the schools would enroll a large majority of boys anyway. I have adopted this term and distinguish between these community-led efforts and a second wave of Black male academies that emerged about fifteen years later under neoliberal educational policies. Another group of single-sex schools opened in the late 1990s in California. While some of these schools were targeted to at-risk students, none enrolled a majority Black population. For an analysis of these California schools, see Datnow, Hubbard, and Woody, *Is Single Gender Schooling Viable in the Public Sector?*
7. Klein, Lee, McKinsey, and Archer, *Identifying U.S. K-12 Public Schools with Deliberate Sex Segregation.* The Department of Education does not keep reliable records of single-sex arrangements nationwide; see J. Williams, *Separation Solution?* There are estimated to be hundreds of single-sex academic classrooms in otherwise coed schools, some of which have remained hidden from public view and have therefore managed to avoid legal scrutiny. There is evidence that many of these classrooms targeting Black youth existed prior to the first wave of Black male academies in the early 1990s. In *Educating Black Males*, Ronnie Hopkins does not hide his disappointment over legal opposition to the original male academy efforts. He endorses single-sex classrooms for being "a successful technique for parents, school administrators, and other school people to avoid civil rights discrimination suits," 32.

8. All names of locations, schools, and individuals at my field site are pseudonyms.

9. At both schools, it was common for adults to refer to one another as "Mr." or "Mrs." in the presence of students. Some male academies, such as Chicago's Urban Prep Academies, even require their students to refer to one another using "Mr."; see Bonner, *Building on Resilience*. The mandatory use of this salutation adds to the respectable character of these schools.

10. Although the school had two middle school grades (seventh and eighth), the community viewed the school as a high school, and I will refer to it as such throughout the book.

11. About one-third of the staff members I interviewed at both schools attended a private single-sex school—either high school or college—or had worked at one prior to working at Perry High or Northside Academy.

12. S. Hall, *Cultural Studies 1983*, 156.

13. "Civil Rights Data Collection."

14. Schott Foundation for Public Education, "Black Lives Matter."

15. According to the American Psychological Association (see the report "Eliminating Health Disparities among Boys and Men"), Black men have the lowest life expectancy rate among all major ethnic groups, and Black men who have sex with men (MSM) are more likely than other groups to contract HIV.

16. Fergus, Noguera, and Martin, *Schooling for Resilience*. The authors provide the first comprehensive analysis of all-male schools. Compared to other researchers on second-wave academies, these authors are less enthusiastic overall about these schools. The success rate varied widely at their seven schools, as several were forced to shut down (as did Perry High School in this book). The authors ask proponents of these schools to learn from past school-reform efforts and not "to simply embrace single-sex education as a panacea," 203. Yet they do not reject these schools outright, and they even appear to support single-sex models so long as they are effective. For example, in a review of Orlando Patterson and Ethan Fosse's book *Cultural Matrix*, Pedro Noguera maintains that Black male academies can reduce "oppositional culture" and raise achievement through excellent instruction and by protecting students from the threat of the streets. Edward Fergus, in a *New York Times* op-ed, "The Freeing Powers of Single-Sex Education," offers an even stronger defense of these schools as spaces where young men of color are liberated from narrow masculine norms. I have similarly argued that these schools promote progressive and flexible gender identities (see Oeur, "Single-Sex Schooling Can Empower Black Boys"). This book softens that endorsement by situating all-male schooling in a larger neoliberal and historical context.

17. R. W. Connell, *Masculinities*, 205.

18. Fergus, Noguera, and Martin, *Schooling for Resilience*.

19. Foucault, *Birth of Biopolitics*.

20. See Noguera, "Responding to the Crisis Confronting California's Black Male Youth." Pedro Noguera argues that "crisis" misdirects attention from the chronic nature of Black disadvantage. See also Lozenski, "Beyond Mediocrity," for an excellent analysis of how ubiquitous crisis narratives disguise the long-term historical causes of today's racial disparities in education.

21. Du Bois, "Editorial," 10 (emphasis added).

22. Quantitative analyses of single-sex public education provide a mixed story, though the weight of the evidence is against these schools having significant impact. No existing meta-analyses include studies of only single-sex public schools, but rather include a mix of public, private, and parochial schools. The first meta-analysis of quantitative research of single-sex schools was conducted by the Department of Education in 2005; see Mael et al., "Single-Sex versus Coeducational Schooling." The report concluded that there is modest support for "academic achievement and more positive academic aspirations," x. While some have interpreted the report as a defense of single-sex education, the report has also been strongly denounced as unreliable; see Rivers and Barnett, *Truth about Girls and Boys,* for a critique. In 2014, drawing on a larger collection of studies (184 compared to the forty used in Mael et al.'s study), Erin Pahlke and colleagues conducted another meta-analysis of studies on single-sex education, "The Effects of Single-Sex Compared with Coeducational Schooling on Students' Performance and Attitudes." They found no significant academic and social benefits for attending single-sex schools. Cornelius Riordan, one of the earliest proponents of single-sex public education, has offered a more optimistic reading of the findings of Pahlke and her colleagues; see Riordan, *Single-Sex Schools.* Riordan rejects claims that student performance in Catholic schools cannot be used to generalize to those in the public sector and has argued since his 1990 text *Girls and Boys in School* that single-sex schools (public or not) are especially beneficial for at-risk youth of color. In *Schooling for Resilience,* Fergus, Noguera, and Martin find only minimal academic growth (as measured by grade point average) at seven male academies.

23. Brooms, "'We Didn't Let the Neighborhood Win.'" Since, from the resilience perspective, the schools effectively seek to shut out a desolate urban landscape, there is little evidence of how the larger community can be empowering.

24. M. James, "Never Quit." James calls this a "power-based" approach. Despite relying heavily on the resilience perspective, in *Schooling for Resilience* Fergus and colleagues overlook James's work, one of the earliest accounts of resiliency in all-male education. This omission reflects their tendency to overlook key literatures on the history of single-sex public education. This includes research on the first-wave academies (see Hopkins, *Educating Black Males;* Murtadha-Watts, "Theorizing Urban Black Masculinity Construction in an African-Centered School"; and Watson and Smitherman, *Educating African-American Males*), legal-historical accounts (see Salomone, *Same, Different, Equal*), and general overviews of

single-sex education (see Datnow and Hubbard, *Gender in Policy and Practice;* and Riordan, *Girls and Boys in School*).

25. "Never quit" is a line from Marlon James's article of the same name. "Never give up" is a line from Joseph Nelson's book of the same name.

26. Saltman, "The Austerity School," 52. The psychologist Angela Duckworth has led the charge in promoting grit; see her book, *Grit*. Some educational literature has capitalized on this new grit industry to update the familiar feel-good narrative of a few heroic "at-risk" youth who beat the odds. For instance, in *Grit and Hope,* Barbara Davenport chronicles a California-based program for Latino youth called Reality Changers. While an inspiration, the successful youth are "respectable" exceptions to the rule. The inflexible program closely monitors the character of the young people (for example, they are prohibited from having sex) and the youth can be expelled for any transgressions.

27. Wacquant, "Scrutinizing the Street."

28. Dumas, "My Brother as 'Problem.'"

29. This terminology is common in Fergus, Noguera, and Martin's *Schooling for Resilience*. Meanwhile, in "'We Didn't Let the Neighborhood Win,'" Brooms restricts neighborhood characteristics to "perils," "challenges," "dangers," and "environmental blight."

30. Fergus, Noguera, and Martin, *Schooling for Resilience,* 39.

31. Brooms, "'We Didn't Let the Neighborhood Win,'" 278.

32. Given that these researchers largely conflate the worldviews of their study participants with their own conceptual framework, they are unable to fully critique the assumptions behind those worldviews. For instance, the authors write that there are structural and cultural explanations for the disadvantage of young men of color "from our vantage point," then write that "both" these explanations have "influenced the development" of these schools from the perspective of their study participants, 14. Later, the authors even suggest that researchers have followed the lead of the study participants in *Schooling for Resilience:* "Like the educators described in this study, a growing number of researchers are trying to find ways to work in the middle ground of the debate between structuralists and culturalists," 18. Yet if the perspectives of the authors' respondents are taken to be the very theory that the authors themselves adopt, then it is unclear how that common sense can be evaluated. In other words, a wider historical view of these schools is needed to develop a *sociological truth* that can explain and, where necessary, critique, the *participant truth* of the people being studied; see Burawoy, "On Desmond," for a discussion of the theoretical demands placed on researchers. Fergus and colleagues appear to attempt to disentangle their analysis from their participants' worldviews by applying reproduction theory, yet the authors never clarify how they will use this framework, and a more concise use of it is especially necessary because none of the works of reproduction theory they cite analyze race (see *Schooling for Resilience,* 231nn31–32). Examples of works that make sharper use of reproduction

theory, assess race, and avoid the victim-blaming characteristic of culturalist accounts include Carter, *Keepin' It Real;* A. Ferguson, *Bad Boys;* and MacLeod, *Ain't No Makin' It.*

33. Hall, "Gramsci's Relevance for the Study of Race and Ethnicity," 20.

34. Without acknowledging this history, in *Schooling for Resilience,* Fergus and colleagues draw a parallel between today's male academies and efforts "to assist girls in science and math during the 1980s and 1990s," 52. Yet comparing single-sex schools *for young men of color* to efforts to assist girls *taken to be a homogeneous group* disguises the racialized and gendered differences in the root causes of disadvantage between these two populations. The authors also argue that the precursors to these schools are community interventions like Big Brothers Big Sisters, but they never compare today's schools to schools in the past. As I have argued, particularly important in this history is how sex separation is linked to racial segregation, and how sex-separate education has been used as a strategy to stabilize gender inequalities. For a historical overview of the relationship between race, gender, and segregation in single-sex schooling, see Salomone, *Same, Different, Equal;* and J. Williams, *Separation Solution?*

35. In *Schooling for Resilience,* Fergus and colleagues write that single-sex schools have only been embraced since 2003. Yet this only marks the emergence of second-wave academies following the passage of No Child Left Behind. I agree with Lisa Stulberg, who writes in *Race, Schools, and Hope* that the first-wave academies (in Milwaukee and Detroit) join a community-control tradition that dates back to the Civil Rights era.

36. In *Schooling for Resilience,* Fergus and colleagues found that "behavioral engagement was the single most important contributor to academic performance," 188, more than other factors such as the quality of instruction, the cultural relevance of the curricula, and relationships among students and between students and staff members. This means that schools primarily reward students who follow the rules. I argue that male academies recruit and attract the very rule-abiding Black male "schoolboys" who fit this profile while deriding their more "delinquent" peers who do not.

37. Collins, *Black Sexual Politics.*

38. Griffin, "Black Feminists and Du Bois," 34. Racial uplift ideology was also paternalistic. Anna Julia Cooper, an early Black feminist and a figure who returns in chapter 1, argued that the advancement of Blacks depended on reforming Black homes. The goal of a domestic Black womanhood was to help groom a patriarchal masculinity that would allow Black men to assume their rightful place at the head of the household.

39. Summers, *Manliness and Its Discontents,* 43.

40. F. Harris, "The Rise of Respectability Politics." For example, the conservative periodical *National Review* has offered a warped history that likens the promotion of good manners to the opposition of slavery. Rather than address the

structural inequalities that divide affluent and poor youth, the magazine provides a rosy picture where having good social skills (such as having a firm handshake) can level the playing field. See Hudson, "Why Manners Matter." Alexandra Hudson, in fact, misrepresents Anthony Jack's sociological research on disadvantaged Black youth as an endorsement of modern finishing schools. Hudson's myopic humanism, which extols valuing everyone's "inherent" worth, is at odds with Jack's larger recognition of unequal social categories and his proposal that elite institutions should change their culture (for example, by prioritizing collaboration and interdependence). See Jack, "Culture Shock Revisited" and "(No) Harm in Asking."

    41. Grundy, "'An Air of Expectancy,'" 46.

    42. Bonner, *Building on Resilience.*

    43. Ross, *Manning the Race,* 9 (emphasis added).

    44. Spence, *Knocking the Hustle;* Dumas, "My Brother as 'Problem'"; F. Harris, "The Rise of Respectability Politics."

    45. Dumas, "My Brother as 'Problem,'" 96.

    46. Hursh, "Assessing No Child Left Behind and the Rise of Neoliberal Education Policies."

    47. R. W. Connell, *Masculinities.*

    48. de Boise, "I'm Not Homophobic, 'I've Got Gay Friends.'"

    49. Frequent crisis tendencies underscore how hegemony is always in an "unstable equilibrium"; see Omi and Winant, *Racial Formation in the United States.*

    50. Tyack and Hansot, *Learning Together.*

    51. Messner, "Gender Ideologies, Youth Sports, and the Production of Soft Essentialism."

    52. Bederman, *Manliness and Civilization,* 12.

    53. J. Williams, *Separation Solution?*

    54. Bederman, *Manliness and Civilization.*

    55. Kimmel, "The Cult of Masculinity."

    56. Bederman, *Manliness and Civilization;* Rotundo, *American Manhood.*

    57. However, during the Reconstruction period, the separate-spheres ideology largely did not apply to Black children. The brutal subjugation of Blacks tended to diminish clear gender roles for Black men and women (who, for example, shared much of the same labor during slavery); see V. Williams, "Reform or Retrenchment."

    58. See Higginbotham, *Righteous Discontent,* for a rich discussion of how a respectability politics and the project of racial uplift at the turn of the twentieth century impacted Black men and women differently.

    59. V. Williams, "Reform or Retrenchment," 51.

    60. Collins, "Intersectionality's Definitional Dilemmas."

    61. V. Williams, "Reform or Retrenchment."

    62. Stulberg, "African American School Choice and the Current Race Politics of Charter Schooling," 38.

63. Sheils, "Segregation by Sex." Quoted in V. Williams, "Reform or Retrenchment," 62. Other historical examples shed light on this strategy. During times of war—periods of crisis in which the security of the nation was perceived to be threatened—the U.S. government has drummed up support through propaganda with explicit visual representations of racial Others who pose a sexual threat to white women.

64. Logan, "Personal Characteristics, Sexual Behaviors, and Male Sex Work." Following desegregation through to the end of the twentieth century, the "gender gap" in education was equated more with disadvantages facing *girls*. Feminist groups called attention to how schools, much like workplaces, were sites of gender discrimination. Turning the "different and unequal" maxim on its head, these groups asserted principles of "sameness" and "equality" and fought for equal treatment and access for women and girls. These findings supported larger worries that adolescence was a toxic period during which the self-esteem of girls plummeted. These worries circulated in a number of widely read "girls-movement" books during this time, most notably Mary Pipher's 1995 best seller *Reviving Ophelia*. Despite gains, a high-profile report, *How Schools Shortchange Girls* by the American Association of University Women Educational Foundation (1992), asserted that progress for girls had stalled. For a critique of these findings, see Kleinfeld, *Myth That Schools Shortchange Girls*.

65. Lingard, "Where to in Gender Policy in Education after Recuperative Masculinity Politics?"

66. Weaver-Hightower, "Issues of Boys' Education in the United States."

67. See, for example, Sax, *Why Gender Matters;* and Gurian, *Boys and Girls Learn Differently!*

68. Bridges and Kimmel, "Engaging Men in the United States," 160. The authors discuss the relationship between "soft essentialism" and boy-crisis narratives.

69. Watson and Smitherman, *Educating African American Males,* 96.

70. Stetser and Stillwell, *Public High School Four-Year On-Time Graduation Rates and Event Dropout Rates.*

71. Cohen, "'End of Men' Is Not True," 1177. The author is critiquing Hanna Rosin's book, *End of Men.*

72. R.W. Connell, *Masculinities.*

73. Bridges and Kimmel, "Engaging Men in the United States."

74. Halpern et al., "Pseudoscience of Single-Sex Schooling."

75. Eliot, "Single-Sex Education and the Brain," 375.

76. Liben, "Probability Values and Human Values in Evaluating Single-Sex Education."

77. American Civil Liberties Union, *Preliminary Findings of ACLU "Teach Kids, Not Stereotypes" Campaign.* Research in psychology has also hypothesized that single-sex classrooms and schools that make gender salient will result in

gender stereotyping; see Bigler and Liben, "Developmental Intergroup Theory of Social Stereotypes and Prejudice."

78. Weaver-Hightower, "Issues of Boys' Education in the United States," 5. In their study of single-sex schools in California in the late 1990s, "Do Single-Sex Schools Improve the Education of Low-Income and Minority Students?," Hubbard and Datnow found that, in the absence of a shared understanding of why single-sex schooling was needed, educators defaulted to gender stereotypes to guide their instruction.

79. J. Williams, *Separation Solution?*

80. In *Separation Solution?*, Juliet Williams also notes that this disguises the fact that white boys still fare better than girls in *other* racial groups.

81. In "Race and Essentialism in Feminist Legal Theory," Angela P. Harris argues that traditional feminist critiques of the law incorrectly assume similarities between Black and white women's experiences and have therefore conceptualized racial differences as being no more than issues of nuance.

82. J. Williams, "Thinking through the 'Boy Crisis,'" 175.

83. Salomone, *Same, Different, Equal.*

84. Hooks, "Publisher's Foreword," 3.

85. Marable, *Black Leadership,* 43.

86. Du Bois, "Editorial," 10.

87. Watson and Smitherman, *Educating African American Males.*

88. R. Ferguson, "'W. E. B. Du Bois,'" 269.

89. The quotation is from David Levering Lewis's book *W. E. B. Du Bois,* 569. This position would soon force Du Bois out of the very organization he had helped found, as other NAACP leaders refused to endorse separation of any kind. See Alridge, "On the Education of Black Folk." Alridge describes how Du Bois drew on Hegelian dialectics to advocate for a productive synthesis between voluntary separation and integration into mainstream institutions. The community control tradition has promoted this synthesis as well as a blending (however odd) between democratic empowerment and corporate interests; see Stulberg, *Race, Schools, and Hope.*

90. For endorsements of Black all-male education from the perspective of critical race theory, see Mitchell and Stewart, "The Efficacy of All-Male Academies"; and Terry et al., "Does the 'Negro' *Still* Need Separate Schools?" Critical race theory interrogates the racism that is endemic to U.S. institutions. A progressive educational perspective, on the other hand, supports Black-controlled schooling and access to charter schools for Black families; see Rofes and Stulberg, *Emancipatory Promise of Charter Schools.*

91. Van Deburg, *Modern Black Nationalism,* 3.

92. Van Deburg, *Modern Black Nationalism,* 3. "Territorial nationalism" is the particular strand of Black Nationalism that supports community schools.

93. Stulberg, "African American School Choice and the Current Race Politics of Charter Schooling," 32.

94. Pedroni, *Market Movements*, 4.

95. Stulberg, *Race, Schools, and Hope,* 20. The Nation of Islam is a territorial nationalist organization. Detroit's Malcolm X Academy was named after the Nation of Islam leader.

96. Salomone, *Same, Different, Equal.*

97. P. Jones, "Educating Black Males."

98. Terry et al., "Does the 'Negro' *Still* Need Separate Schools?," 669.

99. Du Bois, "Does the Negro Need Separate Schools?," 333.

100. Du Bois, "Does the Negro Need Separate Schools?," 335.

101. K. J. Cooper, "Scholars Debate Effectiveness of Single Sex Classes," 15.

102. Zamir, *Dark Voices.* Feminist scholars have critiqued the tendency among male intellectuals to view Du Bois in heroic terms. See Carby, *Race Men;* and J. James, *Transcending the Talented Tenth.*

103. Gaines, *Uplifting the Race.*

104. Foucault, *Birth of Biopolitics.* For a comprehensive overview of the topic, see Dean, *Governmentality.*

105. Carlson, "States, Subjects and Sovereign Power"; Fraser, "Foucault on Modern Power."

106. Garland, "'Governmentality' and the Problem of Crime," 175.

107. McRobbie, "Notes on the Perfect," 10. Some critics have observed how neoliberalism has coopted feminism and produced a "neoliberal feminism." According to this ideology, women accept complete responsibility for striking a perfect work–life balance; see Rottenberg, "The Rise of Neoliberal Feminism." For an insightful analysis of the gendered articulations of neoliberal governmentality in an international context, see Roychowdhury, "Victims to Saviors." I find the author's definition of neoliberal governmentality especially useful: "a historically new modality of power that works through the devolution of risk onto private enterprises," 796.

108. Bettie, *Women without Class.* This theory of identity construction is similar to that in feminist post-structuralism, where subjects are produced through discourses, or those knowledges, practices, and techniques that organize power. Or as Amy Best writes in *Fast Cars, Cool Rides,* identities are "emergent features of ongoing social interaction, set within a set of structural relations, formed out of the discursive repertoires youth use to make sense of, interpret, and narrate their worlds," 17.

109. Dumas, "My Brother as 'Problem,'" 95. Michael Dumas's definition of neoliberal governmentality draws on the work of Lester Spence in "The Neoliberal Turn in Black Politics."

110. R. Ferguson, "'W. E. B. Du Bois,'" 277.

111. Du Bois, "The Talented Tenth," 33.

112. Gaines, *Uplifting the Race.*

113. Summers, "Manhood Rights in the Age of Jim Crow," 755.

114. J. James, *Transcending the Talented Tenth*. In helping to situate Du Bois in larger issues of Black manhood, education, racial uplift, race leadership, and respectability, I will also draw on insights from what could be called "critical Black masculinity studies," which span the fields of history, African American studies, and cultural studies. This includes the work of James, cited here, as well as Hazel Carby *(Race Men)*; Kevin Gaines *(Uplifting the Race)*; Martin Summers *(Manliness and Its Discontents)*; Manning Marable *(Black Leadership)*; and Marlon Ross *(Manning the Race)*. Based primarily, though not exclusively, on intellectual histories of Black male elites, this work has viewed Black manhood reform as a revisionist and "self-conflicting process of cultural-historical transformation"; Ross, *Manning the Race*, 8.

115. See, for example, Mitchell Duneier's book *Slim's Table*, a study of how older working-class Black men distinguish themselves from both middle-class Blacks and younger "ghetto" Blacks; and Amy Wilkins's article, "Stigma and Status."

116. Collins, *Black Feminist Thought*.

117. A. Ferguson, *Bad Boys*; Gunn, "Inner-City 'Schoolboy' Life."

118. In "Problematizing Contemporary Men/Masculinities Theorizing," Chris Beasley shows how critical studies of men and masculinities (CSMM) are largely incompatible with current gender/sexuality (GS) theorizing. CSMM has a solidly *modernist* outlook on gender and identity. A paradigmatic CSMM framework such as hegemonic masculinity assumes a dialectical interplay between agents and structures. Importantly, individuals are intentional agents whose identities are "unified and stable platforms for action," 755. This unity has resulted in one of this framework's stubborn limitations: a seemingly endless list of "categories" of men, a framing that disguises the relational character of gender formation. Contemporary GS theorizing, on the other hand, has a distinctly *postmodern* outlook. A typical post-structural approach does not view subjects as distinct from structures (or discourses, in the language of post-structuralism), or as preexisting those discourses, but are only ever produced through discourses. Therefore, identity and gender formation are constructed through repetitive acts, and often unconsciously. Beasley is skeptical of analyses that wed concepts from CSMM and GS that do not address their conceptual incompatibility. Suffice it to say, my own analysis draws inspiration from both traditions, and I find in their imperfect synthesis the need to take seriously how marginalized actors act strategically within constrained conditions. (Chapter 2 describes this process in greater detail.) Following Hae Yeon Choo and Myra Marx Ferree (see their article "Practicing Intersectionality in Sociological Research") I investigate how actors are "recruited to" discourses, "yet have choices in the 'subject positions' they adopt in these complex locations" and are "political subjects" in "a contested process of self-creation in a field of power relations," 134.

119. Summers, *Manliness and Its Discontents*, 14.

120. In *Black Leadership*, Manning Marable describes how Black political history is characterized by a dialectic between resistance and accommodation. This tension sheds light on the famous debate between the accommodationist orientation of Booker T. Washington's Tuskegee Institute and Du Bois's belief in the training of an elite class of Blacks, as well as the persistent tension between integrationist and separatist ideals in Du Bois's own ideological framework.

121. Crenshaw, "Race, Reform, and Retrenchment." Drawing on Kimberlé Crenshaw's work, Sabina Vaught has argued for a more sophisticated understanding of coercion and consent in explanations of contemporary racism; see her book, *Compulsory*. While racism surely is a "deep-structure feature of society and the state," Vaught writes, the experience of oppression encompasses far more than "psychopolitical processes of consent" by the victimized, 15. Consent operates at the level of those in power, who view the domination of oppressed others as natural and therefore legitimate. In this case, dominant groups, laws, and regulations (such as tactics by police officers) *consent to the legitimate use of force (or coercion)*. This understanding of coercion and consent corrects a tendency in the masculinities literature, where applications of hegemonic masculinity have leaned too heavily on consent at the expense of coercion.

122. Summers, *Manliness and Its Discontents*, 14 (emphasis in the original).

123. Gramsci, *Selections from the Prison Notebooks*. As Gramsci writes, hegemony is not merely the "'spontaneous' consent" offered by the masses, but "the apparatus of state coercive power which 'legally' enforces discipline on those groups who do not 'consent' either actively or passively," 12.

124. See, for example, K. Nolan, *Police in the Hallways*; and Rios, *Punished*. Foucault makes a similar claim that one form of power (such as governmentality) does not replace another (such as sovereign power), but that they coexist. For further discussion, see Carlson, "States, Subjects and Sovereign Power."

125. J. Williams, "The Possibilities and Perils of Social Justice Feminism."

126. Watson and Smitherman, *Educating African American Males*, 46.

127. See, for example, a debate sponsored by the American Enterprise Institute, "Should Single-Sex Schooling Be Eliminated?" In it, Christina Hoff Sommers maintains that it is "misguided" to equate separation by gender with segregation by race. Sommers has been especially critical of the feminist response to single-sex education.

128. A.N.A. et al. v. Breckinridge Co. (KY) Board of Education, 833 F. Supp. 2d, 673, https://www.casemine.com/judgement/us/5914aefdadd7b0493474a61e# (June 13, 2011). For a discussion of this case, see C. Brown, "Legal Issues Surrounding Single-Sex Schools in the U.S." The court also dismissed the charges of the plaintiffs (who were represented by the ACLU) on the grounds that families freely chose to enroll their children in the classes and that the single-sex classes offered an "equivalent education" to the coed classes. And to date, there has been no finding

in federal courts that single-sex education violates the Equal Protection Clause or Title IX.

129. hooks, *Ain't I a Woman?* and *Feminist Theory;* Collins, *Black Feminist Thought.*

130. Collins, *Black Sexual Politics;* Grundy, " 'An Air of Expectancy.' " In a related argument, Juliet Williams asks in *Separation Solution?* whether the claim that all-boys schools will improve the self-esteem of boys "emanates from a superiority complex or, rather, from a foundation of mutual respect for others," 156.

131. J. Williams, "The Possibilities and Perils of Social Justice Feminism," 99.

132. Collins, *From Black Power to Hip Hop,* 106.

133. Gaines, *Uplifting the Race,* 13.

134. Crenshaw, "The Girls Obama Forgot."

135. J. Williams, *Separation Solution?,* 146

136. E. Morris, *Learning the Hard Way,* 15.

137. E. Morris, *Learning the Hard Way.*

138. Berg, *Qualitative Research Methods for the Social Sciences.*

139. For instance, in *Schooling for Resilience,* Fergus, Noguera, and Martin find that teaching "resilience" is the "implicit theory" that drives their sample of seven schools, but we hear less about their differences. In seeking not generalizability but societal significance, feminist scholars have found the extended case method to be a particularly useful methodology; see, for example, Kang, "Managed Hand."

140. Burawoy, "Extended Case Method," (1991), 281.

141. Burawoy, "Extended Case Method," (1998).

142. Taft, "Racing Age." At Perry and Northside, I found that school officials—perhaps because they held positions of authority—appeared eager to satiate my curiosity by "tell[ing] it like it is" in an all-male school, as one administrator put it. In a separate instance, I understood that a "big-man bias" might lead me to focus my attention on popular students, and so I asked teachers for help in recruiting students from a broad range of backgrounds for interviews. For more on adult biases in ethnographic research with children, see Barrie Thorne's book, *Gender Play.*

143. Tavory and Timmermans, "Two Cases of Ethnography," 247.

144. Burawoy, "Extended Case Method," (1998), 5. My engagement with critical Black masculinity studies was especially helpful in this pursuit. My use of the extended case method was therefore a methodological alternative to a reliance on *grounded theory* in resilience perspectives on male academies. In their comparison of grounded theory and the extended case method ("Two Cases of Ethnography"), Iddo Tavory and Stefan Timmermans note that the former builds "ethnonarratives" that take "theoretical clues" from "the lived experience of a people as bounded by various structures and processes," 244–45. The extended case method, on the other hand, at times contests the narratives of informants, who may be

unaware of the historical, macro forces at play. The extended case method therefore prioritizes theoretical narratives over ethnonarratives.

145. For more on feminist standpoint epistemology, see Collins, *Black Feminist Thought*; and Naples, "Towards Comparative Analyses of Women's Political Praxis." Accordingly, I felt it was important to view the school community members as *engaged theorists*. I sometimes shared conceptual language with people I met at the two schools. Staff members, for example, sometimes explicitly drew on their own engagement with critical educational theories from their graduate school training, some of which I draw on in *Black Boys Apart*. My task, then, was to adjudicate between theoretical narratives and the ethnonarratives of those I met; see Tavory and Timmermans, "Two Cases of Ethnography."

146. Du Bois, *Darkwater*, 11. Being modest and perhaps unaware of the impact *Philadelphia Negro* would have, Du Bois described how "[n]obody ever reads that fat volume."

147. Uprichard, "Children as 'Being and Becomings.'"

148. A. Young, *Minds of Marginalized Black Men*.

149. Bettie, *Women without Class*.

1. A Tale of Two (Neoliberal) Schools

1. Wilkerson, *The Warmth of Other Suns*.

2. For a discussion of the impact of middle-class white flight on city governments and school systems, see Cucchiara, *Marketing Schools, Marketing Cities*.

3. As Pauline Lipman argues in *New Political Economy of Urban Education*, the privatization of schools is part and parcel of destructive "urban renewal" efforts under neoliberalism. Lipman argues that community members have "the right to the city," or public access to basic, essential goods such as education, health care, and affordable housing. Lipman, however, is sympathetic to the Black community control tradition and recognizes a history featuring an odd mingling of corporate interests and Black mobilization. I agree with Lipman that "in the big picture, charter schools are another arena for capital accumulation facilitated by the cycle of racialized disinvestment, devaluation, and reinvestment in urban areas," 144. However, on the ground, at the level of "actually existing neoliberalism," we find "marginalized and oppressed people acting in conditions not of their own making," who would prefer to be dignified educational consumers rather than helpless victims of failing school systems, 145.

4. Moore, "Gentrification in Black Face?"

5. Camp, *Incarcerating the Crisis*, 139.

6. Pew Research Center, "Wealth Gaps Rise to Record Highs between Whites, Blacks, and Hispanics."

7. Kuehn, *Labor Market Performance of Young Black Men in the Great Recession*.

8. Duggan, *Twilight of Equality?* Or as Cedric Johnson writes in *Neoliberal Deluge,* neoliberalism "is essentially the ideological rejection of the planner state (both the Soviet socialist model and the Keynesian welfare state alternative) and the activist promotion of a new order of market rule," xx–xxi.

9. Camp, *Incarcerating the Crisis;* Wells, Slayton, and Scott, "Defining Democracy in the Neoliberal Age." This conservative backlash during the 1980s mirrors the retaliation against the gains by Blacks following the Civil War, as described in W. E. B. Du Bois's exquisite 1935 book, *Black Reconstruction in America.* In it, the scholar offers a searing critique of the interconnectedness of racism and capitalism in the United States. Du Bois describes how working-class solidarity was severed by an alliance between a white Southern aristocracy and Northern industrialists.

10. Silva, *Coming Up Short,* 110.

11. Spence, "Neoliberal Turn in Black Politics," 140 (emphasis in the original).

12. National Commission on Excellence in Education, *Nation at Risk,* 112.

13. Hursh, "Assessing No Child Left Behind and the Rise of Neoliberal Education Policies."

14. Berends, "Sociology and School Choice."

15. National Alliance for Public Charter Schools, "Charter School Data Dashboard."

16. Salomone, *Same, Different, Equal.*

17. Thus far, "choice" remains a trump card for single-sex advocates. In a telling example, Leonard Sax again changed the name of the National Association for Single-Sex Public Education—this time, to the National Association for Choice in Education.

18. By law, if a school district offers an all-boys school, then it must also offer a "substantially equal" all-girls or coed option for families. The requirement that sex-separate institutions be equal in every material respect was articulated by the Supreme Court in *United States v. Virginia* (1996). In it, the Court struck down all-male education at the Virginia Military Institute (VMI) under the Equal Protection Clause of the Fourteenth Amendment. The university had hastily created a women's program that fell far short of VMI's own offerings. Opponents had also claimed that a sister institution would inevitably be viewed as inferior to VMI. Notably, VMI attorneys had argued, in defending the institution's all-male student body, that men and women have different developmental characteristics. For a discussion, see Salomone, *Same, Different, Equal.*

19. U.S. Department of Education, *Questions and Answers on Title IX and Single-Sex Elementary and Secondary Classes and Extracurricular Activities.* On the topic of gender essentialism, the DOE stated that "evidence of general biological differences is not sufficient to allow teachers to select different teaching methods or strategies for boys and girls," 22.

20. Duncan's words are quoted in Lipman, *New Political Economy of Urban Education,* 161–62 (emphasis added). As Lipman writes, at the end of his life,

Dr. King warned that profit should not be viewed as more important than people.

21. Brooms, "'We Didn't Let the Neighborhood Win.'"

22. Lubienski, "Innovation in Education Markets," 398.

23. Lipman, *New Political Economy of Urban Education*.

24. Foucault, *Birth of Biopolitics*. As Foucault writes, eighteenth-century liberalism was defined "on the basis of free exchange between two partners who through this exchange establish the equivalence of two values," 119. Foucault recognized that the appeal of competition, in part, was that it is taken to be a "natural" product of "appetites, instincts, behavior," 120. However, he argued, competition is "artificially constructed," so that pure (or "equal") competition is simply a ruse that disguises the unequal foundations on which competition rests. As he writes, competition is "a formal game between inequalities; it is not a natural game between individuals and behaviors," 120.

25. Camp, *Incarcerating the Crisis*, 10. For a summary, see also Rios, *Punished*.

26. Perry and Morris, "Suspending Progress," 1068.

27. K. Nolan, *Police in the Hallways*.

28. Meiners, *Right to Be Hostile;* Rios, *Punished*.

29. Wells, Slayton, and Scott, "Defining Democracy in the Neoliberal Age," 340.

30. Pedroni, *Market Movements*, 141.

31. Pattillo, "Everyday Politics of School Choice in the Black Community." Mary Pattillo writes that "the word control focuses on parents' ability to control *where* their children will attend school, thereby controlling *what* they learn in school," 44–45 (emphasis added). I use "how" instead of "what" as a more expansive term that includes academic curricula as well as school discipline and how schools promote student belonging, the topics of chapters 3 and 4.

32. Stulberg, "African American School Choice and the Current Race Politics of Charter Schooling."

33. E. Morris, *Learning the Hard Way*.

34. The federal government deems as "working poor" those household adults who spend at least twenty-seven weeks of the year working or looking for work, but with incomes still at or below the poverty line. The distinction between the working poor and the poor highlights "two fractions of the Black proletariat," with the former "at the cusp of the formal wage economy and tenuously oriented toward the official structures of white-dominated society (the school, the law, marriage)"; see Wacquant, "Scrutinizing the Street," 1500. For my earlier analysis of Northside Academy, see Oeur, "Respectable Brotherhood."

35. This information was gathered from press releases following Excel's takeover of the school. Teachers likely also left Perry because the teachers' union had opposed the privatization model, citing potential infringement on teachers' rights with the involvement of a third-party firm.

36. Swidler, *Talk of Love*.

37. Although staff members told me about past attempts to bring the students at both schools together for social and extracurricular events, during my year of fieldwork I only observed a few instances of these. Interestingly, they were not even official activities sponsored by both schools. For one meeting of Perry's first-ever gay–straight alliance (GSA) student group, the members of Thompson's GSA were invited to attend. Perry's GSA members attended later meetings at Thompson High.

38. See Salomone, *Different, Same, Equal,* for a history of TYWLS. The school, which itself had drawn stiff opposition from the ACLU and NOW, has experienced academic success since its founding in 1996.

39. Datnow, Hubbard, and Woody, *Is Single Gender Schooling Viable in the Public Sector?*

40. Meyer and Scott, "The Organization of Societal Sectors."

41. See Weil, "Teaching Boys and Girls Separately." In "Six Degrees of Separation," Leonard Sax argues that "the ambient room temperature for learning differs for girls and boys," 194. The optimal temperature for girls is 75 degrees, and for boys, 69 degrees. In "Single-Sex Education and the Brain," Lise Eliot rejects Sax's claim and notes that body mass index is a greater determinant of thermal comfort than gender.

42. Gurian, *Fine Young Man,* 185.

43. Some school officials were also disappointed that the boys would not be able to use Thompson's superior gymnasium.

44. Weil, "Teaching Boys and Girls Separately."

45. Anderson, *Code of the Street.*

46. Perry and Morris, "Suspending Progress."

47. Giroux, *Youth in a Suspect Society,* 20.

48. Noguera, "Saving Black and Latino Boys."

49. Wacquant, *Punishing the Poor.*

50. A. Ferguson, *Bad Boys,* 231.

51. DiMaggio and Powell, "The Iron Cage Revisited"; Lubienski, "Innovation in Education Markets."

52. Lubienski, "Innovation in Education Markets," 243.

53. A. Ferguson, *Bad Boys.*

54. In *Building on Resilience,* Bonner concedes that "gifted" and "high achieving" students are a "consistent theme" across research on resilience in young Black men, 4. As an example, in his study of one Black male academy, "'We Didn't Let the Neighborhood Win,'" Brooms focuses only on "young men who successfully navigated the streets . . . and are thriving academically," 270. Yet he leaves unexamined how this exceptional group of students and their families may have possessed the buy-in important for success *prior* to attending the school, compared to young men who did *not* attend the school. In "'I Want to Be a Soccer Player or a Mathematician,'" Joseph Nelson provides an excellent analysis of

all-male schools as products of neoliberalism, yet his focus is also on a comparatively privileged group of young Black men: academically talented students at a private all-male school.

55. Watson and Smitherman, *Educating African American Males,* 41.

56. Du Bois, "The College-Bred Community," 51.

57. Dunbar's graduates included Edward Brook, the first Black senator after Reconstruction; and Edward Hastie, the first Black federal judge. For a history of Dunbar High, see Stewart, *First Class.*

58. Coulson, *Market Education,* back cover.

59. Stewart, *First Class,* 90.

60. Stewart, *First Class,* 91.

61. Stewart, *First Class,* 90–91.

62. Sowell, "Black Excellence," 18.

63. Gaines, *Uplifting the Race.*

64. Collins, *Black Sexual Politics.*

65. Griffin, "Black Feminists and Du Bois," 34. While critics have debated whether gender was ever a central analytic category in Du Bois's work, Black feminists such as Farah Jasmine Griffin acknowledge Du Bois as an ancestor to intersectional theorizing. For a longer discussion of the place of gender in Du Boisian work, see also Gillman and Weinbaum, *Next to the Color Line;* and Rabaka, *Against Epistemic Apartheid.*

66. Du Bois, "Training of Negroes for Social Power," 67.

67. R. Ferguson, "'W. E. B. Du Bois.'"

68. Ross, *Manning the Race.*

69. Summers, *Manliness and Its Discontents,* 43.

70. Grundy, "'An Air of Expectancy,'" 46.

71. "Race men" is a term from St. Clair Drake and Horace Cayton's classic text, *Black Metropolis.* In my book, I use this term to refer to those who are members of the Talented Tenth in Du Bois's original formulation, with its distinct elitist overtones. While this is the term that is most often associated with Drake and Cayton's text, the authors, in fact, identify three ideal types of Black male leaders. *Race leaders* are those men who aggressively fight for their race and are sincerely dedicated to the cause but may also denounce the moral inferiority of their less privileged brethren. The most admired leaders, however, are *race heroes,* who fight unconditionally against white racism. Interestingly, in this typology Drake and Cayton assign *race men* a slightly negative connotation, writing that suspicious intentions may underlie the work of these leaders (who, for example, tend to be businessmen and may pursue the work for their own personal gain).

72. Grundy, "'An Air of Expectancy.'"

73. J. James, *Transcending the Talented Tenth.*

74. J. James, *Transcending the Talented Tenth.*

75. J. James, *Transcending the Talented Tenth,* 18.

76. A. Cooper, "The Status of Women in America."

77. Hallett, "The Myth Incarnate," 53.

78. Goodkind et al., "Providing New Opportunities or Reinforcing Old Stereotypes?," 1174.

79. Garcia and Stigler, "Closed," 214. Similarly, in "Everyday Politics of School Choice in the Black Community," Mary Pattillo writes that "Black pro-school-choice advocacy is not rooted in free market ideology of privatization, deregulation, and competition, and thus these terms are not common tropes in this context," 44. My findings, however, suggest that competition and empowerment can exist as odd bedfellows.

80. Wacquant, "Scrutinizing the Street," 1500. Based on this insight, I classified the parents and guardians I interviewed into working poor and poor. The Morgan School District described students who qualify for free or reduced-price lunch as coming from "economically disadvantaged families," or those living at or below the federal poverty line. From my interviews with parents and guardians, I was able to roughly determine how many of my respondents were working poor. I suspect there were more working poor and working-class families at Northside than at Perry High. Five of the nine parents (56 percent) I interviewed at Perry High held low-wage jobs at the time I interviewed them; I am classifying them as working poor. Three of the four remaining parents who had each been unemployed for at least nine months told me that they were receiving government assistance. I am unsure of the class position of the last parent. At Northside, I interviewed thirteen parents/guardians (two additional respondents were grandparents and were retired). Of the thirteen, eight (62 percent) were employed in low-wage jobs, and I am classifying them as working poor. Of the remaining five, three parents self-identified as working-class (one of these three was the only parent I interviewed at Northside Academy who had earned a college degree; I also interviewed only one mother at Perry who had earned a college degree). The last two had each been unemployed for over six months. Therefore, while the samples are small, I had a slightly higher percentage of working poor among the families I interviewed at Northside, as well as the only working-class families.

81. "Essentially damaged" is from Michael Dumas's definition of neoliberal governmentality in "My Brother as 'Problem,'" 95.

2. Contradictory Discourses

1. The film is a dramatized account of Joe Clark, a principal (played by Morgan Freeman) who is brought in to turn around Eastside, a high school in New Jersey. While the film was mostly well received, it led to some controversy for its exaggerated portrayal of a renegade principal who stopped at nothing to achieve success. At the start of the film, we learn that the school's fate hangs in the balance: without a dramatic change (in test scores, of course) the state will take over

the school. Clark's tactics of intimidation and humiliation work, but viewers are left to wonder if it was worth it. In a review of the film, the movie critic Roger Ebert writes, "One of the sneaky, uneasy feelings I got while watching 'Lean on Me' is that the movie makes a subtle appeal to those who are afraid of unruly, loud, violent black teenagers. As Clark takes a baseball bat and begins to whip them into shape (at one point even physically fighting a student), the audience is cheered, not because education is being served, but because Clark is a combination of Dirty Harry and Billy Jack, enforcing the law on his own terms." (See the review at http://www.rogerebert.com/reviews/lean-on-me-1989.) To put it differently, the film satiates a mainstream, white audience's desire to control the bodies of Black and Brown children (and to be entertained by the institutional control of Black and Brown children) through aggressive disciplinary tactics. Complicating the story, of course, is that the disciplinarian is a Black man who at the end of the film has won over many people, and the film is not shy about depicting him as a savior of sorts. This reinforces the "father figure" discourse that youth of color (and especially young men) require a stern authority figure, under the assumption that these youth lack a father at home. (At the end of the film, Clark is thrown in jail for chaining the doors to the school. Students and staff demand his release, which marks his own liberation just as the school is metaphorically reborn as a "good" school with the news that enough students have passed a required exam.) In many respects, the film, which was released just as the country was being introduced to the language of charters and experimentation, was a window into a sea change in public education over the next two decades.

2. Fergus, Noguera, and Martin, *Schooling for Resilience,* 18. While scholars have tended to stress either cultural or structural explanations for disadvantage, characterizing them as opposing explanations is a tired debate. As Marcus Hunter and Zandria Robinson write in "The Sociology of Black Urban America," researchers have "worked to reconcile the dialectical interplay of structure and culture and generally see both forces as interacting to produce outcomes," 385. Indeed, William Julius Wilson, whom Fergus and Noguera cite as a structuralist researcher, writes that structural disadvantage and cultural adaptations are inextricably linked, as groups over time acquire behaviors and values that are outgrowths of extreme structural marginality, or "dislocation." See Wilson, "Studying Inner-City Dislocations" and "Why Both Social Structure and Culture Matter in a Holistic Analysis of Inner-City Poverty."

3. Fergus, Noguera, and Martin, *Schooling for Resilience,* 15.

4. Fergus, Noguera, and Martin, *Schooling for Resilience,* 16. The authors cite John Ogbu (see "Variability in Minority School Performance") as a leading culturalist thinker.

5. These ideas were made popular in the 1960s through the work of Oscar Lewis and the controversial Moynihan Report. While the Moynihan Report was for a long time denigrated in academic circles, some researchers believe that history

will prove kind to the report. For instance, in *Cultural Matrix,* Orlando Patterson and Ethan Fosse argue that Moynihan was attentive to structural causes of Black disadvantage.

6. As I explain in the introduction, my book's particular structural orientation is in its adoption of hegemonic masculinity and other tools from the critical study of men and masculinities. I also draw inspiration from a feminist post-structural approach that addresses limitations in structural approaches and also helps us move beyond a tired debate between cultural and structural explanations of disadvantage. (For an analysis of the dissonance between these structural and post-structural approaches, see Beasley, "Problematizing Contemporary Men/Masculinities Theorizing.") Moreover, by retaining the important insight that Black youth at times contest discourses and are therefore agentic and creative persons, my analysis makes space for how youth draw on heterogeneous cultural repertoires to make sense of their worlds and to act.

7. While the design of the seven schools was mostly similar, the authors' more interesting finding is how the schools differed in their implementation of strategies and in their success rates. Some schools were forced to close due to low student achievement. However, since the authors do not address the differences among incoming cohorts across the schools, it is not clear the degree to which student success was based on student selection effects or on the actual work of the schools themselves. Their own descriptions of the schools suggest important selection effects such as buy-in and perhaps even the academic preparedness of the incoming students.

8. See Harding, *Living the Drama,* for a critique of social isolation theory.

9. Wacquant, "Scrutinizing the Street."

10. Wacquant, "Scrutinizing the Street," 1489.

11. Mijs, Bakhtiari, and Lamont, "Neoliberalism and Symbolic Boundaries in Europe," 2.

12. See Harding, *Living the Drama;* Hunter and Robinson, "The Sociology of Urban Black America"; Patterson and Fosse, *Cultural Matrix.* While this research deploys varied theoretical tools, the authors agree that heterogeneity has long been a central feature of Black communities. Within the study of education, a sociocultural approach similarly conceptualizes culture as a dynamic construct and in particular demonstrates how youth deploy cultural artifacts in shaping their racial identities. See, for example, Nasir and Hand, "Exploring Sociocultural Perspectives on Race, Culture, and Learning." This approach resonates with sociological research that views culture as a "tool kit"; see Swidler, "Culture in Action."

13. Harding, "Cultural Context, Sexual Behavior, and Romantic Relationships in Disadvantaged Neighborhoods." A heterogeneous approach helps identify a diversity of experiences and outcomes within urban communities and schools.

14. As Fergus and colleagues write in *Schooling for Resilience,* "most of the boys at the seven schools embraced fairly traditional ideas of manhood," 157.

15. Carter, *Keepin' It Real,* 6. Prudence Carter's research complicates the "acting white" and "oppositional culture" theses associated with the work of John Ogbu.

16. Fergus, Noguera, and Martin, *Schooling for Resilience.*

17. Anderson, *Code of the Street.*

18. A. Ferguson, *Bad Boys;* Carter, *Keepin' It Real.* See also Gunn, "Inner-City 'Schoolboy' Life."

19. McRobbie, "Notes on the Perfect."

20. A. Ferguson, *Bad Boys,* 171.

21. Bettie, *Women without Class.*

22. Pattillo, Delale-O'Connor, and Butts, "High-Stakes Choosing."

23. Phoenix, "Neoliberalism and Masculinity."

24. Choo and Ferree, "Practicing Intersectionality in Sociological Research," 134.

25. Woody, "Homophobia and Heterosexism in Public School Reform."

26. West and Zimmerman, "Doing Gender."

27. Majors and Billson, *Cool Pose.*

28. I followed up with Mr. Green after the assembly. He had recently completed his doctoral training and a separate program to prepare him to be a school leader. He was deliberate about using existing research on learning ("proven methods" was the phrase I heard again and again) in the school and carefully (obsessively, as some staff members saw it) measured student progress. While Mr. Green was correct that existing research (the "theory" in his statement about "theory into practice") generally hypothesized that boys and girls distract one another in school, it was the school's thinking on the "practice" side that I found especially interesting. Here, the school took the discourse of distractions and used it strategically, saying that it did not square with the image of respectable young Black men.

29. Harding, *Living the Drama.*

30. N. Jones, *Between Good and Ghetto.*

31. Collins, *Black Sexual Politics.*

32. For a thorough discussion of Black sexuality and single-sex education, see V. Williams, "Reform or Retrenchment."

33. Bettie, *Women without Class,* 46.

34. U.S. Department of Health and Human Services, "Trends in Teen Pregnancy and Childbearing." In 2014, there were 34.9 births per 1,000 adolescent Black girls aged fifteen to nineteen in the United States, compared to 17.3 births per 1,000 adolescent white girls.

35. Chapter 5 says more about how the young men (some of whom were already fathers) integrated fatherhood into their long-term visions of manhood.

36. Griffin, "Black Feminists and Du Bois."

37. Communities in the South resisted the Supreme Court's *Brown v. Board of Education* ruling by avoiding schooling arrangements that would mix Black boys with their white daughters.

38. Foucault, *Discipline and Punish*. See also A. Ferguson, *Bad Boys*. While Tre was speaking seriously in this instance, the boys also used the language of No Child Left Behind mockingly. For instance, I once heard a Perry High student poke fun at another high school for being full of students whose fighting ability was "below basic." In the language of school reform, "below basic" refers to the bottom quartile of academic performance.

39. N. Jones, *Between Good and Ghetto*.

40. E. Morris, *Learning the Hard Way*.

41. West and Zimmerman, "Doing Gender."

42. Collins, *Black Sexual Politics*, 204.

43. In "Practicing Intersectionality in Sociological Research," Hae Yeon Choo and Myra Marx Ferree detail how "process-centered" approaches to intersectionality recognize that while actors are "recruited to" discourses, they are also able to challenge their subject positions and to assert alternative ones.

44. Froyum, "'At Least I'm Not Gay.'" Fergus, Noguera, and Martin, in *Schooling for Resilience,* also found that young men feared that they would be viewed as being gay for attending an all-male school.

45. Sabo, Kupers, and London, "Gender and the Politics of Punishment."

46. Messerschmidt, "Masculinities, Crime and Prison."

47. A later episode reprised this topic. For a program intended to "scare" them into avoiding incarceration, a group of boys visited a prison and learned about the sexual abuse they could endure as prisoners.

48. Miller, "Incarcerated Masculinities."

49. Beck et al., *Sexual Victimization in Juvenile Facilities Reported by Youth, 2012.*

50. A. Ferguson, *Bad Boys*. Adultification is the process of treating and punishing children as if they were adults and assuming that these children have genuine sinister intentions.

51. Stoudt, "'You're Either In or You're Out.'"

52. Froyum, "'At Least I'm Not Gay,'" 619.

53. Pascoe, *Dude, You're a Fag*.

54. Pascoe, *Dude, You're a Fag*.

55. Majors and Billson, *Cool Pose*, 63.

56. Scheff, "Shame and Conformity."

57. A. Ferguson, *Bad Boys,* 216. These interactions created a harmful environment for non-straight-identifying young men. Adults rarely reprimanded the boys for using homophobic language.

58. I understand that the boys may have been performing masculinity in front of their friends in these joint interviews, but I found these were common sentiments throughout the school.

59. Pascoe, *Dude, You're a Fag.*

60. Froyum, "'At Least I'm Not Gay.'"

61. Skeggs, *Formations of Class and Gender.*

62. Bettie, *Women without Class,* xxxiii.

3. Teaching Black Boys

1. Translation: "Welcome, students." "Hello, teacher."

2. My field notes and interviews are full of times when students would convey to me how difficult Latin was. Some stories were funny, if unintentionally. For example, Burton told me, "I didn't know much about Latin, but this boy around my way used to speak pig latin," he said. "It sounded weird. And I tried it and it was hard. Latin is like pig latin, but weirder and harder." I caught up with Burton seven months later after he had nearly a full academic year of Latin under his belt. Latin was still hard. "But it's *taking me places,*" he said confidently.

3. For an excellent overview of the hidden curriculum with a neo-Marxist emphasis, see Giroux and Penna, "Social Education in the Classroom."

4. Summers, *Manliness and Its Discontents,* 1.

5. Alridge, "Conceptualizing a Du Boisian Philosophy of Education."

6. Watson and Smitherman, *Educating African American Males,* 55. Smitherman recalls "being on a natural high" when she taught Black authors to a group of Black children; the authors included Du Bois: her "man," as she describes him.

7. Leake and Leake, "Islands of Hope," 26.

8. Cobb, "Out of Africa."

9. In *Schooling for Resilience,* Fergus and colleagues also found that aiming for cultural relevance is a major objective of male academies. There are two important frameworks at play: cultural responsiveness and cultural relevance. While there are differences, I categorize them both as cultural relevance (because the term is the more common of the two) and stress the common themes of pedagogy and content. On culturally relevant pedagogy, see Ladson-Billings, "Toward a Theory of Culturally Relevant Pedagogy"; on cultural responsiveness, see Gay, "Preparing for Culturally Responsive Teaching." While I find Gloria Ladson-Billings's framework to be more comprehensive (and more relevant, as it draws inspiration from Black feminism, especially the work of Patricia Hill Collins in *Black Feminist Thought*), Geneva Gay provides a succinct and helpful definition: "using cultural characteristics, experiences, and perspectives of ethnically diverse students as conduits for teaching them more effectively," 106.

10. Du Bois, "Does the Negro Need Separate Schools?," 335.

11. Du Bois, "Does the Negro Need Separate Schools?," 333.

12. According to Gloria Ladson-Billings in "Toward a Theory of Culturally Relevant Pedagogy," a culturally relevant pedagogy has three interrelated propositions. The first is a *conception of self and others.* Here, teachers immerse themselves in the

communities of their students and view their students not as problems, but as children with great potential for success. The second proposition centers on *social relations*. Teachers provide ample opportunities for students to work collaboratively and to act as teachers themselves. This discourages competition by creating an environment where all students feel they are valued members of a learning community. The final proposition is *conceptions of knowledge*. This stresses that educators should ground the content and curriculum in the racial and cultural background of the students.

13. For two main reasons, staff members at both schools strongly preferred teaching boys to girls. First, boys were in dire need of help. Some staff members acknowledged the unique hardships faced by Black girls, but the consensus was that boys were doing worse. (See chapter 2, as well as J. Williams, *Separation Solution?*, for a discussion.) Second, teachers preferred boys to girls because they felt girls were more "catty": they held grudges, had more "attitude," and were "louder." For a discussion of how school teachers interact with Black girls in schools, and the gender performativity of these young women, see Lei, "(Un)Necessary Toughness?"

14. D. Lewis, *W. E. B. Du Bois*. In *Darkwater*, Du Bois admits that he "did not know anything of Latin and Greek" when he was offered the job at Wilberforce, 10; but it is likely he encountered these languages growing up in Great Barrington, Massachusetts.

15. Warren, "The Utility of Empathy for White Female Teachers' Culturally Responsive Interactions with Black Male Students."

16. Cookson and Persell, *Preparing for Power*.

17. Holliday, "The Benefits of Latin?"

18. Bourdieu and Passeron, *Reproduction in Education, Culture, and Society;* Carter, *Keepin' It Real*.

19. Cambridge Coaching, "College Admissions." William Fitzsimmons, director of undergraduate admissions at Harvard University, commented, "Because so few students these days master Latin, it can help an applicant. . . . We certainly do take notice." Andrea Thomas of Hamilton College said, "I was particularly impressed by a student with average test scores and grades who had taken Latin throughout middle and high school. We ended up offering the student admission, and I think it is fair to say that it was his commitment to Latin that tipped the scales."

20. Cookson and Persell, *Preparing for Power*, 74.

21. Cookson and Persell, *Preparing for Power*, 73.

22. I asked Jack about the comment later. He felt the culture of testing treated them like robots. More so than his classmates, Jack described the impersonal nature of testing, an observation shared by many critics of school privatization. See, for example, Ravitch, *Reign of Error*.

23. In "The Myth Incarnate," Tim Hallett also describes how new school administrators cause turmoil when they try to implement strict accountability regimes.

24. Desroche, *Sociology of Hope*.

25. Stulberg, *Race, Schools, and Hope*.

26. Spencer, "Spiritual Politics," 107.

27. Duncan-Andrade, "Note to Educators."

28. This conceptualization of hope is inspired by work in the sociology of culture, which documents the moral force behind persistent optimism. As Margaret Frye writes in "Bright Futures in Malawi's New Dawn," disadvantaged youth are not necessarily "rational" actors who accept likely future outcomes and in turn level their educational expectations. Rather, high aspirations both represent a claim to being virtuous and expand a belief in one's self-efficacy. In these ways, it is possible to view hope as a resource that helps actors clarify problems and overcome those problems, which accords with an understanding of culture as a frame or a tool kit. For a longer exposition of this view of culture, see Harding, *Living the Drama*; and Swidler, "Culture in Action."

29. Du Bois, "The College-Bred Community." A college-bred community linked closely to Du Bois's early thinking on racial uplift and the Talented Tenth. Du Bois tasked Black universities in the South with grooming a distinguished class of Blacks to lead the masses. As he wrote, "The *community* must be able to take hold of its individuals and give them such a social heritage, such present social teachings and such compelling social customs as will force them along the lines of progress, and not into the great forests of death," 57 (emphasis in the original).

30. Berends, "Sociology and School Choice."

31. Mische, "Projects and Possibilities." Ann Mische advocates for greater attention to how "imagined futures" shape action. This chapter is most inspired by her notion of how *volition*—a sense of movement with respect to the future—shapes human behavior. Volition focuses attention on how Northside Academy's race to college had a *pace*: it was not a sprint, but a test of endurance.

32. Hall and Lamont, *Social Resilience in the Neoliberal Era*.

33. Grundy, "'An Air of Expectancy,'" 47.

34. Cookson and Persell, *Preparing for Power*, 73–74.

35. I had experience teaching with a similar population of students (in a middle school), and Mr. Madsen often asked me for my honest, critical feedback on his teaching. Given that he graciously invited me into his classroom and was supportive of my research, I was happy to speak with him about his teaching.

36. Mattingly, *Paradox of Hope*, 3.

37. Desroche, *Sociology of Hope*, 21.

38. Mische, "Projects and Possibilities," 701.

39. Lamont and Molnár, "The Study of Boundaries in the Social Sciences." The authors define *symbolic boundaries* as conceptual or moral distinctions, and *social boundaries* as the "objectified forms of social differences" that result in unequal access to resources, 168.

40. Lubienski, "Innovation in Education Markets."

41. However, elite Black colleges once had strict dress codes. These served a dual purpose, both of which resonate in how Northside understood its own uniform. Reflecting on the dress code at Fisk University in the early 1900s, Martin Summers, in *Manliness and Its Discontents*, writes, "Beyond seeking to level the playing field among middle- and working-class students, the strictures placed on fashion at Fisk were influenced by the connection educators perceived between dress and disposition. Fisk officials took pride in the fact that the institutions' [*sic*] dress code was both a reflection, and a facilitator, of its students' good character," 257.

42. Cookson and Persell, *Preparing for Power*, 29.

43. Given that I dressed professionally, the young men often asked me about the brands I wore and where I shopped. In the city of Morgan, there has been a marked shift away from Black urban brands (such as FUBU and Rocawear) to preppy mainstream brands such as Ralph Lauren and Tommy Hilfiger. For an excellent analysis of consumption in poor Black neighborhoods, see Nightingale, *On the Edge*. For a discussion of urban fashion, race, and masculinity, see Majors and Billson, *Cool Pose*.

44. In "'I Don't Like to Dream about Getting Paid,'" Christopher Holmes Smith calls hip-hop moguls "captains of industry" who first reached ubiquitous acclaim during the economic expansion at the end of the twentieth century. Smith offers a nuanced portrait of how placing moguls into categories of celebrity and commodity culture disguises their meaningful achievements, yet he also warns that the hip-hop elite have an "ethical responsibility" to poorer Blacks. Smith is hopeful that these moguls can help heal rather than exacerbate divisions within the Black community: "The ascension of the hip-hop mogul has gone a long way toward opening up space in working-class and poor minority communities to view mainstream corporate enterprise with more than absolute suspicion and disdain. These openings may enable new progressive coalitions to proceed with building their proposed agendas without being hamstrung by the class-based friction that has typically plagued the hip-hop generation from within," 90–91.

45. Higginbotham, *Righteous Discontent*, 187.

46. A. Ferguson, *Bad Boys*, 216.

47. A. Ferguson, *Bad Boys*, 108.

48. Gaines, *Uplifting the Race*, 2.

49. More than any scholar of his generation, Du Bois convincingly explained the disadvantage of Blacks as a function of historical and structural oppression, yet his early writings still contain morally laden language about the cultural deficiencies within the Black community. In *Philadelphia Negro*, for example, he characterizes the submerged tenth as full of "baffling and sinister phenomena: shrewd laziness, shameless lewdness, cunning crime," 311–12.

50. There was wide consensus that Mr. Reagan, who was white, deserved to be promoted to an administrator position at Perry. He had been passed over, however, because of the school's desire for an entirely Black male leadership, a commitment

that the district shared. In chapter 4, I discuss the "race men" who comprised this Black male leadership and their contentious relationship with white women in the building.

51. See Fergus, Noguera, and Martin, *Schooling for Resilience*, for a discussion of how low schooling expectations harm young men of color. In their study of seven male academies, these authors develop a "theory of change" to make explicit the assumptions schools make about boys of color. The schools, the authors found, located problems in two categories: school- and community-based (e.g., lack of cultural relevancy) and social-emotional (e.g., lack of self-esteem). But less clear are the *sources* of those assumptions. Did the staff members learn these in professional development? From the research they encountered in graduate courses they took to earn a certification to teach? From the media, movies, and television? In my conversations with the adults at Northside and Perry, I found that there were various sources for these assumptions. The first was research teachers encountered in their graduate classes and professional development. Teachers were particularly inspired by older and popular books on racism, poverty, and education (e.g., *Other People's Children* by Lisa Delpit, *Savage Inequalities* by Jonathan Kozol, *Code of the Street* by Elijah Anderson, and *The Dreamkeepers* by Gloria Ladson-Billings). Teach For America teachers pulled out binders of materials covering the importance of cultural relevance. Others did not refer to scholarship but based their explanations on experience working with children and explained how they recalibrated their thoughts on Black male disadvantage once they had a chance to work closely with these young men. Black men told me they drew on their own personal experiences to make sense of why their own students were struggling.

52. Ladson-Billings, "Toward a Theory of Culturally Relevant Pedagogy."

53. See also Fergus, Noguera, and Martin, *Schooling for Resilience*, for a comprehensive discussion of culturally relevant instruction.

54. Rosenbaum, *Beyond College for All.*

55. Rosenbaum, *Beyond College for All.*

56. Title I is the first section of the landmark Elementary and Secondary Education Act of 1965. It provides financial assistance for schools with student populations that are at least 40 percent low-income. Ms. Valenzuela was one of two school assistants—the other being Mr. Jeffries, profiled in chapter 4—who epitomized the organic intellectual. They both grew up in the neighborhood, suffered personal hardships, and were recovering from drug addictions. Doing far more than was required in their job descriptions, Ms. Valenzuela and Mr. Jeffries became strong advocates for their young men, helping articulate for them and those in the community what Gramsci, in *Selections from the Prison Notebooks*, calls "good sense," the seeds of social transformation and counter-hegemonic struggle.

57. Gramsci, *Selections from the Prison Notebooks.*

58. High-stakes, standardized testing has come under heavy fire by critics. For a critique, see Carter and Welner, *Closing the Opportunity Gap.* As the authors

recommend, "Instead of continuous batteries of high-stakes tests, the focus should be on low-stakes, informative testing that enables teachers to understand how well their students are learning. The focus should be on the portfolio of work that expects students to use a range of critical thinking skills," 225.

59. Jerrim, "The Unrealistic Educational Expectations of High School Pupils."

60. "Controlling image" is a term used by Collins in *Black Feminist Thought* to refer to historically specific, socially constructed, and externally created images used to reinforce the subordination of Black women.

61. Duggan, *Twilight of Equality?*, 16 (emphasis in the original).

62. In *Philadelphia Negro,* Du Bois already suspected the limitations of uplift ideology even as he continued to lobby for strong Black leadership and especially vibrant Black-controlled institutions such as schools. As Kevin Gaines writes in *Uplifting the Race,* even in Du Bois's early work, the scholar was attuned to the oppressive conditions that befell Blacks under racial capitalism. These observations on the interlocking nature of racial and social class oppression would coalesce years later in his magnum opus, *Black Reconstruction.*

63. Rosenbaum, "Complexities of College for All," 114.

64. The new Academic Resource Center did provide tutoring assistance and help with college applications, but Larry thought twelfth graders could take a class devoted to applying to college.

65. Du Bois, "College-Bred Community," 51.

66. Marable, *Black Leadership,* 27.

67. Du Bois, "Does the Negro Need Separate Schools?," 335.

68. J. Nolan, "Kaine to Introduce Legislation on High School Career and Technical Education."

69. "Kaine Leads Bipartisan Effort." Todd Young, a Republican Senator from Indiana and member of the CTE caucus, has said, "Strong CTE programs are a critical part of equipping students with the skills they need in tomorrow's workforce. With almost half of employers nationwide experiencing a lack of skilled workers, this legislation is a positive step forward in closing the skills gap and addressing the needs of our local communities."

70. M. James, "Never Quit," 186.

71. For an overview, see Duckworth, *Grit.*

72. Saltman, "Austerity School," 52.

73. Weber, "Class, Status, Party," 117.

74. Northside at first struggled with retention. About 50 percent of the students in the inaugural cohort transferred to another school. Beginning with the second cohort, the attrition rate dropped precipitously; officials believed this was because Northside was more successful in attracting students who had bought into the school's academic culture. By 2013 (the graduation year for the students who were ninth graders when I started my research), the school's attrition rate had been cut in half. Northside's college matriculation rate was considerably higher than the

city average. Fewer than 30 percent of eligible young Black men across Morgan enrolled in college after high school, and less than 5 percent go on to earn a bachelor's degree.

4. Black Male Belonging

1. Boastin' and bussin' were ubiquitous, and it was hard to avoid being the target of bussin' after spending time with the students. Most of this was innocuous. The older boys especially teased me about women and not "gettin' girls," and I normally just smiled and did not respond. The boys also sometimes teased me about my clothes (a wrinkled shirt, for example), and here I felt more comfortable with modestly boastin' about what I was wearing.

2. Marable, *Black Leadership*. As Manning Marable writes, Du Bois was at times a fierce critic of the Black church, but he still saw in it a "radical commitment to serve humanity" that was less present in white Christianity, 73.

3. Du Bois, *Philadelphia Negro,* 203.

4. Lincoln and Mamiya, *Black Church in the African American Experience.*

5. Du Bois, *Souls of Black Folk.* In *Philadelphia Negro,* however, Du Bois questioned the moral compass of the Black church leadership, which he claimed had been sullied by business interests. This was troubling above all because it harmed the church's ability to transmit positive values to the patriarchal family, which Du Bois saw as the ultimate measure of Black respectability. See Gaines, *Uplifting the Race,* for an analysis of Du Bois's thoughts on the Black church within the context of uplift ideology.

6. Pattillo-McCoy, "Church Culture as a Strategy of Action in the Black Community."

7. Lincoln and Mamiya, *Black Church in the African American Experience.*

8. Mr. Bradley estimated that less than 10 percent of the male mentors that day were the students' biological fathers.

9. Pugh, *Longing and Belonging,* 7.

10. Stack, *All Our Kin.*

11. Gaines, *Uplifting the Race,* 169.

12. O. Lewis, *Children of Sánchez.*

13. Collins, *Black Sexual Politics.* For a comprehensive discussion of the racist and sexist features of the Moynihan Report, see J. Williams, *Separation Solution?*

14. Anderson, *Code of the Street.*

15. Officer Sherman implied that greater parental involvement would benefit the young men. In *Broken Compass,* however, Keith Robinson and Angel L. Harris find weak evidence for the claim that parental involvement improves academic achievement.

16. Urban ethnographers have debated the ethics of close relationships between researchers and informants they meet in the field, or "insiders." I kept in touch with

Mr. Jeffries after my research ended and, given how much of an influence he was on the project, shared portions of written drafts with him. A well-known insider in urban ethnography is Doc from Harrison Whyte's classic book *Street Corner Society*. For a discussion of the ethical implications behind Whyte's relationship with Doc, see Whyte, "Revisiting 'Street Corner Society.' "

17. Noddings, *Caring*; Valenzuela, *Subtractive Schooling*.

18. Collins, *Black Feminist Thought*.

19. L. Bass, "When Care Trumps Justice."

20. For example, see Holland, "Positive Role Models for Primary-Grade Black Inner-City Males." As Spencer Holland writes, "The single-parent, female-headed households in this nation's urban communities deny the young Black male child a major vehicle necessary in the socialization process of all boys, an adult male," 40. Later in the article, Holland writes that boys are the "*major* victims" of poor urban schooling. It is precisely this assertion of young Black men as more disadvantaged than their female peers (and by extension, more deserving of special educational programs) that feminists have contested. For a discussion, see J. Williams, *Separation Solution?*

21. Ingersoll, Merrill, and Stuckey, "Seven Trends."

22. Collins, *Black Sexual Politics*. As Patricia Hill Collins writes, a related, troublesome "weak men, strong women" thesis valorizes Black women's strength (as caregivers for their families and fictive kin) but leaves these women vulnerable to exploitation. Collins suggests that we foreground and critique a capitalist and racist gender ideology that pits Black men and women against one another. This insight is helpful for understanding the impulse to separate Black boys and girls in schools.

23. Tronto, *Caring Democracy*.

24. Gaines, *Uplifting the Race*, 157.

25. Drake and Cayton, *Black Metropolis*, 393.

26. Drake and Cayton, *Black Metropolis*. In "The Talented Tenth," a lecture given at the end of his life, Du Bois also recognized how the Talented Tenth could be selfish men. I revisit this issue in the Conclusion.

27. Collins, *Black Feminist Thought*.

28. Tronto, *Caring Democracy*.

29. The phrase "school-to-prison pipeline" (and its variants, such as "cradle-to-prison pipeline") was well known at the two schools, but opinions about it varied widely. In his capacity as prison minister, Mr. Youseff viewed himself as a mentor for incarcerated men.

30. hooks, *We Real Cool*.

31. Reese was a popular class clown. His joking in this example joined a long African American tradition of using humor to discuss "deeper truths with impunity," as Richard Majors and Janet Billson write in *Cool Pose*, 63. The meaning behind Reese's "formal" voice becomes legible when we interpret his joke as a matter of respectability politics. It intentionally rejected the language and tone of the

streets, and Reese came across as polite and obedient. I noticed the boys sometimes used this mocking tone when they criticized something regarding whiteness. The students also sometimes turned the formal voice on me, meaning they were critical of my own identity as a researcher. For example, one time Reese, whom I did not get to know well, said aloud when I entered his classroom, "The researcher has arrived to continue his report on Black males. Are there any Black males here he can report on?" The other boys laughed. Embarrassed, I took a seat immediately and wondered how I should respond. I decided to try and follow up with Reese to discuss the ethics around my research. He never seemed interested in chatting with me, which I understood and accepted. At other times, students adopted a "surfer voice" when they learned I had come from California, and said phrases like "awesome, dude!" and "cool, dude!" For more on "clownin'" and "riffin'" (or as I call it, bussin' and boastin'), see E. Morris, *Learning the Hard Way.*

32. Harding, *Living the Drama,* 56.

33. Harding, *Living the Drama.*

34. Terry et al., "Does the 'Negro' *Still* Need Separate Schools?"

35. "Transcript: Barack Obama's Speech on Race."

36. Mr. Jeffries asked me to be a mentor. At first I was not sure if it was right for me to take responsibility for mentoring a young person in the middle of research, particularly because I would eventually return to Berkeley after my fieldwork was completed. I agreed in the end because I knew it meant a lot to Mr. Jeffries and because it would allow me to become fully immersed in the program. My mentee knew about my research, and we agreed I would not interview him for the book nor share anything here about our time together. I had gladly accepted requests to help around the school: to help with after-school tutoring, to drive students to college fairs, and to lead a résumé-building workshop. By the end of the year, I was actively seeking ways to help out in the school. I admired a culture there of adults extending a hand whenever they could, beyond their classrooms, and so I was happy to make an effort to do the same. I volunteered far less at Northside. This was because fewer people asked that of me, but also because the students there simply had more resources and more adults available to help them. I also suspected the school saw me more as strictly a researcher, which may have helped the school with its self-conscious branding and desire for legitimacy.

37. The quote is from Jon Zaff, a researcher at Tufts University, who was quoted in Willens's article, "Ninth Grade." The article cites research from McCallumore and Sparapani, "The Importance of the Ninth Grade on High School Graduation Rates and Student Success in High School."

38. In some respects, the mentoring program nurtured what Iesha Jackson, Yolanda Sealey-Ruiz, and Wanda Watson have called "reciprocal love"; see their article of the same name. In their observations of a mentoring program for Black and Latino youth, the researchers found that a reciprocal love is nourished whenever personal well-being grows healthier through the strength of a community's well-being.

39. In "Suspending Progress," however, Brea Perry and Edward Morris found that excessive levels of punishment may dampen academic achievement *for all children* because students come to question the moral authority of their schools. For a discussion of morality and school punishment, see Durkheim, *Moral Education*.

40. K. Nolan, *Police in the Hallways*, 102.

41. In "When Care Trumps Justice," Lisa Bass describes how Black female administrators sometimes refused to follow an institutional "ethic of justice" and practiced a personal "ethic of care" that was fairer to their students.

42. I have written in greater detail about Perry High's GSA in my book chapter, "It's Not How Regular Boys Are Supposed to Act." Due to a scheduling conflict, I was unable to spend much time observing the GSA at Northside. There, the organization started when an eleventh grader approached Ms. Spring about starting one because he wanted it to be his "legacy" and "way of giving back" to the school, as Ms. Spring told me during our interview.

43. This is known as the Matthew Shepard and James Byrd, Jr., Hate Crimes Prevention Act (2009). Byrd was brutally murdered by white supremacists in Texas in 1998, when the state had no hate crimes legislation.

44. It was not uncommon, for example, for mentors to broach conversations about relationships with women and girls, while some mentors bonded with their mentees by joking that they were single because they were unattractive to girls.

45. Finn, "Preparing for Power in Elite Boarding Schools and in Working-Class Schools," 58.

46. In " 'Trust Me, You Are Going to College,' " Rhoden shows that a Black male academy promoted solidarity and a sense of school belonging by building three forms of trust: trust in oneself, trust in close others, and institutional trust.

47. A. Ferguson, *Bad Boys*, 208.

48. Desroche, *Sociology of Hope*.

49. Mische, "Projects and Possibilities," 698.

50. Pattillo-McCoy, "Church Culture as a Strategy of Action in the Black Community," 769. The description of the church here is telling: in Christian imagery, an anchor is a symbol of hope.

51. Pattillo-McCoy, "Church Culture as a Strategy of Action in the Black Community," 782.

52. See Brooms, " 'We Didn't Let the Neighborhood Win,' " for an excellent discussion of how Black male academy students feel pressured to defend their masculinity.

53. Duncan-Andrade, "Note to Educators." Borrowing a line from the legendary hip-hop artist Tupac Shakur, Duncan-Andrade writes that the phrase "roses in concrete" refers "to young people who emerge in defiance of socially toxic environments as the 'roses that grow from concrete.' Concrete is one of the worst imaginable surfaces in which to grow, devoid of essential nutrients and frequently contaminated by

pollutants. Any growth in such an environment is painful because all of the basic requirements for healthy development (sun, water, and nutrient-rich soil) must be hard-won. The ability to control, in a material way, the litany of social stressors that result from growing up in concrete is nearly impossible for urban youth," 186.

54. Lamont and Molnár, "The Study of Boundaries in the Social Sciences," 168.

55. Rios, *Punished.*

56. Rios, *Punished,* 147.

57. E. Morris, "'Snitches End Up in Ditches,' and Other Cautionary Tales."

58. Rios, *Punished,* 146.

59. This translates as "in place of the parent."

60. Durkheim, *Moral Education.* For applications of Durkheim's model of moral authority in schools, see Arum, *Judging School Discipline;* and Perry and Morris, "Suspending Progress."

61. Garcia and Stigler, "Closed."

62. See K. Nolan, *Police in the Hallways,* for a historical overview of zero-tolerance policies in public schools.

63. Summers, *Manliness and Its Discontents,* 242.

64. Golann, "The Paradox of Success at a No-Excuses School." The author argues that the heavy emphasis on maintaining order at these schools tends to cultivate worker-learners rather than lifelong learners.

65. For instance, Fayette McKenzie, an early white president of Fisk University, was proud to call the school a military institution: "The essential principles of efficiency exemplified in the military have been absorbed into the university. These principles include concentration of effort, unremitting toil, elimination of all unnecessary activities and motions, regular and insistent schedule of life, promptness, accuracy, reliability, thoroughness, instant and complete obedience." Quoted in Summers, *Manliness and Its Discontents,* 250.

66. Stewart, *First Class.* There were striking parallels between the management of student conduct at Dunbar High School and at Black colleges such as Fisk and Howard (for a summary of the latter, see Summers, *Manliness and Its Discontents*). This went far beyond classroom expectations. For example, Dunbar High pupils were instructed to "avoid loud talking and boisterous laughter" on the streets and to refrain from chewing gum, 92–93. The expectations were also strongly gendered. And perhaps the most important part of Dunbar High's curriculum was the "Gospel of the Toothbrush," which it adopted from the teachings of Booker T. Washington. The school demanded the students adhere to the strictest guidelines for hygiene to set the students apart from the "sullied" reputations of the Eastern European immigrants and poor Blacks in the community.

67. In his critique of grit, "The Austerity School," Kenneth Saltman contends that grit's mandate of strict self-control has gone hand in hand with the rise of "no excuses" public schools, which demand complete submission to authority. I agree

with Saltman that a key assumption behind grit and its close kin, resilience, is a rejection of local communities thought to do nothing else but hold young people back. It is precisely this kind of logic that impedes the progressive alliances of urban social movements that I describe in the Conclusion.

68. Du Bois gave a speech at his alma mater, Fisk University, in 1924. In a happy coincidence for this book, Du Bois's speech was titled "Diuturni Silenti," which is Latin for "continued silence." Du Bois explained to those in attendance that "diuturni silenti" was a line from the speech "Pro Marcelo" (46 B.C.) by Cicero, the renowned Roman politician. In it, Cicero speaks up in defense of his fellow politician Marcus Claudius Marcellus, who was in exile for opposing Julius Caesar during the Roman Civil War (49–45 B.C.). Fisk officials were caught off guard as Du Bois used this slice of Roman history to indicate that he could no longer remain silent about his opposition to the strict methods in which his alma mater was disciplining its students. As Du Bois wrote, the school's strict methods were stunting male development. As Ronald Ferguson writes in "'W. E. B. Du Bois,'" Fisk University students rallied behind Du Bois while protesting the administration. Du Bois had provided them with the language for reclaiming their bodies during a post-Victorian era that swapped self-discipline for a freer consumer culture and liberating music like jazz and the blues.

69. Fergus, "The Freeing Powers of Single-Sex Education."

70. The rowing team (one of the few in the city), perhaps more than any other activity at the school, linked the charter school to elite boys' schools.

71. Dumas and Nelson, "(Re)Imagining Black Boyhood."

72. This included one Asian teacher at Perry High who was close to a small number of white teachers in the building.

73. Picower, "The Unexamined Whiteness of Teaching," 199. And as I described in the Introduction, historical controlling images of Black men have been implicated in tropes of white female victimhood.

74. Hughey, "White Savior Film and Reviewers' Reception," 475.

75. Given the tendency of young men to gravitate toward female teachers instead of male teachers, it is likely that these women did a disproportionate share of the emotional labor in the building, which reinforces the perception that women are naturally more caring than men. For a discussion of caring in the context of education, see Noddings, *Caring.*

76. Saltman, "Austerity School," 52.

77. W. Morris, "'Blind Side' Sticks to the Playbook on Race and Renewal."

78. For an overview of oppositional culture theory, see A. L. Harris, *Kids Don't Want to Fail.*

79. Higginbotham, *Righteous Discontent.*

80. Tilly, "Changing Forms of Inequality," 34.

5. Heroic Family Men and Ambitious Entrepreneurs

1. Anderson, *Code of the Street.*

2. Mische, "Projects and Possibilities."

3. Ann Arnett Ferguson discusses the process of "adultification" in *Bad Boys.*

4. In "(Re)Imagining Black Boyhood," Michael Dumas and Joseph Nelson provide a convincing analysis of how Black boyhood is a seemingly inconceivable state of affairs. They ask that researchers focus especially on how younger boys make and inhabit their social worlds.

5. Randles and Woodward, "Learning to Labor, Love, and Live."

6. A few teachers believed that boys misbehaved in the days leading up to a long holiday because they were stressed about having to be away from school for so long. School was a relatively safe and structured place in a community that otherwise provided few certainties and safety nets. One teacher was even sure some boys pretended to act out so that they could be reprimanded, receiving attention (albeit negative) from adults and perhaps even seeking a detention to delay the start of the long holiday break.

7. A. Young, *Minds of Marginalized Black Men.*

8. Fader, *Falling Back,* 180.

9. Lamont, *Dignity of Working Men,* 2.

10. Carlson, *Citizen-Protectors.*

11. Western et al., "Stress and Hardship after Prison," 540.

12. Fader, *Falling Back.*

13. Anderson, *Code of the Street.* For a longer discussion of how young Black men seek multiple forms of dignity, see Oeur, "Recognizing Dignity." In that article, I develop a threefold model of dignity. Social dignity refers to a sense of worth that varies by time and place and is unevenly distributed in status hierarchies. A second is inherent dignity, or the basic humanity of all people irrespective of status differences. Substantive dignity is a third form that refers to a self-worth that comes from a sense of belonging in wider communities.

14. Rios, *Punished.*

15. Ray and Rosow, "Two Different Worlds of Black and White Fraternity Men," 167.

16. Ross, "In Search of Black Men's Masculinities."

17. In *Between Good and Ghetto,* Nikki Jones found that poor Black girls sometimes navigated difficult relationships with the fathers of their children. Jones describes how young men can exploit these relationships because their partners would tolerate a lot from them, not wanting to appear less-than-respectable for being young, unattached mothers. But she also found that some young men were caught between being involved with the drug economy and being more active in their sons' lives. Even if some of the young fathers at Perry High wished to help raise their children, the pressure to hustle drugs remained. In another instance, Jones describes a young woman who tolerated abuse from her boyfriend because she did

not want to contact the authorities and thereby "participate in a process that re-sults in the incarceration of yet another young Black man," 148. The young woman also depended on the father of the child for financial support.

18. Anderson, *Code of the Street*, 149.

19. Edin and Nelson, *Doing the Best I Can*, 204.

20. Edin and Nelson, *Doing the Best I Can*, 204. For more on teenage father-hood and inner-city young men, see Harding, *Living the Drama*. In this qualitative study, David Harding found that some young men embraced a "frame" (or a per-spective that guides action) of responsible fatherhood in order to contest main-stream narratives of irresponsible fathers of color.

21. Edin and Nelson, *Doing the Best I Can*, 102.

22. Edin and Nelson, *Doing the Best I Can*, 207.

23. I. Young, "Logic of Masculinist Protection," 4.

24. Griffin, "Black Feminists and Du Bois."

25. Griffin, "Black Feminists and Du Bois," 35. Indeed, Farah Jasmine Griffin quotes Du Bois for his understanding of the need to protect in a manner that *liber-ates* the needy: "Not by guarding the weak in weakness do we gain strength, but by making weakness free and strong," 35–36.

26. N. Jones, *Between Good and Ghetto*.

27. Tronto, *Caring Democracy*.

28. In *Schooling for Resilience*, Fergus and colleagues also note that young men of color are socialized into "traditional male roles" in a manner that proves "prob-lematic," 156.

29. Quoted in V. Williams, "Reform or Retrenchment," 22n36.

30. Tocqueville, *Democracy in America*. While Ms. Holden portrayed the text as an enthusiastic defense of democracy, Tocqueville was also an early critic of the U.S. political economy; for a recent exposition of the book and Tocqueville's visit to the United States, see J. L. Nolan, *What They Saw in America*.

31. This is a cultural and political history defined by the dominance of the American dream, the belief that one's fate was not tied to hereditary titles, and the vital presence of immigrants and democratic ideals; see Kimmel, *Manhood in Amer-ica*, 13.

32. Kimmel, *Manhood in America*, 13.

33. Gaines, *Uplifting the Race*, 84.

34. R. Connell, "Masculinities in Global Perspective," 310.

35. R. Connell, "Masculinities in Global Perspective," 312. Raewyn Connell has also referred to this hegemonic entrepreneurialism as "transnational business masculinity." See her coauthored article with Julian Wood, "Globalization and Business Masculinities," for a longer discussion. There are important connections between Tocqueville's early observations and Connell's analysis of contemporary entrepreneurial masculinities. Tocqueville also observed in the American na-tional character a "mercantilist spirit" driven by profit-seeking. Furthermore, the

Frenchman warned that this material greediness could give rise to an industrial elite that would threaten American democracy; see J. L. Nolan, *What They Saw in America.*

36. See Connell and Wood, "Globalization and Business Masculinities."

37. Du Gay, *Consumption and Identity at Work.*

38. Mische, "Projects and Possibilities."

39. A college counselor and other adults informed the young men that college students struggle to graduate within four years, and some take up to six. Thus, graduating within four years became an important goal.

40. To accentuate how dominant this narrative of global competition has become, some teachers at Perry also conveyed this message to students. As Mr. Youseff said, "You've got to look way beyond just Perry, way beyond East Morgan and see that you're truly in the global marketplace. That's why I say all they learn academically, that's small. How they learn to think of themselves and what role they have in the world is going to be bigger." Mr. Youseff's thinking here was strongly inspired by his time teaching outside the United States and by his conviction that American students were falling further and further behind their international counterparts, especially in math and science, the subjects he taught.

41. Teachers sometimes used the phrase "getting left behind," clearly reminiscent of No Child Left Behind. Mr. Davidson, another Northside teacher, used this phrase to warn students to not get left behind in the next great "scientific revolution" happening around the world.

42. Summers, *Manliness and Its Discontents.*

43. Randles and Woodward, "Learning to Labor, Love, and Live," 12.

44. More subtle was how Mr. Davidson's comments were racialized. The high-achieving international students he spoke of primarily come from China and India. Mr. Davidson positioned them against American students as a group and indirectly against his own Black students.

45. Dumas, "My Brother as 'Problem,'" 96.

46. Watson and Smitherman, *Educating African American Males.*

47. Uprichard, "Children as 'Being and Becomings.'"

Conclusion

1. Jeremiah introduced me to friends and classmates and promised to always give me "the lowdown."

2. Jeremiah had overheard a teacher refer to another teacher as a "seasoned vet," and he adopted the title for himself.

3. In *Minds of Marginalized Black Men*, Alford Young Jr. describes how having a job provides the lives of poor Black men a sense of order and meaning.

4. The full text of the bill is available at https://leginfo.legislature.ca.gov/faces /billTextClient.xhtml?bill_id=201720180AB23.

5. Crenshaw, Halpern, and Williams, "Single-Sex Schools Are a Civil Rights Assault."

6. Gramsci, *Selections from the Prison Notebooks*. In this book, I have advanced two claims regarding common sense. The first is that resilience has become commonsense thinking among policy makers and practitioners who work with poor youth of color and that this thinking has become more ensconced with the surge in popularity of its more controversial cousin, grit. (For a critique of grit, see Saltman, "Austerity School.") The second claim is that a dominant research perspective on Black male academies has uncritically accepted this perspective, when it is precisely resilience and its consequences for Black male subjectivity that deserve critique. Stuart Hall, drawing on Gramsci, has written that the development of good sense is necessary for counter-hegemonic struggle. As Hall writes in "Gramsci's Relevance for the Study of Race and Ethnicity," "It always requires a further work of political education and cultural politics to renovate and clarify these constructions of popular thought—"common sense"—into a more coherent political theory or philosophical current. This 'raising of popular thought' is part and parcel of the process by which a collective will is constructed, and requires extensive work of intellectual organization—an essential part of any hegemonic political strategy. Popular beliefs, the culture of a people—Gramsci argues—are not arenas of struggle which can be left to look after themselves," 21.

7. Spence, "Neoliberal Turn in Black Politics."

8. F. Harris, "Rise of Respectability Politics," 33.

9. Dumas, "My Brother as 'Problem,'" 110 (emphasis in the original).

10. Weber, *Protestant Ethic and the "Spirit" of Capitalism*. For an excellent analysis of the historical underpinnings of Weber's use of "elective affinity," see McKinnon, "Elective Affinities of the Protestant Ethic."

11. For example, in "School Choice, Charter Schools, and White Flight," educational sociologists Linda Renzulli and Lorraine Evans have argued that with increased competition, "charter schools left to their own devices may promote racial segregation in the public schools," with "whites avoiding their nonwhite counterparts," 413.

12. Keith and Herring, "Skin Tone and Stratification in the Black Community," 775.

13. Harvey, "Neoliberalism as Creative Destruction."

14. See especially W. Brown, *Undoing the Demos*.

15. As Lisa Duggan writes in *Twilight of Equality?*, "really existing" neoliberalism contradicts the framing "in theory" of the market as opposed to the state. The same applies for people's actual experiences of markets and democratic institutions, which may have at times an uneasy relationship but still coexist in people's cultural and ideological frames, as with the Black community control tradition. For background on this tradition, see Stulberg, *Race, Schools, and Hope*.

16. Stulberg, *Race, Schools, and Hope*.

17. C. Johnson, "An Open Letter to Ta-Nehisi Coates and the Liberals Who Love Him."

18. Dumas, "My Brother as 'Problem.'"

19. They include the deaths of Michael Brown in 2014 in Ferguson, Missouri; Alton Sterling, 2016, Baton Rouge, Louisiana; Philando Castile, 2016, Falcon Heights, Minnesota; and Terence Crutcher, 2016, Tulsa, Oklahoma. The "Say Her Name" campaign has raised awareness of police violence against Black women. For a discussion, see M. Brown et al., "#SayHerName."

20. Cornwall, Karioris, and Lindisfarne, *Masculinities under Neoliberalism.*

21. R. Connell, "Masculinities in Global Perspective," 314. Future research should also examine other seemingly progressive initiatives that have been swept up by the neoliberal tide. It remains to be seen how the current presidential administration will handle this program, but there are high hopes for the My Brother's Keeper initiative, which Barack Obama rolled out in the waning days of his presidency. My Brother's Keeper, run by the White House's Office of African American Achievement, is a public-private venture that aims to nurture community- and individual-level interventions for young men of color. As Michael Dumas observes in "My Brother as 'Problem,'" despite its good intentions, the program is an example of neoliberal governmentality. Not only is it funded entirely by private-sector organizations, but it draws strength from a politics of respectability.

22. U.S. Department of Education, *Questions and Answers on Title IX and Single-Sex Elementary and Secondary Classes and Extracurricular Activities,* 25. Also of note is the OCR's concern with sex stereotyping in single-sex arrangements. The document recommends that educators be aware of the risk of sex stereotyping and how generalizations may "ignore the differences among students of the same sex," 21.

23. Gershenson et al., "The Long-Run Impacts of Same-Race Teachers." The study sample includes one hundred thousand low-income Black third graders in North Carolina, who largely struggled as a cohort. About 13 percent dropped out of high school, and half of the students graduated with no plans of attending college. However, the Black boys who had at least one Black teacher showed a 29 percent increased interest in college and had a 39 percent lower chance of dropping out of high school.

24. Fergus, Noguera, and Martin, *Schooling for Resilience.*

25. Executive Office of the President, "Every Student Succeeds Act," 7.

26. DeVos called for more "innovation disruptors."

27. Wells, Slayton, and Scott, "Defining Democracy in the Neoliberal Age," 343.

28. "Pure competition" is a term from Foucault's *Birth of Biopolitics,* 120. As Joan Tronto writes in *Caring Democracy,* choices are not completely free if they are made within systems of oppression.

29. See Smith, "Shared, Collaborative, and On Demand," a report by the Pew Research Center. Only 15 percent of Americans have ever used ridesharing, while

33 percent have never heard of it. Ridesharing users tend to be educated and financially well-off. College graduates are nearly six times more likely to use ridesharing than those with only a high school degree, while the largest share of those polled by the Pew Research Center had an annual household income of at least $75,000. Data available at http://www.pewinternet.org/2016/05/19/on-demand-ride-hailing-apps.

30. See http://www.governing.com/topics/transportation-infrastructure/gov -public-transportation-riders-demographic-divide-for-cities.html#data.

31. Rofes and Stulberg, *Emancipatory Promise of Charter Schools*, 281.

32. Quoted in Gross, "Benefit of Racial Isolation."

33. D. Lewis, *W. E. B. Du Bois*, 281. Quoted in Olson, *Abolition of White Democracy*, 132.

34. Garcia and Stigler, "Closed," 214.

35. R. Ferguson, "'W. E. B. Du Bois.'"

36. Reed, *W. E. B. Du Bois and American Political Thought*, 4.

37. The notion of "freezing" Du Boisian ideas comes from Joy James's book, *Transcending the Talented Tenth*.

38. Carby, *Race Men*, 12. As Juliet Williams similarly writes in *Separation Solution?*, "If the merits of single-sex initiatives are to be engaged on their own terms, surely it is incumbent on proponents to supply some kind of rationale for excluding similarly disadvantaged girls from such opportunities," 147.

39. Gaines, *Uplifting the Race*, 3.

40. Gaines, *Uplifting the Race*, 3.

41. For a discussion, see the many excellent chapters in *Progressive Black Masculinities*, edited by Athena Mutua. For an analysis of how Black male academies undermine the construction of progressive Black masculinities, see Laing, "Black Masculinities Expressed through, and Constrained by, Brotherhood."

42. Dumas and Nelson, "(Re)Imagining Black Boyhood." This framework also demands that children, as vulnerable persons, be viewed as worthy of protection and care. (I also discuss this in my article, "Recognizing Dignity.") My analysis has revealed that a neoliberal respectability politics splinters Black communities and assumes that some Black children are more worthy of protection than others.

43. Fetner and Elafros, "The GSA Difference."

44. Silva, *Coming Up Short*, 18.

45. Brooms, "'We Didn't Let the Neighborhood Win.'"

46. Olson, *Abolition of White Democracy*, 142. See also Davis, *Abolition Democracy*.

47. Lipman, *New Political Economy of Urban Education*.

48. Du Bois, "Talented Tenth," 347.

49. Du Bois, "Talented Tenth," 349. Using phrases that apply just as easily to neoliberalism's zero-sum politics, Du Bois described how a Talented Tenth would encourage a "free-for-all" with the "devil taking the hindmost." Du Bois suggested that just as science had evolved greatly over the first half of the twentieth century,

that so must he himself make a "conscious, continuous, and determined effort to keep abreast with the development of knowledge," 347.

50. Du Bois, "Talented Tenth," 353.

51. For a comprehensive discussion of the significance of the Guiding Hundredth for Du Bois's critical pedagogy, see Rabaka, *Against Epistemic Apartheid*.

52. Lozenski, "Beyond Mediocrity," 181. The author argues that the notion of an "achievement gap" ignores the historical causes of contemporary racial inequalities and that privatized efforts to reform education are unlikely to lead to meaningful progress.

53. Garza, "A Herstory of the #BlackLivesMatter Movement," 23.

54. Harris-Perry, "How to Save the N.A.A.C.P. from Irrelevance." Melissa Harris-Perry suggests that the NAACP can again become a central player in the antiracist struggle by changing its traditional elite leadership style to fit contemporary times: "This will happen only if the organization commits itself to making substantive change that disrupts the balance of power for the most vulnerable. To get there, the NAACP must search for its new president not in the highest places, but rather in the lowest. Is the NAACP ready to follow the leadership of undocumented women? Queer women? Black women? Is it ready to listen to those who have been incarcerated? Those who are H.I.V. positive? Is it ready to have as its president a young person just out of foster care who, because he is transgender and black, lived with vulnerabilities many can't imagine? These are the kinds of leaders capable of offering a radical new direction for an organization that has been irrelevant for far too long."

55. Spence, *Knocking the Hustle*, 139. Lester Spence writes that "respectable" figures (such as Rosa Parks) have often been held up as the face of civil rights struggles. For Black Lives Matter supporters, a respectability politics is dangerous because it judges the deaths of some (the "less respectable") to be more justifiable than the deaths of others at the hands of law enforcement. For these activists, law enforcement should be held accountable in *all* cases, and how victims "behaved should not have any bearing on how they were treated by police," 139. Spence finds fault in Du Bois's elitist ideologies of racial uplift, claiming that they undermine true democratic mobilization. Du Bois's notion of abolition democracy, however, seems to me to lay the groundwork for the kind of counter-hegemonic struggle that Spence has in mind.

56. Garza, "A Herstory of the #BlackLivesMatter Movement," 24. For an excellent critique of the veneration of charismatic male leadership in the Black freedom movement, see Edwards, *Charisma and the Fictions of Black Leadership*.

57. The island metaphor is taken from Donald Leake and Brenda Leake's description of the Milwaukee first-wave academy as an "island of hope in a sea of indifference"; see "Islands of Hope," 25.

58. Camp, *Incarcerating the Crisis*, 148.

59. Ochoa, *Academic Profiling*, 4 (emphasis in the original).

60. Giroux, "White Nationalism, Armed Culture and State Violence in the Age of Donald Trump." As Henry Giroux argues, a "blend of neo-liberal orthodoxy, religious fundamentalism, educational repression and an accelerating militarism found its end point in the election of Donald Trump," 889. In response to Attorney General Jeff Sessions's mandate for stricter sentencing in criminal cases, Sherrilyn Ifill, the president of the NAACP Legal Defense and Educational Fund, said in May 2017, "When President Trump asked Black Americans what we have to lose by electing him, the answer is all the gains we've made in advancing justice and fairness." See Jarrett and Scott, "AG Sessions Paves Way for Stricter Sentencing in Criminal Cases."

61. Tronto, *Caring Democracy.*

62. Quoted in A. Bass, *Those About Him Remained Silent*, 47. Wilkins observed how Du Bois's embrace of Communism had guided him away from the civil rights establishment in the United States. On the day he died, Du Bois sent to Washington, D.C. a telegram in support of the Civil Rights March.

63. Heim, "Country's Newest All-Boys Public School Opens Its Doors."

64. Bama, "Morehouse Men Visit 'Young Kings' of Ron Brown College Prep High School in DC."

65. Du Bois, "Does the Negro Need Separate Schools?," 334–35.

66. Du Bois, *Prayers for Dark People,* 36.

Alridge, Derrick P. "Conceptualizing a Du Boisian Philosophy of Education: Toward a Model for African-American Education." *Educational Theory* 49, no. 3 (1999): 359–79.

Alridge, Derrick P. "On the Education of Black Folk: W. E. B. Du Bois and the Paradox of Segregation." *Journal of African American History* 100, no. 3 (2015): 473–93.

American Association of University Women Educational Foundation. *How Schools Shortchange Girls.* Washington, D.C.: American Association of University Women, 1992.

American Civil Liberties Union. *Preliminary Findings of ACLU "Teach Kids, Not Stereotypes" Campaign.* New York: American Civil Liberties Union, 2012.

American Enterprise Institute. "Should Single-Sex Schooling Be Eliminated?" August 28, 2013. Transcript.

American Psychological Association. *Eliminating Health Disparities among Boys and Men.* May 24, 2016. Presentation slides. https://www.apa.org/topics/health-disparities/boys-and-men.pdf.

Anderson, Elijah. *Code of the Street: Decency, Violence, and the Moral Life of the Inner City.* New York: W. W. Norton, 2000.

Arum, Richard. *Judging School Discipline: The Crisis of Moral Authority.* Cambridge, Mass.: Harvard University Press, 2005.

Bama, East Texas. "Morehouse Men Visit 'Young Kings' of Ron Brown College Prep High School in DC." *Rolling Out,* September 24, 2016. http://rollingout.com/2016/09/24/morehouse-men-visit-young-kings-ron-brown-college-prep-high-school-dc.

Bass, Amy. *Those About Him Remained Silent: The Battle over W. E. B. Du Bois.* Minneapolis: University of Minnesota Press, 2012.

Bass, Lisa. "When Care Trumps Justice: The Operationalization of Black Feminist Caring in Educational Leadership." *International Journal of Qualitative Studies in Education* 25, no. 1 (2012): 73–87.

Beasley, Chris. "Problematizing Contemporary Men/Masculinities Theorizing: The Contribution of Raewyn Connell and Conceptual-Terminological Tensions Today." *British Journal of Sociology* 63, no. 4 (2012): 747–65.

Beck, Allen J., David Cantor, John Hartge, and Tim Smith. *Sexual Victimization in Juvenile Facilities Reported by Youth, 2012*. Washington, D.C.: Bureau of Justice Statistics, 2013. https://www.bjs.gov/content/pub/pdf/svjfry12.pdf.

Bederman, Gail. *Manliness and Civilization: A Cultural History of Gender and Race in the United States, 1880–1917*. Chicago: University of Chicago Press, 1995.

Berends, Mark. "Sociology and School Choice: What We Know after Two Decades of Charter Schools." *Annual Review of Sociology* 41 (2015): 159–80.

Berg, Bruce L. *Qualitative Research Methods for the Social Sciences*. 7th ed. Boston, Mass.: Allyn and Bacon, 2007.

Best, Amy L. *Fast Cars, Cool Rides: The Accelerating World of Youth and Their Cars*. New York: New York University Press, 2005.

Bettie, Julie. *Women without Class: Girls, Race, and Identity*. 2nd ed. Oakland: University of California Press, 2014.

Bigler, Rebecca S., and Lynn S. Liben. "A Developmental Intergroup Theory of Social Stereotypes and Prejudice." *Advances in Child Development and Behavior* 34 (2006): 39–89.

Bonner, Fred A. *Building on Resilience: Models and Frameworks of Black Male Success across the P-20 Pipeline*. Sterling, Va.: Stylus, 2015.

Bourdieu, Pierre, and Jean-Claude Passeron. *Reproduction in Education, Society, and Culture*. 2nd ed. London: Sage, 1990.

Bridges, Tristan S., and Michael Kimmel. "Engaging Men in the United States: Soft Essentialism and the Obstacles to Coherent Initiatives in Education and Family Policy." In *Men and Masculinities around the World: Transforming Men's Practices*, edited by Elisabetta Ruspini, Jeff Hearn, Bob Pease, and Keith Pringle, 159–73. New York: Springer, 2011.

Brooms, Derrick R. "'We Didn't Let the Neighborhood Win': Black Male Students' Experiences in Negotiating and Navigating an Urban Neighborhood." *Journal of Negro Education* 84, no. 3 (2015): 269–81.

Brown, Christina Spears. "Legal Issues Surrounding Single-Sex Schools in the U.S.: Trends, Court Cases, and Conflicting Laws." *Sex Roles* 69, nos. 7–8 (2013): 356–62.

Brown, Melissa, Rashawn Ray, Ed Summers, and Neil Fraistat. "#SayHerName: A Case Study of Intersectional Social Media Activism." *Ethnic and Racial Studies* 40, no. 11 (2017): 1831–46.

Brown, Wendy. *Undoing the Demos: Neoliberalism's Stealth Revolution*. New York: Zone Books, 2015.

Burawoy, Michael. "The Extended Case Method." In *Ethnography Unbound: Power and Resistance in the Modern Metropolis*, edited by Michael Burawoy et al., 271–87. Berkeley: University of California Press, 1991.

Burawoy, Michael. "The Extended Case Method." *Sociological Theory* 16, no. 1 (1998): 4–33.

Burawoy, Michael. "On Desmond: The Limits of Spontaneous Sociology." *Theory and Society* 46, no. 4 (2017): 261–84.

Cambridge Coaching. "College Admissions: The Benefit of Taking Latin in High School," March 17, 2014. http://blog.cambridgecoaching.com/blog/bid/339190/College-Admissions-The-Benefits-of-Taking-Latin-in-High-School.

Camp, Jordan T. *Incarcerating the Crisis: Freedom Struggles and the Rise of the Neoliberal State.* Oakland: University of California Press, 2016.

Carby, Hazel V. *Race Men.* Cambridge, Mass.: Harvard University Press, 2010.

Carlson, Jennifer. *Citizen-Protectors: The Everyday Politics of Guns in an Age of Decline.* New York: Oxford University Press, 2015.

Carlson, Jennifer. "States, Subjects and Sovereign Power: Lessons from Global Gun Cultures." *Theoretical Criminology* 18, no. 3 (2014): 335–53.

Carter, Prudence L. *Keepin' It Real: School Success beyond Black and White.* New York: Oxford University Press, 2005.

Carter, Prudence L., and Kevin G. Welner. *Closing the Opportunity Gap: What America Must Do to Give Every Child an Even Chance.* New York: Oxford University Press, 2013.

Choo, Hae Yeon, and Myra Marx Ferree. "Practicing Intersectionality in Sociological Research: A Critical Analysis of Inclusions, Interactions, and Institutions in the Study of Inequalities." *Sociological Theory* 28, no. 2 (2010): 129–49.

"Civil Rights Data Collection." *Data Snapshot: School Discipline.* Washington, D.C.: Office for Civil Rights, U.S. Department of Education, 2014.

Cobb, William, Jr. "Out of Africa: The Dilemmas of Afrocentricity." *Journal of Negro History* 82, no. 1 (1997): 122–32.

Cohen, Philip N. "The 'End of Men' Is Not True: What Is Not and What Might Be on the Road toward Gender Equality." *Boston University Law Review* 93, no. 3 (2013): 1159–84.

Collins, Patricia Hill. *Black Feminist Thought: Knowledge, Consciousness, and the Politics of Empowerment.* New York: Routledge, 2000.

Collins, Patricia Hill. *Black Sexual Politics: African Americans, Gender, and the New Racism.* New York: Routledge, 2004.

Collins, Patricia Hill. *From Black Power to Hip Hop: Racism, Nationalism, and Feminism.* Philadelphia: Temple University Press, 2006.

Collins, Patricia Hill. "Intersectionality's Definitional Dilemmas." *Annual Review of Sociology* 41 (2015): 1–20.

Connell, R. W. *Masculinities.* 2nd ed. Berkeley: University of California Press, 2005.

Connell, R. W., and Julian Wood. "Globalization and Business Masculinities." *Men and Masculinities* 7, no. 4 (2005): 347–64.

Connell, Raewyn. "Masculinities in Global Perspective: Hegemony, Contestation, and Changing Structures of Power." *Theory and Society* 45, no. 4 (2016): 303–18.

Cookson, Peter W., Jr., and Caroline Hodges Persell. *Preparing for Power: America's Elite Boarding Schools.* New York: Basic Books, 1985.

Cooper, Anna Julia. "The Status of Women in America." In *A Voice from the South,* edited by Charles Lemert and Esme Bhan, 109–17. Lanham, Md.: Rowman and Littlefield, 1988.

Cooper, K. J. "Scholars Debate Effectiveness of Single-Sex Classes." *Diverse Issues in Higher Education* 23, no. 21 (2006): 14–15.

Cornwall, Andrea, Frank G. Karioris, and Nancy Lindisfarne. *Masculinities under Neoliberalism.* London: Zed Books, 2016.

Coulson, Andrew J. *Market Education: The Unknown History.* Piscataway, N.J.: Transaction, 1999.

Crenshaw, Kimberlé. "The Girls Obama Forgot." *New York Times,* July 29, 2014. https://www.nytimes.com/2014/07/30/opinion/Kimberl-Williams-Crenshaw -My-Brothers-Keeper-Ignores-Young-Black-Women.html?_r=0&mtrref=www .google.com&gwh=EE29A5DE2970B77C7C8C333B3794D05F&gwt=pay &assetType=opinion.

Crenshaw, Kimberlé. "Race, Reform, and Retrenchment: Transformation and Legitimation in Antidiscrimination Law." *Harvard Law Review* 101, no. 7 (1988): 1331–87.

Crenshaw, Kimberlé, Diane Halpern, and Juliet A. Williams. "Single-Sex Schools Are a Civil Rights Assault." *Education Week,* May 21, 2017. http://blogs.edweek.org .ezproxy.library.tufts.edu/edweek/on_california/2017/05/single_sex_schools_a _civil_rights_assault.html?qs=Single+Sex+Schools+a+Civil+Rights+Assault.

Cucchiara, Maia Bloomfield. *Marketing Schools, Marketing Cities: Who Wins and Who Loses When Schools Become Urban Amenities.* Chicago: University of Chicago Press, 2013.

Datnow, Amanda, and Lea Hubbard, eds. *Gender in Policy and Practice: Perspectives on Single-Sex and Coeducational Schooling.* New York: RoutledgeFalmer, 2002.

Datnow, Amanda, Lea Hubbard, and Elisabeth Woody. *Is Single Gender Schooling Viable in the Public Sector? Lessons from California's Pilot Program.* Ontario: Ontario Institute for Studies in Education, University of Toronto, 2001.

Davenport, Barbara. *Grit and Hope: A Year with Five Latino Students and the Program that Helped Them Aim for College.* Oakland: University of California Press, 2016.

Davis, Angela. *Abolition Democracy: Beyond Empire, Prisons, and Torture.* New York: Seven Stories Press, 2005.

Dean, Mitchell. *Governmentality: Power and Rule in Modern Society.* 2nd ed. Los Angeles: Sage, 2010.

de Boise, Sam. "'I'm Not Homophobic, 'I've Got Gay Friends': Evaluating the Validity of Inclusive Masculinity." *Men and Masculinities* 18, no. 3 (2015): 318–39.

Delpit, Lisa. *Other People's Children: Cultural Conflict in the Classroom.* New York: New Press, 2006.

Desroche, Henri. *The Sociology of Hope.* Translated by Carol Martin-Sperry. London: Routledge and Kegan Paul, 1979.

DiMaggio, Paul J., and Walter W. Powell. "The Iron Cage Revisited: Institutional Isomorphism and Collective Rationality in Organizational Fields." *American Sociological Review* 48, no. 2 (1983): 147–60.

Drake, St. Clair, and Horace R. Cayton. *Black Metropolis: A Study of Negro Life in a Northern City.* 2nd ed. New York: Harper and Row, 1962.

Du Bois, W. E. B. *Black Reconstruction in America: Toward a History of the Part Which Black Folk Played in the Attempt to Reconstruct Democracy in America, 1860–1880.* New York: Free Press, 1992.

Du Bois, W. E. B. "The College-Bred Community." In *The Education of Black People: Ten Critiques, 1906–1960,* edited by Herbert Aptheker, 49–60. New York: Monthly Review, 2001.

Du Bois, W. E. B. *Darkwater: Voices from Within the Veil.* Mineola, N.Y.: Dover, 1999.

Du Bois, W. E. B. "Does the Negro Need Separate Schools?" *Journal of Negro Education* 4, no. 3 (1935): 328–35.

Du Bois, W. E. B. "Editorial." *The Crisis: Record of the Darker Races* 1, no. 1 (1910): 1–20.

Du Bois, W. E. B. *The Philadelphia Negro: A Social Study.* Philadelphia: University of Pennsylvania Press, 1995.

Du Bois, W. E. B. *Prayers for Dark People.* Amherst: University of Massachusetts Press, 1980.

Du Bois, W. E. B. *The Souls of Black Folk.* New York: Dover, 1994.

Du Bois, W. E. B. "The Talented Tenth: Memorial Address." In *W. E. B. Du Bois: A Reader,* edited by David Levering Lewis, 347–53. New York: Henry Holt and Co., 1995.

Du Bois, W. E. B. "The Training of Negroes for Social Power." In *Du Bois on Education,* edited by Eugene F. Provenzo, 65–74. Walnut Creek, Calif.: Altamira, 2002.

Du Gay, Paul. *Consumption and Identity at Work.* London: Sage, 1996.

Duckworth, Angela. *Grit: The Power of Passion and Perseverance.* New York: Simon and Schuster, 2016.

Duggan, Lisa. *The Twilight of Equality? Neoliberalism, Cultural Politics, and the Attack on Democracy.* Boston: Beacon Press, 2004.

Dumas, Michael J. "My Brother as 'Problem': Neoliberal Governmentality and Interventions for Black Young Men and Boys." *Educational Policy* 30, no. 1 (2016): 94–113.

Dumas, Michael J., and Joseph Nelson. "(Re)Imagining Black Boyhood: Toward a Critical Framework for Educational Research." *Harvard Educational Review* 86, no. 1 (2016): 27–47.

Duncan-Andrade, Jeffrey M. R. "Note to Educators: Hope Required When Growing Roses in Concrete." *Harvard Educational Review* 79, no. 2 (2009): 181–94.

Duneier, Mitchell. *Slim's Table: Race, Respectability, and Masculinity.* Chicago: University of Chicago Press, 2015.

Durkheim, Émile. *Moral Education.* Translated by Everett K. Wilson and Herman Shurer. Mineola, N.Y.: Dover, 2002.

Edin, Kathryn, and Timothy J. Nelson. *Doing the Best I Can: Fatherhood in the Inner City.* Berkeley: University of California Press, 2013.

Edwards, Erica R. *Charisma and the Fictions of Black Leadership.* Minneapolis: University of Minnesota Press, 2012.

Eliot, Lise. "Single-Sex Education and the Brain." *Sex Roles* 69, nos. 7–8 (2013): 363–81.

Executive Office of the President. "Every Student Succeeds Act: A Progress Report on Elementary and Secondary Education." Washington, D.C.: The White House, 2015. https://obamawhitehouse.archives.gov/sites/whitehouse.gov/files/docu ments/ESSA_Progress_Report.pdf.

Fader, Jamie J. *Falling Back: Incarceration and Transitions to Adulthood among Urban Youth.* New Brunswick, N.J.: Rutgers University Press, 2013.

Fergus, Edward. "The Freeing Powers of Single-Sex Education." *New York Times,* March 10, 2015. https://www.nytimes.com/roomfordebate/2015/03/10/are-same-sex-colleges-still-relevant/the-freeing-powers-of-single-sex-education.

Fergus, Edward, Pedro Noguera, and Margary Martin. *Schooling for Resilience: Improving the Life Trajectory of Black and Latino Boys.* Cambridge, Mass.: Harvard University Press, 2014.

Ferguson, Ann Arnett. *Bad Boys: Public Schools in the Making of Black Masculinity.* Ann Arbor: University of Michigan Press, 2000.

Ferguson, Roderick A. "'W. E. B. Du Bois': Biography of a Discourse." In *Next to the Color Line: Gender, Sexuality, and W. E. B. Du Bois,* edited by Susan Gillman and Alys Eve Weinbaum, 269–88. Minneapolis: University of Minnesota Press, 2007.

Fetner, Tina, and Athena Elafros. "The GSA Difference: LGBTQ and Ally Experiences in High Schools with and without Gay-Straight Alliances." *Social Sciences* 4, no. 3 (2015): 563–81.

Finn, Patrick J. "Preparing for Power in Elite Boarding Schools and in Working-Class Schools." *Theory into Practice* 51, no. 1 (2012): 57–63.

Foucault, Michel. *The Birth of Biopolitics: Lectures at the Collège de France, 1978–1979.* New York: Picador, 2008.

Foucault, Michel. *Discipline and Punish: The Birth of the Prison.* 2nd ed. Translated by Alan Sheridan. New York: Vintage, 1995.

Fraser, Nancy. "Foucault on Modern Power: Empirical Insights and Normative Confusions." *Praxis International* 1, no. 3 (1981): 272–87.

Froyum, Carissa. "'At Least I'm Not Gay': Heterosexual Identity Making among Poor Black Teens." *Sexualities* 10, no. 5 (2007): 603–22.

Frye, Margaret. "Bright Futures in Malawi's New Dawn: Educational Aspirations as Assertions of Identity." *American Journal of Sociology* 117, no. 6 (2012): 1565–624.

Gaines, Kevin K. *Uplifting the Race: Black Leadership, Politics, and Culture in the Twentieth Century.* Chapel Hill: University of North Carolina Press, 2012.

Garcia, David R., and Monica L. Stigler. "Closed: Competition, Segregation, and the Black Student Experience in Charter Schools." In *Black Educational Choice: Assessing the Public and Private Alternatives to Traditional K-12 Schools,* edited by Diana T. Slaughter-Defoe, Howard C. Stevenson, Edith G. Arrington, and Deborah J. Johnson, 205–16. Santa Barbara, Calif.: Praeger, 2012.

Garland, David. "'Governmentality' and the Problem of Crime: Foucault, Criminology, Sociology." *Theoretical Criminology* 1, no. 2 (1997): 173–214.

Garza, Alicia. "A Herstory of the #BlackLivesMatter Movement." In *Are All the Women Still White? Rethinking Race, Expanding Feminisms,* edited by Janelle Hobson, 23–28. Albany, N.Y.: State University of New York Press, 2016.

Gay, Geneva. "Preparing for Culturally Responsive Teaching." *Journal of Teacher Education* 53, no. 2 (2002): 106–16.

Gershenson, Seth, Cassandra Hart, Constance Lindsay, and Nicholas W. Papageorge. 2017. "The Long-Run Impacts of Same-Race Teachers." IZA Institute of Labor Economics Discussion Paper Series no. 10630.

Gillman, Susan, and Alys Weinbaum, eds. *Next to the Color Line: Gender, Sexuality, and W. E. B. Du Bois.* Minneapolis: University of Minnesota Press, 2007.

Giroux, Henry A. "White Nationalism, Armed Culture and State Violence in the Age of Donald Trump." *Philosophy & Social Criticism* 43, no. 9 (2017): 887–910.

Giroux, Henry A. *Youth in a Suspect Society: Democracy or Disposability?* New York: Palgrave Macmillan, 2009.

Giroux, Henry A., and Anthony N. Penna. "Social Education in the Classroom: The Dynamics of the Hidden Curriculum." *Theory and Research in Social Education* 7, no. 1 (1979): 21–42.

Golann, Joanne W. "The Paradox of Success at a No Excuses School." *Sociology of Education* 88, no. 2 (2015): 103–19.

Goodkind, Sara, Lisa Schelbe, Andrea A. Joseph, Daphne E. Beers, and Stephanie L. Pinsky. "Providing New Opportunities or Reinforcing Old Stereotypes? Perceptions and Experiences of Single-Sex Public Education." *Children and Youth Services Review* 35, no. 8 (2013): 1174–81.

Gramsci, Antonio. *Selections from the Prison Notebooks.* Edited and translated by Quintin Hoare and Geoffrey Nowell Smith. New York: International Publishers, 1971.

Griffin, Farah Jasmine. "Black Feminists and Du Bois: Respectability, Protection, and Beyond." *ANNALS of the American Academy of Political and Social Science* 568, no. 1 (2000): 28–40.

Gross, Natalie. "The Benefit of Racial Isolation." *Atlantic,* February 8, 2017. https:// www.theatlantic.com/education/archive/2017/02/the-benefit-of-racial-isolation /516018/

Grundy, Saida. "'An Air of Expectancy': Class, Crisis, and the Making of Manhood at a Historically Black College for Men." *ANNALS of the American Academy of Political and Social Science* 642, no. 1 (2012): 43–60.

Gunn, Raymond. "Inner-City 'Schoolboy' Life." *ANNALS of the American Academy of Political and Social Science* 595, no. 1 (2004): 63–79.

Gurian, Michael. *Boys and Girls Learn Differently! A Guide for Parents and Teachers.* 2nd ed. New York: Jossey-Bass, 2010.

Gurian, Michael. *A Fine Young Man: What Parents, Mentors, and Educators Can Do to Shape Adolescent Boys into Exceptional Men.* New York: Jeremy P. Tarcher/Putnam, 1998.

Hall, Peter A., and Michèle Lamont. *Social Resilience in the Neoliberal Era.* New York: Cambridge University Press, 2013.

Hall, Stuart. *Cultural Studies 1983: A Theoretical History.* Durham, N.C.: Duke University Press, 2016.

Hall, Stuart. "Gramsci's Relevance for the Study of Race and Ethnicity." *Journal of Communication Inquiry* 10, no. 2 (1986): 5–27.

Hallett, Tim. "The Myth Incarnate: Recoupling Processes, Turmoil, and Inhabited Institutions in an Urban Elementary School." *American Sociological Review* 75, no. 1 (2010): 52–74.

Halpern, Diane, Lise Eliot, Rebecca S. Bigler, Richard A. Fabes, Laura D. Hanish, Janet Hyde, Lynn S. Liben, and Carol Martin. "The Pseudoscience of Single-Sex Schooling." *Science* 333 (2011): 1706–7.

Harding, David. "Cultural Context, Sexual Behavior, and Romantic Relationships in Disadvantaged Neighborhoods." *American Sociological Review* 72, no. 3 (2007): 341–64.

Harding, David. *Living the Drama: Community, Conflict, and Culture among Inner-City Boys.* Chicago: University of Chicago Press, 2010.

Harris, Angel L. *Kids Don't Want to Fail: Oppositional Culture and the Black-White Achievement Gap.* Cambridge, Mass.: Harvard University Press, 2011.

Harris, Angela P. "Race and Essentialism in Feminist Legal Theory." *Stanford Law Review* 42, no. 3 (1990): 581–616.

Harris, Fredrick. "The Rise of Respectability Politics." *Dissent* 61, no. 1 (2014): 33–37.

Harris-Perry, Melissa. "How to Save the N.A.A.C.P. from Irrelevance." *New York Times,* May 30, 2017. https://www.nytimes.com/2017/05/30/opinion/melissa -harris-perry-naacp.html.

Harvey, David. "Neoliberalism as Creative Destruction." *ANNALS of the American Academy of Political and Social Science* 610, no. 1 (2007): 21–44.

Heim, Joe. "The Country's Newest All-Boys Public School Opens Its Doors." *Washington Post*, August 22, 2016. https://www.washingtonpost.com/local/education /the-countrys-newest-all-boys-public-high-school-opens-its-doors/2016/08/22/ a09a78e6–688d-11e6–99bf-f0cf3a6449a6_story.html?utm_term=.205364347d8c.

Higginbotham, Evelyn Brooks. *Righteous Discontent: The Women's Movement in the Black Baptist Church, 1880–1920.* Cambridge, Mass.: Harvard University Press, 1993.

Holland, Spencer H. "Positive Role Models for Primary-Grade Black Inner-City Males." *Equity and Excellence in Education* 25, no. 1 (1991): 40–44.

Holliday, Lisa R. "The Benefits of Latin?" *Educational Research Quarterly* 36, no. 1 (2012): 3–12.

hooks, bell. *Ain't I a Woman?: Black Women and Feminism.* Boston: South End, 1981.

hooks, bell. *Feminist Theory: From Margin to Center.* 2nd ed. Cambridge, Mass.: South End, 2000.

hooks, bell. *We Real Cool: Black Men and Masculinity.* New York: Routledge, 2004.

Hooks, Benjamin. "Publisher's Foreword." *The Crisis* 98, no. 8 (1991): 3.

Hopkins, Ronnie. *Educating Black Males: Critical Lessons in Schooling, Community, and Power.* Albany, N.Y.: State University of New York Press, 1997.

"Hostility Greets Students at Black School in White Area of Detroit." *New York Times*, December 2, 1992. https://www.nytimes.com/1992/12/02/education/hos tility-greets-students-at-black-school-in-white-area-of-detroit.html.

Hubbard, Lea, and Amanda Datnow. "Do Single-Sex Schools Improve the Education of Low-Income and Minority Students? An Investigation of California's Single-Gender Academies." *Anthropology and Education Quarterly* 36, no. 2 (2005): 115–31.

Hudson, Alexandra. "Why Manners Matter." *National Review*, April 27, 2016. https://www.nationalreview.com/2016/04/why-good-manners-matter-they -help-disadvantaged-kids-climb-ladder-success/.

Hughey, Matthew W. "The White Savior Film and Reviewers' Reception." *Symbolic Interaction* 33, no. 3 (2010): 475–96.

Hunter, Marcus Anthony, and Zandria F. Robinson. "The Sociology of Urban Black America." *Annual Review of Sociology* 42 (2016): 385–405.

Hursh, David. "Assessing No Child Left Behind and the Rise of Neoliberal Education Policies." *American Educational Research Journal* 44, no. 3 (2007): 493–518.

Ingersoll, Richard, Lisa Merrill, and Daniel Stuckey. "Seven Trends: The Transformation of the Teaching Force." Philadelphia: Consortium for Policy Research in Education, University of Pennsylvania. http://www.cpre.org/sites/default/files /workingpapers/1506_7trendsapril2014.pdf.

Jack, Anthony Abraham. "Culture Shock Revisited: The Social and Cultural Contingencies to Class Marginality." *Sociological Forum* 29, no. 2 (2014): 453–75.

Jack, Anthony Abraham. "(No) Harm in Asking: Class, Acquired Cultural Capital, and Academic Engagement at an Elite University." *Sociology of Education* 89, no. 1 (2016): 1–19.

Jackson, Iesha, Yolanda Sealey-Ruiz, and Wanda Watson. "Reciprocal Love: Mentoring Black and Latino Males through an Ethos of Care." *Urban Education* 49, no. 4 (2014): 394–417.

James, Joy. *Transcending the Talented Tenth: Black Leaders and American Intellectuals.* New York: Routledge, 1996.

James, Marlon. "Never Quit: The Complexities of Promoting Social and Academic Excellence at a Single-Gender School for Urban American American Males." *Journal of African American Males in Education* 1, no. 3 (2010): 167–95.

Jarrett, Laura, and Eugene Scott. "AG Sessions Paves Way for Stricter Sentencing in Criminal Cases." CNN, May 12, 2017. http://www.cnn.com/2017/05/12/poli tics/sessions-criminal-charging-memo/index.html.

Jerrim, John. "The Unrealistic Educational Expectations of High School Pupils: Is America Exceptional?" *Sociological Quarterly* 55, no. 2 (2014): 196–231.

Johnson, Cedric. *The Neoliberal Deluge: Hurricane Katrina, Late Capitalism, and the Remaking of New Orleans.* Minneapolis: University of Minnesota Press, 2011.

Johnson, Cedric. "An Open Letter to Ta-Nehisi Coates and the Liberals Who Love Him." *Jacobin,* February 3, 2016. https://www.jacobinmag.com/2016/02/ta -nehisi-coates-case-for-reparations-bernie-sanders-racism.

Johnson, Dirk. "Milwaukee Creating 2 Schools for Black Boys." *New York Times,* September 30, 1990. http://www.nytimes.com/1990/09/30/us/milwaukee-creat ing-2-schools-for-black-boys.html.

Jones, Nikki. *Between Good and Ghetto: African American Girls and Inner-City Violence.* New Brunswick, N.J.: Rutgers University Press, 2010.

Jones, Patricia A. "Educating Black Males: Several Solutions, but No Solution." *The Crisis* 98, no. 8 (1991): 12–18.

"Kaine Leads Bipartisan Effort." Press release, March 14, 2017. https://www.kaine .senate.gov/press-releases/kaine-leads-bipartisan-effort-to-raise-the-quality -of-career-and-technical-education-hosts-career-tech-fair.

Kang, Miliann. "The Managed Hand: The Commercialization of Bodies and Emotions in Korean Immigrant–Owned Nail Salons." *Gender and Society* 17, no. 6 (2003): 820–39.

Keith, Verna, and Cedric Herring. "Skin Tone and Stratification in the Black Community." *American Journal of Sociology* 97, no. 3 (1991): 760–78.

Kimmel, Michael S. "The Cult of Masculinity: American Social Character and the Legacy of the Cowboy." In *Beyond Patriarchy: Essays by Men,* edited by Michael Kaufman, 235–49. Toronto: Oxford University Press, 1987.

Kimmel, Michael S. *Manhood in America: A Cultural History.* 2nd ed. New York: Oxford University Press, 2006.

Klein, Sue, Jennifer Lee, Paige McKinsey, and Charmaine Archer. *Identifying U.S. K-12 Public Schools with Deliberate Sex Segregation.* Arlington, Va.: Feminist Majority Foundation, 2014.

Kleinfeld, Judith. *The Myth That Schools Shortchange Girls: Social Science in the Service of Deception.* Washington, D.C.: Women's Freedom Network, 1998.

Kozol, Jonathan. *Savage Inequalities: Children in America's Schools.* New York: Harper Perennial, 1992.

Kuehn, Daniel. *The Labor Market Performance of Young Black Men in the Great Recession.* Washington, D.C.: Urban Institute, 2013.

Ladson-Billings, Gloria. *The Dreamkeepers: Successful Teachers of African American Children.* San Francisco: Jossey-Bass, 2009.

Ladson-Billings, Gloria. "Toward a Theory of Culturally Relevant Pedagogy." *American Educational Research Journal* 32, no. 3 (1995): 465–91.

Laing, Tony. "Black Masculinities Expressed through, and Constrained by, Brotherhood." *Journal of Men's Studies* 25, no. 2 (2017): 168–97.

Lamont, Michèle. *The Dignity of Working Men: Morality and the Boundaries of Race, Class, and Immigration.* 2nd ed. Cambridge, Mass.: Harvard University Press, 2009.

Lamont, Michèle, and Virág Molnár. "The Study of Boundaries in the Social Sciences." *Annual Review of Sociology* 28 (2002): 167–95.

Leake, Donald O., and Brenda L. Leake. "Islands of Hope: Milwaukee's African American Immersion Schools." *Journal of Negro Education* 61, no. 1 (1992): 24–29.

Lei, Joy L. "(Un)Necessary Toughness?: Those 'Loud Black Girls' and Those 'Quiet Asian Boys.'" *Anthropology and Education Quarterly* 34, no. 2 (2003): 158–81.

Lewis, David Levering. *W. E. B. Du Bois: Biography of a Race, 1868–1919.* New York: Holt, 1993.

Lewis, Oscar. *The Children of Sánchez: Autobiography of a Mexican Family.* New York: Vintage, 2011.

Liben, Lynn S. "Probability Values and Human Values in Evaluating Single-Sex Education." *Sex Roles* 72 (2015): 401–26.

Lincoln, C. Eric, and Lawrence H. Mamiya. *The Black Church in the African American Experience.* Durham, N.C.: Duke University Press, 1990.

Lingard, Bob. "Where to in Gender Policy in Education after Recuperative Masculinity Politics?" *International Journal of Inclusive Education* 7, no. 1 (2003): 33–56.

Lipman, Pauline. *The New Political Economy of Urban Education: Neoliberalism, Race, and the Right to the City.* New York: Routledge, 2011.

Logan, Trevon D. "Personal Characteristics, Sexual Behaviors, and Male Sex Work: A Quantitative Approach." *American Sociological Review* 75, no. 5 (2010): 679–704.

Lozenski, Brian D. "Beyond Mediocrity: The Dialectics of Crisis in the Continuing Miseducation of Black Youth." *Harvard Educational Review* 87, no. 2 (2017): 161–85.

Lubienski, Christopher. "Innovation in Education Markets: Theory and Evidence on the Impact of Competition and Choice in Charter Schools." *American Educational Research Journal* 40, no. 2 (2003): 395–443.

MacLeod, Jay. *Ain't No Makin' It: Leveled Aspirations in a Low-Income Neighborhood.* 2nd ed. Boulder, Colo.: Westview, 1995.

Mael, Fred, Alex Alonso, Doug Gibson, Kelly Rogers, and Mark Smith. *Single-Sex versus Coeducational Schooling: A Systematic Review.* Document no. 2005–01. Washington, D.C.: U.S. Department of Education, 2005.

Majors, Richard, and Janet M. Billson. *Cool Pose: The Dilemmas of Black Manhood in America.* New York: Touchstone, 1993.

Marable, Manning. *Black Leadership: Four Great American Leaders and the Struggle for Civil Rights.* New York: Penguin, 1999.

Mattingly, Cheryl. *The Paradox of Hope: Journeys through a Clinical Borderland.* Berkeley: University of California Press, 2010.

McCallumore, Kyle M., and Ervin F. Sparapani. "The Importance of the Ninth Grade on High School Graduation Rates and Student Success in High School." *Education* 130, no. 3 (2010): 447–57.

McKinnon, Andrew M. "Elective Affinities of the Protestant Ethic: Weber and the Chemistry of Capitalism." *Sociological Theory* 28, no. 1 (2010): 108–26.

McRobbie, Angela. "Notes on the Perfect: Competitive Femininity in Neoliberal Times." *Australian Feminist Studies* 30, no. 83 (2015): 3–20.

Meiners, Erica R. *Right to Be Hostile: Schools, Prisons, and the Making of Public Enemies.* New York: Routledge, 2010.

Messerschmidt, James W. "Masculinities, Crime and Prison." In *Prison Masculinities,* edited by Don Sabo, Terry A. Kupers, and Willie James London, 67–72. Philadelphia: Temple University Press, 2001.

Messner, Michael. "Gender Ideologies, Youth Sports, and the Production of Soft Essentialism." *Sociology of Sport Journal* 28, no. 2 (2011): 151–70.

Meyer, John W., and W. Richard Scott. "The Organization of Societal Sectors: Propositions and Early Evidence." In *The New Institutionalism in Organizational Analysis,* edited by Walter W. Powell and Paul Dimaggio, 108–40. Chicago: University of Chicago Press, 1991.

Mijs, Jonathan, Elyas Bakhtiari, and Michèle Lamont. "Neoliberalism and Symbolic Boundaries in Europe: Global Diffusion, Local Context, Regional Variation." *Socius: Sociological Research for a Dynamic World* 2 (2016): 1–8.

Miller, Teresa A. "Incarcerated Masculinities." In *Progressive Black Masculinities,* edited by Athena D. Mutua, 155–74. New York: Routledge, 2006.

Mische, Ann. "Projects and Possibilities: Researching Futures in Action." *Sociological Forum* 24, no. 3 (2009): 694–704.

Mitchell, Anthony B., and James B. Stewart. "The Efficacy of All-Male Academies: Insights from Critical Race Theory (CRT)." *Sex Roles* 69, nos. 7–8 (2013): 382–92.

Moore, Kesha S. "Gentrification in Black Face? The Return of the Black Middle Class to Urban Neighborhoods." *Urban Geography* 30, no. 2 (2009): 118–42.

Morris, Edward W. *Learning the Hard Way: Masculinity, Place, and the Gender Gap in Education.* New Brunswick, N.J.: Rutgers University Press, 2012.

Morris, Edward W. "'Snitches End Up in Ditches' and Other Cautionary Tales." *Journal of Contemporary Criminal Justice* 26, no. 3 (2010): 254–72.

Morris, Wesley. "'The Blind Side' Sticks to the Playbook on Race and Renewal." *Boston Globe,* November 20, 2009. http://archive.boston.com/ae/movies/articles /2009/11/20/blind_side_sticks_to_the_playbook_on_race_and_renewal.

Moynihan, Daniel P. *The Negro Family: The Case for National Action.* Washington, D.C.: Office of Policy Planning and Research, U.S. Department of Labor, 1965.

Murtadha-Watts, Khaula. "Theorizing Urban Black Masculinity Construction in an African-Centered School." In *Masculinities at School,* edited by Nancy Lesko, 49–74. New York: Sage, 2000.

Mutua, Athena D., ed. *Progressive Black Masculinities.* New York: Routledge, 2006.

Naples, Nancy A. "Towards Comparative Analyses of Women's Political Praxis: Explicating Multiple Dimensions of Standpoint Epistemology for Feminist Ethnography." *Women and Politics* 20, no. 1 (1999): 29–57.

Nasir, Na'ilah Suad, and Victoria M. Hand. "Exploring Sociocultural Perspectives on Race, Culture, and Learning." *Review of Educational Research* 76, no. 4 (2006): 449–76.

National Alliance for Public Charter Schools. "Charter School Data Dashboard." https://data.publiccharters.org/.

National Commission on Excellence in Education. *A Nation at Risk: The Imperative for Educational Reform.* Washington, D.C.: National Commission on Excellence in Education, 1983.

Nelson, Joseph. "'I Want to Be a Soccer Player or a Mathematician': Fifth-Grade Black Boys' Aspirations at a 'Neoliberal' Single-Sex School." In *Masculinity and Aspiration in an Era of Neoliberal Education: International Perspectives,* edited by Garth Stahl, Joseph Nelson, and Deron Wallace, 108–25. London: Routledge, 2017.

Nelson, Joseph. *Never Give Up: Resilience, Academic Success, and Middle School Boys.* Cambridge, Mass.: Harvard University Press, forthcoming.

Nightingale, Carl Husemoller. *On the Edge: A History of Poor Black Children and Their American Dreams.* New York: Basic Books, 1993.

Noddings, Nel. *Caring: A Feminine Approach to Ethics and Moral Education.* Berkeley: University of California Press, 1984.

Noguera, Pedro A. "Responding to the Crisis Confronting California's Black Male Youth: Providing Support without Furthering Marginalization." *Journal of Negro Education* 65, no. 2 (1996): 219–36.

Noguera, Pedro A. Review of *The Cultural Matrix: Understanding Black Youth,* edited by Orlando Patterson and Ethan Fosse. *American Journal of Sociology* 121, no. 6 (2016): 1940–43.

Noguera, Pedro A. "Saving Black and Latino Boys: What Schools Can Do to Make a Difference." *Kappan* 93, no. 5 (2012): 8–12.

Nolan, Jr., James L. *What They Saw in America: Alexis de Tocqueville, Max Weber, G. K. Chesterton, and Sayyid Qutb.* New York: Cambridge University Press, 2016.

Nolan, Jim. "Kaine to Introduce Legislation on High School Career and Technical Education." *Richmond Times-Dispatch,* March 16, 2016. http://www.richmond .com/news/virginia/government-politics/kaine-to-introduce-legislation-on-high -school-career-and-technical/article_445d6173-b897–5463-b3e4–700f49cf1aa7 .html.

Nolan, Kathleen. *Police in the Hallways: Discipline in an Urban High School.* Minneapolis: University of Minnesota Press, 2011.

Ochoa, Gilda. *Academic Profiling: Latinos, Asian Americans, and the Achievement Gap.* Minneapolis: University of Minnesota Press, 2013.

Oeur, Freeden. "It's Not How Regular Boys Are Supposed to Act: The Nonnormative Sexual Practices of Black Boys in All-Male Public Schools." In *Gender and Sexualities in Education: A Reader,* edited by Elizabeth J. Meyer and Dennis Carlson, 357–69. New York: Peter Lang, 2014.

Oeur, Freeden. "Recognizing Dignity: Young Black Men Growing Up in an Era of Surveillance." *Socius: Sociological Research for a Dynamic World* 2 (2016): 1–15.

Oeur, Freeden. "The Respectable Brotherhood: Young Black Men in an All-Boys Charter High School." *Sociological Perspectives* 60, no. 6 (2017): 1063–81.

Oeur, Freeden. "Single-Sex Schooling Can Empower Black Boys." CNN, May 22, 2014. http://www.cnn.com/2013/10/18/opinion/oeur-same-sex-education/index .html.

Ogbu, John. "Variability in Minority School Performance: A Problem in Search of an Explanation." *Anthropology and Education Quarterly* 18, no. 4 (1987): 312–34.

Olson, Joel. *The Abolition of White Democracy.* Minneapolis: University of Minnesota Press, 2004.

Omi, Michael, and Howard Winant. *Racial Formation in the United States.* 3rd ed. New York: Routledge, 2014.

Pahlke, Erin, Janet Hyde, and Carlie Allison. "The Effects of Single-Sex Compared with Coeducational Schooling on Students' Performance and Attitudes: A Meta-analysis." *Psychological Bulletin* 140, no. 4 (2014): 1042–72.

Pascoe, C. J. *Dude, You're a Fag: Masculinity and Sexuality in High School.* Berkeley: University of California Press, 2007.

Patterson, Orlando, and Ethan Fosse, eds. *The Cultural Matrix: Understanding Black Youth*. Cambridge, Mass.: Harvard University Press, 2015.

Pattillo, Mary. "Everyday Politics of School Choice in the Black Community." *Du Bois Review* 12, no. 1 (2015): 41–71.

Pattillo, Mary, Lori Delale-O'Connor, and Felicia Butts. "High-Stakes Choosing." In *Choosing Homes, Choosing Schools*, edited by Annette Lareau and Kimberly Goyette, 237–67. New York: Russell Sage Foundation, 2014.

Pattillo-McCoy, Mary. "Church Culture as a Strategy of Action in the Black Community." *American Sociological Review* 63, no. 6 (1998): 767–84.

Pedroni, Thomas C. *Market Movements: African American Involvement in School Voucher Reform*. New York: Routledge, 2007.

Perry, Brea L., and Edward W. Morris. "Suspending Progress: Collateral Consequences of Exclusionary Punishment in Public Schools." *American Sociological Review* 79, no. 6 (2014): 1067–87.

Pew Research Center. "Wealth Gaps Rise to Record Highs between Whites, Blacks, and Hispanics." January 11, 2012. http://www.pewresearch.org/fact-tank/2012/01/11/wealth-gaps-rise-to-record-highs-between-whites-blacks-and-hispanics-2/.

Phoenix, Ann. "Neoliberalism and Masculinity: Racialization and the Contradictions of Schooling for 11- to 14-Year-Olds." *Youth and Society* 36, no. 2 (2004): 227–46.

Picower, Bree. "The Unexamined Whiteness of Teaching: How White Teachers Maintain and Enact Dominant Racial Ideologies." *Race Ethnicity and Education* 12, no. 2 (2009): 197–215.

Pipher, Mary. *Reviving Ophelia: Saving the Selves of Adolescent Girls*. New York: Ballantine, 1995.

Pugh, Allison. *Longing and Belonging: Parents, Children, and Consumer Culture*. Berkeley: University of California Press, 2009.

Rabaka, Reiland. *Against Epistemic Apartheid: W. E. B. Du Bois and the Disciplinary Decadence of Sociology*. Lanham, Md.: Lexington Books, 2010.

Randles, Jennifer, and Kerry Woodward. "Learning to Labor, Love, and Live: Shaping the Good Neoliberal Citizen in State Work and Marriage Programs." *Sociological Perspectives* 61, no. 1 (2018): 39–56.

Ravitch, Diane. *Reign of Error: The Hoax of the Privatization Movement and the Danger to America's Public Schools*. New York: Vintage, 2014.

Ray, Rashawn, and Jason A. Rosow. "The Two Different Worlds of Black and White Fraternity Men: Visibility and Accountability as Mechanisms of Privilege." *Journal of Contemporary Ethnography* 41, no. 1 (2012): 66–94.

Reed, Adolph L., Jr. *W. E. B. Du Bois and American Political Thought: Fabianism and the Color Line*. New York: Oxford University Press, 1997.

Renzulli, Linda A., and Lorraine Evans. "School Choice, Charter Schools, and White Flight." *Social Problems* 52, no. 3 (2005): 398–418.

Rhoden, Stuart. "'Trust Me, You Are Going to College': How Trust Influences Academic Achievement in Black Males." *Journal of Negro Education* 86, no. 1 (2017): 52–64.

Riordan, Cornelius. *Girls and Boys in School: Together or Separate?* New York: Teachers College Press, 1990.

Riordan, Cornelius. *Single-Sex Schools: A Place to Learn.* Lanham, Md.: Rowman and Littlefield, 2015.

Rios, Victor. *Punished: Policing the Lives of Black and Latino Boys.* New York: New York University Press, 2011.

Rivers, Caryl, and Rosalind C. Barnett. *The Truth about Girls and Boys: Challenging Toxic Stereotypes about Our Children.* New York: Columbia University Press, 2011.

Robinson, Keith, and Angel L. Harris. *The Broken Compass: Parental Involvement with Children's Education.* Cambridge, Mass.: Harvard University Press, 2014.

Rofes, Eric, and Lisa M. Stulberg. *The Emancipatory Promise of Charter Schools: Toward a Progressive Politics of School Choice.* Albany, N.Y.: State University of New York Press, 2004.

Rosenbaum, James E. *Beyond College for All: Career Paths for the Forgotten Half.* New York: Russell Sage Foundation, 2001.

Rosenbaum, James. E. "The Complexities of College for All: Beyond Fairy-tale Dreams." *Sociology of Education* 84, no. 2 (2011): 113–17.

Rosin, Hanna. *The End of Men: And the Rise of Women.* New York: Riverhead Books, 2012.

Ross, Marlon B. "In Search of Black Men's Masculinities." *Feminist Studies* 24, no. 3 (1998): 599–626.

Ross, Marlon B. *Manning the Race: Reforming Black Men in the Jim Crow Era.* New York: New York University Press, 2005.

Rottenberg, Catherine. "The Rise of Neoliberal Feminism." *Cultural Studies* 28, no. 3 (2014): 418–37.

Rotundo, E. Anthony. *American Manhood: Transformations in Masculinity from the Revolution to the Modern Era.* New York: Basic Books, 1994.

Roychowdhury, Poulami. "Victims to Saviors: Governmentality and the Regendering of Citizenship in India." *Gender and Society* 29, no. 6 (2015): 792–816.

Sabo, Don, Terry Kupers, and Willie London. "Gender and the Politics of Punishment." In *Prison Masculinities,* edited by Don Sabo, Terry A. Kupers, and Willie London, 3–18. Philadelphia: Temple University Press, 2001.

Salomone, Rosemary. *Same, Different, Equal: Rethinking Single-Sex Schooling.* New Haven, Conn.: Yale University Press, 2003.

Saltman, Kenneth J. "The Austerity School: Grit, Character, and the Privatization of Public Education." *symplokē* 22, no. 1 (2014): 41–57.

Sax, Leonard. "Six Degrees of Separation: What Teachers Need to Know about the Emerging Science of Sex Differences." *Educational Horizons* 84, no. 3 (2006): 190–200.

Sax, Leonard. *Why Gender Matters: What Parents and Teachers Need to Know about the Emerging Science of Sex Differences.* New York: Broadway Books.

Scheff, Thomas J. "Shame and Conformity: The Deference-Emotion System." *American Sociological Review* 53, no. 3 (1988): 395–406.

Schott Foundation for Public Education. *Black Lives Matter: The Schott 50 State Report on Public Education and Black Males.* Cambridge, Mass.: Schott Foundation for Public Education, 2015.

Sheils, Merrill. "Segregation by Sex." *Newsweek*, September 19, 1977.

Silva, Jennifer M. *Coming Up Short: Working-Class Adulthood in an Age of Uncertainty.* New York: Oxford University Press, 2013.

Skeggs, Beverley. *Formations of Class and Gender: Becoming Respectable.* London: Sage, 2002.

Smith, Aaron. "Shared, Collaborative, and on Demand: The New Digital Economy." *Pew Research Center,* May 19, 2016. http://www.pewinternet.org/2016/05/19/the-new-digital-economy.

Smith, Christopher Holmes. "'I Don't Like to Dream about Getting Paid': Representations of Social Mobility and the Emergence of the Hip-Hop Mogul." *Social Text* 21, no. 4 (2003): 69–97.

Sowell, Thomas. "Black Excellence: The Case of Dunbar High School." In *The Public Interest on Education,* edited by Nathan Glazer, 1–19. New York: University Press of America, 1984.

Spence, Lester K. *Knocking the Hustle: Against the Neoliberal Turn in Black Politics.* New York: Punctum, 2015.

Spence, Lester K. "The Neoliberal Turn in Black Politics." *Souls: A Critical Journal of Black Politics, Culture, and Society* 14, nos. 3–4 (2012): 139–59.

Spencer, Elaine B. "Spiritual Politics: Politicizing the Black Church Tradition in Anticolonial Praxis." In *Anti-colonialism and Education: The Politics of Resistance,* edited by George J. Sefa Dei and Arlo Kempf, 107–27. Rotterdam: Sense, 2006.

Stack, Carol. *All Our Kin: Strategies for Survival in a Black Community.* New York: Basic Books, 1974.

Stetser, Marie C., and Robert Stillwell. *Public High School Four-Year On-Time Graduation Rates and Event Dropout Rates: School Years 2010–11 and 2011–12. First Look.* NCES 2014–391. Washington, D.C.: National Center for Education Statistics, 2014.

Stewart, Alison. *First Class: The Legacy of Dunbar, America's First Black Public High School.* Chicago: Chicago Review Press, 2013.

Stoudt, Brett G. "'You're Either In or You're Out': School Violence, Peer Discipline, and the (Re)Production of Hegemonic Masculinity." *Men and Masculinities* 8, no. 3 (2006): 273–87.

Stulberg, Lisa M. "African American School Choice and the Current Race Politics of Charter Schooling: Lessons from History." *Race and Social Problems* 7, no. 1 (2015): 31–42.

Stulberg, Lisa M. *Race, Schools, and Hope: African Americans and School Choice After Brown*. New York: Teachers College Press, 2008.

Summers, Martin. "Manhood Rights in the Age of Jim Crow: Evaluating End-of-Men Claims in the Context of African American History." *Boston University Law Review* 93, no. 3 (2013): 745–67.

Summers, Martin. *Manliness and Its Discontents: The Black Middle Class and the Transformation of Masculinity, 1900–1930*. Chapel Hill: University of North Carolina Press, 2005.

Swidler, Ann. "Culture in Action: Symbols and Strategies." *American Sociological Review* 51, no. 2 (1986): 273–86.

Swidler, Ann. *Talk of Love: How Culture Matters*. Chicago: University of Chicago Press, 2001.

Taft, Jessica. "Racing Age: Reflections on Antiracist Research with Teenage Girls." In *Representing Youth: Methodological Issues in Critical Youth Studies*, edited by Amy L. Best, 203–25. New York: New York University Press, 2007.

Tavory, Iddo, and Stefan Timmermans. "Two Cases of Ethnography: Grounded Theory and the Extended Case Method." *Ethnography* 10, no. 3 (2009): 243–63.

Terry, Clarence L., Terry K. Flennaugh, Samarah M. Blackmon, and Tyrone C. Howard. "Does the 'Negro' *Still* Need Separate Schools? Single-Sex Educational Settings as Critical Race Counterspaces." *Urban Education* 49, no. 6 (2013): 666–97.

Thorne, Barrie. *Gender Play: Girls and Boys in School*. New Brunswick, N.J.: Rutgers University Press, 1993.

Tilly, Charles. "Changing Forms of Inequality." *Sociological Theory* 21, no. 1 (2003): 31–36.

Tocqueville, Alexis de. *Democracy in America*. Translated by Harvey C. Mansfield and Delba Winthrop. Chicago: University of Chicago Press, 2012.

"Transcript: Barack Obama's Speech on Race." NPR. March, 18, 2008. http://www.npr.org/templates/story/story.php?storyId=88478467.

Tronto, Joan C. *Caring Democracy: Markets, Equality, and Justice*. New York: New York University Press, 2013.

Tyack, David, and Elizabeth Hansot. *Learning Together: A History of Coeducation in American Public Schools*. New York: Russell Sage Foundation, 1992.

Uprichard, Emma. "Children as 'Being and Becomings': Children, Childhood and Temporality." *Children and Society* 22, no. 4 (2008): 303–13.

U.S. Department of Education. *Questions and Answers on Title IX and Single-Sex Elementary and Secondary Classes and Extracurricular Activities*. Washington, D.C.: U.S. Department of Education, 2014.

U.S. Department of Health and Human Services. "Trends in Teen Pregnancy and Childbearing." June 2, 2016. https://www.hhs.gov/ash/oah/adolescent-develop

ment/reproductive-health-and-teen-pregnancy/teen-pregnancy-and-childbear
ing/trends/index.html.

Valenzuela, Angela. *Subtractive Schooling: U.S.-Mexican Youth and the Politics of Caring.* Albany, N.Y.: State University of New York Press, 1999.

Van Deburg, William L. *Modern Black Nationalism: From Marcus Garvey to Louis Farrakhan.* New York: New York University Press, 1997.

Vaught, Sabina E. *Compulsory: Education and the Dispossession of Youth in a Prison School.* Minneapolis: University of Minnesota Press, 2017.

Wacquant, Loïc. *Punishing the Poor: The Neoliberal Government of Social Insecurity.* Durham, N.C.: Duke University Press, 2009.

Wacquant, Loïc. "Scrutinizing the Street: Poverty, Morality, and the Pitfalls of Urban Ethnography." *American Journal of Sociology* 107, no. 6 (2002): 1468–1532.

Warren, Chezare A. "The Utility of Empathy for White Female Teachers' Culturally Responsive Interactions with Black Male Students." *Interdisciplinary Journal of Teaching and Learning* 3, no. 3 (2013): 175–200.

Watson, Clifford, and Geneva Smitherman. *Educating African American Males: Detroit's Malcolm X Academy.* Chicago: Third World Press, 1996.

Weaver-Hightower, Marcus B. "Issues of Boys' Education in the United States: Diffuse Contexts and Futures." In *The Problem with Boys' Education: Beyond the Backlash,* edited by Wayne Martino, Michael D. Kehler, and Marcus B. Weaver-Hightower, 1–35. New York: Routledge, 2009.

Weber, Max. "Class, Status, Party." In *Social Stratification: Class, Race, and Gender in Sociological Perspective,* edited by David Grusky, 113–22. 4th ed. Boulder, Colo.: Westview, 2014.

Weber, Max. *The Protestant Ethic and the "Spirit" of Capitalism and Other Writings.* Edited and translated by Peter Baehr and Gordon C. Wells. New York: Penguin, 2002.

Weil, Elizabeth. "Teaching Boys and Girls Separately." *New York Times Magazine,* March 2, 2008. http://www.nytimes.com/2008/03/02/magazine/02sex3-t.html.

Wells, Amy Stuart, Julie Slayton, and Janelle Scott. "Defining Democracy in the Neoliberal Age: Charter School Reform and Educational Consumption." *American Educational Research Journal* 39, no. 2 (2002): 337–61.

West, Candace, and Don Zimmerman. "Doing Gender." *Gender and Society* 1, no. 2 (1987): 125–51.

Western, Bruce, Anthony A. Braga, Jaclyn Davis, and Catherine Sirois. "Stress and Hardship after Prison." *American Journal of Sociology* 120, no. 5 (2015): 1512–47.

Whyte, William Foote. "Revisiting 'Street Corner Society.'" *Sociological Forum* 8, no. 2 (1993): 285–98.

Whyte, William Foote. *Street Corner Society: The Social Structure of an Italian Slum.* 4th ed. Chicago: University of Chicago Press, 1993.

Wilkerson, Isabel. *The Warmth of Other Suns: The Epic Story of America's Great Migration*. New York: Random House, 2010.

Wilkins, Amy. "Stigma and Status: Interracial Intimacy and Intersectional Identities among Black College Men." *Gender and Society* 26, no. 2 (2012): 165–89.

Willens, Michelle. "Ninth Grade: The Most Important Year in High School." *Atlantic*, November 1, 2013. https://www.theatlantic.com/education/archive/2013/11/ninth-grade-the-most-important-year-in-high-school/281056.

Williams, Juliet A. "The Possibilities and Perils of Social Justice Feminism: What We Can Learn from the Single-Sex Public Education Debates." *Freedom Center Journal* 5, no. 1 (2014): 87–100.

Williams, Juliet A. *The Separation Solution? Single-Sex Education and the New Politics of Gender Equality*. Oakland: University of California Press, 2016.

Williams, Juliet A. "Thinking through the 'Boy Crisis': From Multiple Masculinities to Intersectionality." In *Exploring Masculinities: Feminist Legal Theory Reflections*, edited by Martha Fineman and Michael Thomson, 163–75. New York: Routledge, 2013.

Williams, Verna. "Reform or Retrenchment: Single Sex Education and the Construction of Race and Gender." *Wisconsin Law Review* 15, no. 1 (2004): 15–80.

Wilson, William Julius. "Studying Inner-City Social Dislocations: The Challenge of Public Agenda Research." *American Sociological Review* 56, no. 1 (1991): 1–14.

Wilson, William Julius. "Why Both Social Structure and Culture Matter in a Holistic Analysis of Inner-City Poverty." *ANNALS of the American Academy of Political and Social Science* 629, no. 1 (2010): 200–19.

Woody, Elisabeth L. "Homophobia and Heterosexism in Public School Reform: Constructions of Gender and Sexuality in California's Single Gender Academies." *Equity and Excellence in Education* 36, no. 2 (2003): 148–60.

Young, Alford, Jr. *The Minds of Marginalized Black Men: Making Sense of Mobility, Opportunity, and Future Life Chances*. Princeton, N.J.: Princeton University Press, 2004.

Young, Iris Marion. "The Logic of Masculinist Protection: Reflections on the Current Security State." *Signs: Journal of Women in Culture and Society* 29, no. 1 (2003): 1–25.

Zamir, Shamoon. *Dark Voices: W. E. B. Du Bois and American Thought, 1888–1903*. Chicago: University of Chicago Press, 1995.

Zinn, Howard. *A Young People's History of the United States: Columbus to the War on Terror*. Adapted by Rebecca Stefoff. New York: Seven Stories, 2009.

FREEDEN BLUME OEUR is associate professor of sociology at Tufts University. With Edward W. Morris, he is coeditor of *Unmasking Masculinities: Men and Society.*